COMMUNICATION
C·A·M·P·A·I·G·N
MANAGEMENT

COMMUNICATION
C·A·M·P·A·I·G·N
MANAGEMENT
A Systems Approach

by

·ROBERT E. SIMMONS·
Boston University

Longman
New York & London

Communication Campaign Management

Longman, 95 Church Street, White Plains, N.Y. 10601

Associated companies:
Longman Group Ltd., London
Longman Cheshire Pty., Melbourne
Longman Paul Pty., Auckland
Copp Clark Pitman, Toronto

Executive editor: Gordon T. R. Anderson
Development editor: Virginia L. Blanford
Production editor: Marie-Josée A. Schorp
Cover design: Kevin C. Kall
Text art: John Hadley
Production supervisor: Kathleen M. Ryan

Library of Congress Cataloging-in-Publication Data

Simmons, Robert E.
    Communication campaign management: a systems approach/by Robert E.
    Simmons.
        p. cm.

    Bibliography: p.
    Includes index.
    ISBN 0-8013-0404-0
    1. Publicity—United States—Management.   I. Title.
HM263.S517   1990   89-36276
659'.068—dc20   CIP

ABCDEFGHIJ-ML-99 98 97 96 95 94 93 92 91 90 89

I dedicate this book to communicators in all parts of the globe who use their talents to make the world better and safer for all of us. Particular gratitude is expressed to those who strive to halt the Acquired Immunodeficiency Syndrome (AIDS) epidemic; I am especially fortunate to have learned from many of them.

Contents

Foreword

"Too soon old, too late smart." That Pennsylvania Dutch adage has a special meaning for the communication professional. All too often, the designers of elaborate communication campaigns for political candidates, charity drives, corporations, or even local community groups find that their learning curves peak after the conclusions of their campaigns.

Communication campaigns are frequently evaluated after the ads have been aired, the media contacted, and the press offensives concluded. They are measured by the final results (votes, money, etc.) or by the media's polls. If the candidate wins or the fund drive exceeds its goals, then the campaign is judged a success. If something goes wrong, angry postmortems drag on into the night.

Recent political campaigns have shed especially bright light on this process, with some candidates producing ads and events that have blundered, backfired, or been ignored. On the other hand, some campaigns have been successful from the start, focusing on and speaking to the needs, aspirations, and desires of the public. One explanation of this phenomenon might be that the winner had better intuition, more creativity, or a better message. A more likely explanation was that the winner had planned, designed, and executed a more sophisticated communication campaign from the very beginning.

Must the candidates and their communication chiefs wait until the polls are closed to know whether they are reaching the voters? Must non-profit campaigners wait until the final tally to tell the tale? Perhaps so a few years ago. Not so today. As Robert Simmons points out in this important volume, communication is a systemic process that requires careful and constant measurement from the outset.

A number of imperatives drive us to this conclusion. First of all, the consumers of information have far more information than they can handle. The clutter of advertising messages and news bytes is now estimated in the thousands of units each day. The sheer volume of media stimuli have blunted the sensitivities of most information consumers. Despite this rather forbidding context, the prime imperative of the communicator remains: he or she must get the audience's attention and hold that attention long enough to get the proper message across and be sure it is understood.

One can try to do this through what Dr. Simmons calls the "creative" approach. This approach is driven by instinct, technique, and intuition. It might produce a great ad that gets strong critical support. But there is no assurance that the communicator's message will get across, getting people to attend to it or getting it shown to the right people at the right time or place.

As any marketer will tell you, the more there is to choose, the more choosy the consumer gets. This certainly is true of the communication product, as it is with any other. We are in a cluttered environment, which means information consumers can pick the kind of stimuli they want when they want it.

Today's information consumers have access to a staggering number of sources. Cable television gives access to more than a hundred channels, many of them with a highly specialized focus on subjects like sports, weather, or health care. Trade and hobby publications abound, serving every interest from computer hacking to pet care. And radio remains as cluttered a medium as it ever was.

Technology has empowered information consumers, who can tune out, zap, or otherwise edit the material that comes their way. They can even use their telephones to respond to media, listen to ads, or purchase products. The old model of the consumer as a passive media captive is as outmoded as the vacuum tube. The contemporary voter–consumer–contributor is active, participating in the communication process rather than being subject to it.

Even without technology, the modern information consumer is so media savvy that he or she will instinctively sort and filter whatever messages do get through. Creativity must be matched with credibility, lest the communicator's efforts win the attention or even the amusement of key audiences, but fail to convince them.

Another critical factor in today's communication process is money. The organizer of a political campaign or a community awareness effort faces a tightening crunch between budgets and media costs. The situation is equally severe for a business trying to mount a communication campaign. Money can't be wasted.

The unimaginable diversity of media sources makes the financial issue even harder to contend with. Saturation bombing of the media is either impossible or extremely expensive. It is also enormously wasteful. Many of the media outlets are of no value to a communication campaign because of their size, their audience's tastes or their programming practices.

The imperatives of consumer choice and cost-effectiveness have governed the makers of products from the earliest days of commerce. They have not had a similar impact in the world of communication until very recently. But now the crunch has come.

The people who pay for communication services are aware of the difficulties of raising money and of reaching their audiences. They are more demanding than ever in both the public and private sector. In other words, people want their money's worth from communication campaigns. They want the system to become rationalized and responsive to budgets. Most importantly, they want results.

Robert Simmons has a profound understanding of today's communication environment and he has developed a sophisticated strategy for dealing with it. And while much of this book deals with management terminology, its principles are derived from common sense. The communication process requires a clear sense of focus, a firm sense of mission, and a precise sense of direction. The proper audiences must be targeted from the outset, and their attitudes and receptivity must be understood before the "creative" process begins.

Another vital element of Dr. Simmons's analysis is his thorough description of the measurement process. He persuasively demonstrates the need for constant feedback and reinforcement, lest messages get lost, forgotten, or misunderstood. He also offers a step-by-step approach for evaluating the impact and effectiveness of a communication campaign. In short, by using a systems approach to managing communication, one can avoid the nasty surprises and disappointments of those failed campaigns that seemed "such a good idea" at the outset.

Admittedly, *Communication Campaign Management: A Systems Approach* is not a remedy for misbegotten ideas. No matter how sophisticated the system, a poor information product will not find a market. Nonetheless, a systems approach can reveal a bad idea before it's too late. It can also make sure that a good idea is properly constructed to get the attention, and the support, of sympathetic and influential information consumers.

Dr. Simmons's system approach is a state-of-the-art approach to a modern problem in a valuable textbook for the student of campaign management methodology and applications. It also is a useful handbook for communication campaign managers that will enable them to work smart soon, before it's too late.

Raymond L. Kotcher
Executive Vice President/U.S.
Ketchum Public Relations

Acknowledgements

The existence of this book owes much to some special people who helped develop my interest in communication management by sharing perspectives or by putting opportunities in my path that gave me opportunities to learn: Dr. William Mindak, whom I encountered during my graduate studies at the University of Minnesota; Marco Antônio Rodrigues Dias, formerly of the Universidade de Brasília and now director of higher education for UNESCO, Paris; Edward L. Bernays, who may be the father of strategic planning in the communication field, and Raymond L. Kotcher, executive vice president/U.S. for Ketchum Public Relations, who first introduced me to Mr. Bernays.

Also, there are persons who helped motivate me during times when inertia set in: Peter E. Sanders, Kees van der Bas and Piet van Straalen, superstars of DATA/GOLD BV, an international advertising and PR firm in Moodrecht (Rotterdam); Dr. H. Joachim Maitre and Walter Lubars of Boston University; and Lois M. Ludeman of OURS Inc., Minneapolis, who contributed extensive time to insightful and beneficial manuscript critiques.

Finally, I acknowledge the unflagging support and humane treatment of the people of Longman: Gordon T. R. Anderson, executive editor, whose good humor often carried the day; Dr. Virginia Blanford, who helped me find my way out of various briarpatch tangles of academic prose; Marie-Josée Schorp, who makes book production seem almost fun; and Jeff Campbell, who worked with me in the early stages to get the book under way.

COMMUNICATION
C·A·M·P·A·I·G·N
MANAGEMENT

CHAPTER 1

Strategic Planning, Systems, and Campaigns

This book addresses the concerns of those who want to be campaign managers or planners and those already responsible for mass communication campaigns who want to be more effective. Its core is strategic planning, which is based on the *general systems model*. Most people are aware of marketing and advertising campaigns that deal with products and services. However, a list of other applications, from public relations to agriculture, reveals the spread of communication campaigns (see Exhibit 1.1). For all of them, the general systems approach integrates activities to provide an effective framework for a comprehensive solution to any communication problem.

EXHIBIT 1.1. Communication Campaign Applications

| Applications | Fields Employing Campaigns | | | | |
	PR	Marketing	Advertising	Agriculture	Education
Products	X	X	X	X	
Services	X	X	X		
Corporate PR	X	X			
Organizational communication	X				
Politics	X		X		
Health	X	X			X
Social services marketing	X	X			
Arts	X	X			
Community development	X	X			X
Agricultural diffusion				X	

In the communication community, many campaigns depend on a *creative model*, which grows out of experiences of those who write, produce, and deliver messages—often with more emphasis on the two former aspects than the latter. Those embracing the creative model tend to believe that when a message displays true "inspiration" in its creation and production, and when an effective mass media plan delivers it, success is virtually guaranteed. They give little more than a nod to problem-analysis research, behavioral and management theory, and evaluation research.

In contrast, clients and upper-level managers tend to view problems in management terms: goals, control, cost effectiveness, and verifiable results. They expect to find a substantial *management* structure underpinning a campaign, said a principal in a successful Canadian communication firm, and any fascination with creativity stems mainly from the hope that it might improve impact or ensure a competitive edge.

Strategic planning is an alternative that represents a powerful fusion of theory, methodologies, principles, and techniques drawn from management, the social sciences (including communication), communication practice, and scientific research. The creative model is not abandoned; strategic planning simply repositions it in a larger managerial framework. The general systems model (Buckley, 1967) contends that all these elements can be considered parts of an integrated process: All must support the central goal or a set of goals. The parts are integrated by communication linkages; in fact, systems cannot exist without communication. That is, communication provides energy and direction and meets needs for corrective feedback.

Systems are adaptive; they continuously require information inputs, including feedback, and then process these inputs to survive, meet goals, function cost effectively, and improve efficiency over time. Units in a managerial system deal with information processing and decision making; thus they are organized around techniques and methodologies that address these ends. *Techniques* are specific procedures for dealing with problems. *Methodologies* incorporate techniques and provide extensive explanations justifying the particular procedures.

Much of the interest in using strategic planning and its supporting systems model stems from a concern with efficiency. Sometimes strategic planning addresses efficient use of resources and profit making, as in business; in nonprofit organizations, it involves stretching limited resources as efficiently as possible to bring about changes that can affect lives, such as in child adoption, health, community education, and food-production programs.

THE QUEST FOR IMPROVED CAMPAIGN RESULTS

The *powerful effects communication model*, of which the creative model is part, has been largely discredited (Severin with Tankard, 1988, pp. 311–330). Even under favorable conditions, measurable campaign effects are likely to

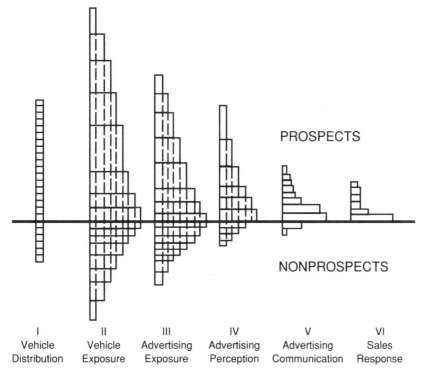

PROSPECTS

NONPROSPECTS

I	II	III	IV	V	VI
Vehicle Distribution	Vehicle Exposure	Advertising Exposure	Advertising Perception	Advertising Communication	Sales Response

EXHIBIT 1.2. Example of drop-off from exposure to response

Source: Reprinted from *Toward Better Media Comparisons.* © Copyright 1961 by the Advertising Research Foundation. Reprinted by Permission.

be small in relation to the amount of communication activity (see Exhibit 1.2). Wasteful activity—for example, media space or time purchases and personal contacts expended on audiences that are not essential to a campaign's success—compounds the problem.

As Atkin (1981, p. 267) observes,

> At this point in time, scientists studying effects of information campaigns and related mass media content can be grouped into two divergent camps. . . . The neo-null effects proponents who adhere to the view that the media are largely impotent . . . [and] the academics and practitioners who hold that the media are potentially influential, especially if a campaign is properly designed and effects are sensitively measured and interpreted. . . . Rather than concentrating on the array of factors that limit effectiveness, [the latter group has] searched for ways to overcome the barriers. . . .

Considerable attention is being given to the comprehensive planning of a campaign. In a review of mass media campaigns that have succeeded or failed, Atkin (1981, pp. 265–279) identifies several elements that contribute to success:

1. Precampaign audience analysis
2. Identification of manifest or latent needs of receivers
3. Relevant message content, as perceived by receivers, as well as entertainment and production value (attractive production)
4. Selection of spokespersons who may improve arousal and credibility in regard to messages
5. Pilot testing of alternative sources, messages, and styles
6. Methodological selection of media or channels—including recognition of the influence of, or interference from, media or interpersonal sources
7. Factors that enhance chances for exposure—access (reach and frequency) and arousal (inclusion of content that is relevant and affect-oriented, i.e., emotionally arousing).

Solomon (1981, pp. 281–292) discusses elements, drawn from social marketing, that were not main points in the Atkin inventory, including

1. A philosophy that marketing [or communication] is an exchange process, that people give their attention when the communicator offers something they want (This observation has been made by Kotler, 1972, and Bauer, 1971.)
2. Hierarchies of effects—essentially decisional process models, such as the Stanford Heart Disease Prevention Program's stages approach: awareness, knowledge, motivation, skills learning, and maintenance/self-maintenance
3. Segmentation: "The key is to consider segmenting the audience, learn about each key segment, and plan a campaign to reach each segment and effectively" (Solomon, 1981, p. 287).
4. Identification of all the relevant markets
5. Analysis of the competitive environment
6. Determination of what expectations for results are realistic

Simmons and Mujica (1987) identify other characteristics of effective campaign planning:

1. Timely intervention
2. Segmentation that not only delivers messages to the particular audiences that are crucial to the problem but also, because of finite campaign resources, does so cost effectively
3. Use of research for tracking campaigns during execution and, at the end, getting feedback that may improve the next planning cycle
4. Allocation of effort to targeted audiences in proportion to their potential impact on the problem

Simmons, Hills, and Lee (1988) suggest other considerations:

1. Need for an understanding of human information processing, particularly motivation, and ways this body of theory might aid in the formulation of campaign strategy
2. Use of behavioral objectives, or *management by objectives (MBO)*, in planning to ensure production of relevant messages and to establish criteria against which campaign results can be measured

A SYSTEMS MODEL FOR THIS BOOK

An integrative model that addresses and focuses the strengths and concerns of management, behavioral theorists, communication practitioners, and researchers is superior to lists of prescriptions. To that end, I have used the systems model shown in Exhibit 1.3 to organize this book. Note that the basic activities, in sequence, are problem analysis, segmentation and analysis of behaviors in the potential audience, validation research, specification of objectives, elaboration of message and media/channel strategies and plans, work planning, budgeting, and evaluation. Later, within the context of the systems model, this book describes methodologies, methods, and techniques you can use in the conceptualization and execution of each of the major activities; they are flexible in application and useful in dealing with many situations.

As the arrows and feedback loops in Exhibit 1.3 suggest, activities build on one another systematically. For example,

1. The initial problem analysis leads toward an audience segmentation scheme, which is then expanded in the next activity.
2. Appraisal of the behaviors and beliefs of individual audience segments suggests the need for empirical verification. The next activity explains how verification research should be implemented.
3. The behaviors and beliefs of specific target audiences, once verified, offer a rational basis for the management by objectives plan.
4. The MBO plan then provides the basis for elaboration of the message strategy and the evaluation strategy.
5. The initial problem analysis provides information about the client's plan or ability to finance the proposed campaign. That, in turn, provides the basis for development of the budget.
6. Conditions established in the problem analysis and in the media/channel analysis identify information needed to expand the work objectives and work plan.
7. Finally, the original problem analysis, the MBO section, the message plan, and the media/channel plan establish the essential elements for evaluating the campaign.

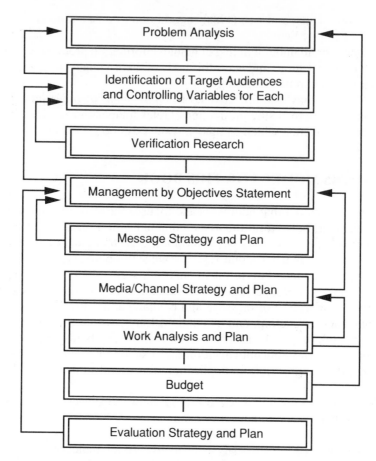

Exhibit 1.3. Communication Campaign Systems Model
Note: Arrows indicate information food and feedback.

Moreover, planning involves feedback loops like those in Exhibit 1.3. They make possible cross-checks that identify deviation from internal consistency—for example, where planned work does not correspond to objectives, such as message elements that do not relate to MBO.

With the systems approach, the management or planning of a campaign can prevent problems that would result from spontaneously generated plans. That is, it helps you to anticipate and avoid flaws in campaign plans, whereas other approaches often create problems that become obvious when it is too late to make corrections. In particular, feedback makes adaptation possible.

Since management systems also require you to record facts, key assumptions, and procedures, the written record helps reduce ambiguity to a minimum. Ambiguity leads to undesired variability in the execution of work; in turn, this almost inevitably produces unforeseen and often undesirable results. When you base work control on a systems model, you reduce uncertainty in work delegation and monitoring; you must state the plan and the underlying facts, assumptions, and strategies as well as the work tasks, the time allocated for each, and the planned end results. You can use this information to assign work and to evaluate it. These factors enhance job satisfaction because the persons who are assigned responsibilities know what they are to do, the deadlines, and the criteria by which they will be evaluated. This approach also makes it easy for you to provide unambiguous explanations to clients or upper-level managers about what must be done, when, and why.

Additionally, the systems approach requires evaluation of a campaign. In particular, statements of intended outcomes that make up MBO specify the observable or measurable criteria against which the campaign's results can be judged. Again, the systems approach helps you to anticipate and eliminate two other major sources of ambiguity: whether a campaign does its job satisfactorily and whether the results might be due to other causes. Moreover, feedback from evaluation research often can show you how to make your next campaign more efficient.

Some campaigns conduct evaluation research not only at the end of a project but also while work is in progress. This additional feedback may make possible mid-course corrections that enhance the success of your campaign.

SUMMARY

Communication activity—message creation, production, and delivery—constitutes only one part of an effective communication campaign. Campaigns' effects on overt behaviors tend to be small in any case, but intuitive planning, as opposed to structured planning, can diminish results even further. Attention to approaches that can improve results is important in both profit-making and nonprofit campaigns. Moreover, clients and upper-level managers are likely to appreciate or insist on a managerially oriented approach to campaigns, like that incorporated in strategic planning and the general systems model.

Strategic planning, which is based on a general systems model, reveals a much more complex array of factors that can affect the success of a campaign. Included are viewpoints from management, behavioral theory, communication practice, and research. As a manager or planner, you must understand how these perspectives are *integrated* as explanations about a campaign develop; strategic planning and a systems model are immeasurably helpful in this respect. In the execution of planning, they make possible not only step-by-step progress but also cross-checks to reassure you that all the content and activities are logically congruent. Another advantage is that feedback can be used to improve the next stage of work.

The chapters that follow demonstrate how strategic planning, the systems model, and related managerial subsystems like methodologies and techniques make the model work. We will begin with problem analysis.

REFERENCES

C. K. Atkin, "Mass Media Information Campaign Effectiveness," in R. E. Rice and W. J. Paisley (eds.), *Public Communication Campaigns* (Beverly Hills, CA: Sage, 1981).

R. A. Bauer, "The Obstinate Audience," in W. Schramm and D. F. Roberts (eds.), *The Process and Effects of Mass Communication* (Urbana: University of Illinois Press, 1971).

Ludwig von Bertalanffy, *General Systems Theory* (New York: Braziller, 1968).

Walter Buckley, *Sociology and Modern Systems Theory* (Englewood Cliffs, NJ: Prentice-Hall, 1967).

Walter Buckley, *Modern Systems Research for the Behavioral Scientist* (Chicago: Aldine, 1968).

Philip Kotler, "A Generic Concept of Marketing," *Journal of Marketing,* 36 (1972): 46–54.

W. J. Severin with J. W. Tankard, Jr., *Communication Theories,* 2nd ed. (White Plains, NY: Longman, 1988).

R. E. Simmons and G. Mujica, "Managerial and Behavioral Problems May Weaken Mass Media Educational Efforts in AIDS Epidemic," *Markeur* (Rotterdam), Fall 1987.

R. E. Simmons, C. L. Hills, and J.-S. Lee, "Behavioral and Managerial Models That Can Help Improve AIDS Campaign Planning," speech to the Health Communication Division, International Communication Assn., New Orleans, May 1988.

D. S. Solomon, "A Social Marketing Perspective on Campaigns," in R. E. Rice and W. J. Paisley (eds.), *Public Communication Campaigns* (Beverly Hills, CA: Sage, 1981).

CHAPTER 2

Conceptualizing
the Problem Analysis

At the outset of any campaign, there always is a perceived problem: A new product needs to be introduced to the public, or a school bond issue must be "sold" to the voters in a school district. The communication campaign is conceived and initiated to deal with the perceived problem. The first step in any campaign, then, is to define and analyze the problem with as much precision as possible.

To intelligently develop a managerial plan for a campaign—any campaign—you must utilize certain modes of thinking and techniques, or procedures. Understanding human information-processing behavior is also essential. This chapter will introduce aspects of management theory and procedures and basic communication behavior theory that you, as a manager or planner, will need to implement strategic planning.

SOME PRELIMINARY OBSERVATIONS

Identifying a problem is relatively simple. However, efficient analysis of a problem requires structure, or more precisely, system:

1. The collected information relating to the problem must be objective— that is, written and available for review at any time—and capable of empirical verification.
2. The research, analysis, and planning methodologies and techniques

and the specific procedures that are used must be standardized. Moreover, the techniques should be widely used in the management community to encourage confidence in the soundness of your overall management effort.

3. There must be a sequenced structure that makes possible both step-by-step elaboration of research, analysis, strategy, and plans and the use of feedback to cross-check and identify inconsistencies.

Even experienced managers and planners may find the analysis of complex cases bewildering at times. The difficulty stems in large part from the mass of information and the need for a way to organize it. Analysis is most difficult when there is extensive information that lacks order. Managers and planners who work intuitively, that is, without a system, are more likely to experience frustration about their inability to find the most important patterns in a large, complex array of information or distinguish the most critical interrelationships. A system also helps ensure that you will investigate relationships fully and articulate a carefully reasoned strategy; this is one of the crucial differences between campaign planning based on strategic planning or managerial systems and a "creative" approach.

Advantages of a Systems Model

A systems model enables you to accomplish the first steps in managerial planning by providing techniques that help you to

1. Reorganize large masses of information into simpler yet more meaningful categories
2. Differentiate important information and eliminate nonessential information
3. View problem-connected events, phenomena, and concepts in an *integrated* context that makes it easier to make sense of, or explain, what is occurring
4. Formulate strategy that can serve as the basis for plans and their implementation.

The approach also has an important long-range benefit. When problem analysis develops an explanation that is empirically testable (testable against real-life conditions), at least a fledgling theory about the problem emerges. Such a theory can be used to deal with not only the problem at hand but also other, similar problems in the future.

The quest for an adequate theory is perhaps even more important for a manager or planner than for the scholar or academician because of the fact that tangible outcomes are involved—money, jobs, and opportunity, to name a few. When theory functions well, it makes it possible to explain and manage any problem cost effectively and also to predict or forecast similar problems. As a manager or planner, you will discover that over time a knowledge of theory increases your efficiency.

Analysis of a problem is a process that leads you to explore, define, and redefine. You investigate and describe phenomena, then attempt to group and classify them; formal research and theory make this activity more effective. As the intellectual analysis progresses and is refined, the factors and relationships that underlie the problem—in this case, your campaign problem—tend to become clearer.

Although it is human to be impatient when seeking solutions, satisfactory or efficient ones emerge less often from such shortcuts as intuitive or trial-and-error approaches. You should resist the temptation to favor a "quick fix" because it pushes you toward oversimplification and bad decisions.

As you collect and analyze information, which often consists of assumptions and anecdotal reports, you should remind yourself constantly to be cautious. You must be careful not to equate assumptions—whether yours or those of your clients, upper-level managers, or colleagues—with facts. You must recognize, too, that anecdotal "evidence" (e.g., "I know someone who . . .") should be considered neither conclusive nor generalizable. A good rule is to insist on proof—preferably from two or more trustworthy sources—to substantiate assumptions or anecdotal reports.

DOCUMENTARY RESEARCH
AND EFFECTIVE MANAGEMENT

One behavior that quickly distinguishes an efficient professional in management or planning activities is the use of published information to learn about the variables or relationships in the problem under investigation. Reliance on less complete knowledge entails managerially unacceptable risks. A basic search through the literature in the field can help you avoid many potential pitfalls:

1. *Rediscovering the wheel*: Your problem might already have one or more solutions that are either workable or close enough conceptually to be adapted. There is no economy in reinventing what already is known.
2. *Already-disproved solutions*: The solution you are considering might have already been proved incorrect, unworkable, or unsatisfactory.
3. *Weaker alternatives*: The existing literature also might help you rule out some explanations or solutions that are relatively weak among the ideas you are considering.

The existing literature can help by providing you with heuristic—that is, idea-generating—inspiration, contributing to new views of the problem, and perhaps, new thoughts about how to solve it. Before we proceed to analysis, an understanding of the techniques of research is in order.

Information-Retrieval Technology

Although knowledge about how to use library card catalogs, indexes, and other resources is invaluable, what used to be a cumbersome process has been made substantially easier and more efficient by new ways of *computer information retrieval.*

Computerized systems offer highly efficient ways to search indexes, periodicals, archives, and library collections. Citations and abstracts pertaining to subject codes specified by the user can be located and scanned or printed quickly.

Information-retrieval services, such as those provided for a fee by MeadDataCentral (particularly Nexis and Medis), Dialog, and BRS Information Technologies, are widely available and widely used.[1] These services tend to be up to date since they tap into many sources, such as publications and wire services, who process their information with computers and then contract to permit transfer of information to retrieval services for access by other users. Some information-retrieval systems provide services internationally. These services, which are available to subscribers directly or through many urban and university research libraries, offer one of the most efficient means to date to gain access to periodical literature and documents.

Some information-retrieval services store text in a file format, including only descriptors, citation information, and abstracts. Because searching in such systems involves the use of the descriptors (content category terms), usually any search can be refined—to make it more cost effective and produce less irrelevant information—by using the connectors *and, or,* or *not.* Descriptors chained with *and* must all be present for a file to meet the search conditions. Descriptors chained with *or* permit substitutions; for example, "magazines or newspapers or television or radio or mass media" would retrieve any file that has any one of those five descriptors. Descriptors chained with *not* specify exclusion rules; for example, "television and violence and children not United States" would exclude files that relate to the United States. Output includes files matching the specified descriptors, citations for the related files, or both citations and abstracts. Moreover, additional connectors permit control over dates for searching, as before or after a specified date or between certain dates. Usually, results can be viewed on a computer video display terminal (VDT) or printed.

Other information-retrieval systems store entire documents and make

---

1 For more details, see *Online Access,* September/October 1987.

possible *full-text searching*. That is, *keywords* (essentially descriptors) can be searched through the entire text of each file—either throughout all sublibraries in a system, in one or more sublibraries, or in specified sources within sublibraries. The great advantage of full-text searching is that if relevant information is buried several paragraphs down within a document file, it still will be found. The disadvantage is that the approach is more costly because of the execution of computer algorithms that control the searching and matching of words within a file against the specified search descriptors. Descriptor chaining conventions beyond "and/or/not" enable you to customize the search more carefully. You can pick levels of display—for example, a list of documents matching the search criteria, partial display of the text, or display of the entire document. What is scanned on a monitor screen can be sent to a printer.

Many countries outside the United States also have national data and information banks or information-retrieval systems. Professional reference librarians in major libraries often can advise you about useful indexes, abstracts, information archives, data banks, and other information-retrieval systems.

Once you have completed a literature search, you can begin to use the information you have gathered. The managerial strategic planning framework for problem analysis is based on the following:

1. *"Real state/ideal state" analyses*: Information about the problem can be selected, structured, and crystallized through *"real state/ideal state" analyses*. This technique helps you to develop a history of what the client or organization has attempted to accomplish in the past (sometimes doing well or not so well), what goals the client or organization has now, and a general strategy to meet these goals.

2. *Audience segmentation*: *Segmentation* provides a process for the identification of those groupings, hereafter called *segments*, within a total audience that pose better opportunities for attaining the intended goals. Segmentation also supports effective media and channel selection.

3. *Behavioral analysis*: This theory-oriented exploration of psychological and sociological factors helps you identify the factors (or variables) that may determine how audience members respond to your campaign's messages. You may also gain insights about how you can *prevent* problems while still in the planning stage.

4. *Force field analysis*: This technique simplifies the inventory of variables that seem to control the behaviors in the important audience segment. Force field analysis helps you to eliminate extraneous variables and differentiate variables that appear to bring about change from those that produce resistance. It also enables you to assess which variables have the strongest effect on behavior. This analysis

technique provides insights about factors that must be addressed by either the message strategy or other interventions, and it helps you to formulate a strategy to motivate and bring about change.

REAL STATE/IDEAL STATE ANALYSES

As you begin developing real state/ideal state analyses, you are certain to discover you need a broader view of the problem and its context. Real state/ideal state analyses are part of a process that can be viewed as a form of needs assessment.

Function of the Two Analyses

At the outset, the client or organization has one or more goals that a campaign is supposed to address. Real state analysis is the beginning of a situational assessment. In effect, it asks, "What are the client's or organization's experiences with the problem, and what can we learn from them?" Real state analysis helps you to make a critical assessment of the history of the problem to aid in problem solving. This may include

1. Experiences of your client or upper-level managers regarding the problem, particularly what things worked or did not work; additional insights may be gained from reported experiences (e.g., research literature) of other organizations' campaigns concerning the same type of problem
2. Interviews with persons who are experts or authorities regarding the problem.
3. Interviews with persons who might be the target of the campaign

Ideal state analysis asks, "Where is the client or organization going, and what general strategy will move things in the desired direction?" It focuses on

1. Goals, the desired end products of the campaign
2. The audience segment that will be addressed, including an indication of what percentage of effort should be allocated to each segment if there is more than one
3. An assessment of factors controlling target audience behaviors affecting the problem—information and motivation as well as enabling factors such as availability, access, cost, and credit
4. The communication strategy—that is, recommendation of a unique and persuasive proposition about benefits, identification of a central theme for messages, and presentation of a concise overview of the mass media or other channels that should be used

5. The time frame for the campaign
6. Recommendations for financing—sometimes including creative solutions

Information Inventory

To make information collection efficient, structure is always better than no structure. And structure suggests the need for *early* thinking about questions that should be investigated.

You might want to consider the following 11 categories in developing the real state/ideal state analyses, although not every one will be addressed in every campaign.

- Global objectives
- History of the client or organization
- How the problem is linked to information
- Audience segmentation
- Factors that control audience segments' behavior
- Messages and appropriateness
- Competition
- Positioning
- Channel and mass media selection
- Budget
- Timing

Let us look at each of these more carefully:

Global Objectives. You must ascertain what it is, in specific terms, that the client or organization hopes to accomplish with the campaign. This information will give you both focus and a context for assessing other information about the problem.

History of the Client or Organization. Development of a brief history of the organization as it has attempted to deal with the problem is essential, as is information about the decision makers—especially if they have predilections about possible courses of action or have special areas of expertise that make them good resources.

How the Problem Is Linked to Information. Sometimes organizations or clients hope for changes that communication cannot produce. For the most part, communication can have impacts on specific classes of outcomes— *knowledge, affect* (feeling), *motivation* (as controlled by beliefs), and *practices*—that are called the *KAMP variables*. Later, they will be supplemented by *demographics* and *media*, two other variables that are instrumental in efficient message-delivery strategies.

Audience Segmentation. You must ascertain whether the client or organization has a clear-cut idea about what audiences are being sought. Do not be surprised if there are indications that your client or organization wants to communicate with "everyone out there." However, for greater effect, some segment of the total audience should be addressed instead. (Segmentation is discussed later in greater detail.)

Factors That Control Audience Segments' Behaviors. You usually will find it necessary to determine which of the KAMP variables or combinations of variables might be controlling the behaviors that are involved. A section on theory perspectives later in this chapter discusses information-processing behaviors that affect what people do.

Messages and Appropriateness. You should ascertain what message themes were used in past campaigns and try to determine whether they accomplished the desired results. Often, this analysis provides cues about the design of better messages and ways of explaining to the client or upper-level managers why your message strategy will avoid repetition of failures. You may find that previous messages are addressed to "everyone," a reason specific audience segments might tune out, or that the messages fail to "sell" the "product" (goods, services, or ideas) in relation to the particular needs or interests of specific audience segments. Also, you might find some messages fail because they are not understandable or persuasive, even though written by professionals.

Competition. Managers and planners in marketing communication and advertising are always concerned with what the competition is doing—for example, how much it is spending, where the expenditures are made, and what the message strategies are. They know their own companies or those of clients do not operate in a vacuum. However, in a broad sense, competition must be considered even by managers and planners in nonprofit organizations because other organizations or groups may compete for the same target audiences, for dominance in the field, or for the philanthropy of the same funding sources.

Furthermore, both profit-making and nonprofit organizations must consider that there may be competition from organized groups that have opposing agendas—for example, citizen action groups or lobbies. In some cases, these can present formidable obstacles to the successful conduct of a communication campaign.

Positioning. Especially in a competitive market, it is vital that you consider *positioning*, or the "offer" (Reeves, 1961; Ries & Trout, 1986). Positioning involves development of a distinctive proposition; better yet, it involves development of a unique proposition. Reeves introduced the concept of a *unique selling proposition* (USP) as an indispensable component of adver-tisements, but USP also can be beneficial in messages for nonprofit groups; too many communicators are competing with the same cry: "Look at us!"

Relating your messages to the motivational interests of any target audi-ence segment can help you isolate some feature, claim, or assertion that you can use in positioning. In turn, that approach may capture the interest of those persons who make up the segment. Another approach is to investigate the benefits that *only* your organization, product, or service can offer. The best positioning strategy is one that is relevant, compelling, and unique. Good positioning improves the chances that members of any desired au-dience segment will expose themselves to the message, attend to the con-tent, and act.

Mass Media and Channel Selection. Frequently, campaigns will fail or be weakened because the mass media or other channels did not reach the intended audience. Perhaps the cost was too high in that a particular medium or channel reached a much larger number of persons who were *not* important to the campaign, while reaching only a relatively small number of those in the targeted audience segment or segments.

The most typical failing is a "shotgun" approach to exposure: The assumption is that if a message is everywhere, any audience segment is bound to be "hit." This premise is doubtful, and often costly as well.

You should address several basic questions here: What are the target audiences and what media or channels have been *proven* to reach them? Is there a minimal spillover to audience segments that are not of interest? You also should reflect on whether the media or channels that were used were appropriate to the messages in terms of credibility, timeliness, availability, accessibility, or relative permanence.

Budget. Two aspects of *budgeting* merit early examination: what your client or organization has been willing to spend on similar campaigns in the past and what is allocated for the current campaign. You might find that the scope of the campaign plan determines the budget; in other cases, the reverse may be the case. You also may find that in competitive situations you must consider what the opposition is spending. More information about how organizations set budgets is presented in Chapter 9.

If the available funds are insufficient, you should investigate whether less important activities of the communication program could be modified or eliminated to free the resources required to mount an effective new cam-paign, or you might look for previously unexplored ways to develop revenues.

Timing. Inappropriate timing in the presentation of a campaign or project or an insufficient period of activity often hampers efforts to deal with the problem. Some human activities are cyclical, and a campaign that addresses the problem at the wrong time can be doomed.

Additionally, some campaigns simply do not last long enough to accomplish the desired results: Some managers or planners believe a brief, intensive period of activity works like a hypodermic needle—the injection of information into a population bringing a rapid effect. However, research shows that instead, impact builds over time, like a slowly rising learning curve.

Also, you should examine the proposed time frame for implementation of the campaign since it may restrict the time available for planning, execution, and exposure.

Format for Ideal and Real State Analyses

Once the information collection is completed, you must synthesize *in writing* the most important findings of the real state analysis and the ideal state analysis. The two should be formulated separately, to help sort out the information.

If at the outset your information—especially in the ideal state analysis— is fairly thorough but not absolutely complete, you should not worry too much. The first versions are tentative, serving mainly to help you organize your ideas. Research feedback and time for reflection will supply new facts and ideas to help refine both the real state and ideal state analyses. Often, the 11 information inventory categories provide sufficient structure to help you sort and group information as you begin to work on synthesis.

The writing should be terse. You should not get bogged down in extraneous information or extensive articulation of detail. Concentrate on the *essence* of each observation. If you cannot write either a real state or an ideal state analysis in two or three typed and single-spaced pages, you probably should consider weeding out information, writing more concisely, or both.

Consider adopting the following general rules for documents that will make up the campaign plan:

- Begin each section on a new page, with a heading.
- Type the text single-spaced.
- Write in a terse, bulletin style, with each new item introduced on a new line and emphasized by a bold square or circle.

If a reader requires more than three minutes to grasp the *main* points— that is, to get an accurate overview—in a particular section, it should be edited or rewritten.

AUDIENCE SEGMENTATION

Audience segmentation is one of the most important concepts in making modern communication campaigns efficient. This strategy recognizes that any total audience is usually made up of subgroups, or segments; in most cases it is neither useful nor economically productive to address campaign messages to all persons in a population.

The important segments must be defined in a way that helps identify them and the means through which each can be reached. Usually, this process involves

1. Identifying the audience segment that will offer the best potential in relation to your problem
2. Ascertaining how each segment can be described in terms of attributes that will help you specify the appropriate mass media or other channels to use

The audience segmentation strategy should be incorporated as part of the ideal state document. Here are factors you should consider:

Identify Segments Concerned with the Issue

Behavioral literature on selective exposure suggests that unless individuals perceive that information offers some utility or gratification, they are likely to ignore the communication (Davison, Boylan, & Yu, 1976). Bauer (1971) compares the situation to a transaction: Your success in transmitting information to other persons depends on knowledge of an audience and its wants; if you do not learn what a targeted audience expects in exchange for its attention to a message and then do not provide it, successful communication is unlikely.

Differentiate Segments in Terms of Impact

Since campaign resources must be used economically, you must determine which segment or segments will merit your principal attention. Try to differentiate individuals or groups in terms of their impact on your problem. For example, persons who make up segments could be differentiated as

1. The end users of the information
2. Persons who make the decisions
3. Persons who demonstrate extensive involvement: For example, if you are dealing with a community development project, you would consider persons who are activitists and organizers. In marketing,

you might consider heavy users. Often a relatively small segment accounts for most of the activity. Pareto's economic principle says that 80 percent of a company's business is attributable to 20 percent of the customers. This principle also seems to apply to other situations, for example, a research organization in which 80 percent of the manuscript production can be traced to about 20 percent of the staff.

4. Opinion leaders (individuals who retransmit information and possibly influence others) or gatekeepers (individuals who select or filter information and then retransmit it) (Severin, with Tankard, 1988, p. 197)
5. Persons who serve as role models or who otherwise influence others through social pressure
6. Persons to whom others refer for risk analysis perspectives, that is, those individuals who are consulted about decisions that involve success, failure, or risks—for example, buying a car, implementing a new practice in business or in farming, or trying a new health practice

Consider the Possibility of More Than One Segment

In some cases, two or more segments might be instrumental in resolving the problem. In some cases two or more potential audience segments form an integrated system in themselves. Remember, such a system, in the terms of the general systems theory (Buckley, 1967), would be made up of units—people, groups, or organizations—that are functionally interrelated in regard to specified goals or activities.

For example, a problem may involve (1) a city's public housing authority, (2) landlords, and (3) renters. Suppose each interacts with each of the other two units or entities, affecting, say, policy formulation. If all three segments are instrumental in resolving the problem, addressing only one would be futile.

Use Demographics to Define Segments

Audience segments are defined in terms of *demographics* (census categories) —for example, income, education, age, gender, race, site of residence, or occupation—that correlate with particular behaviors or *life-styles*. Because mass media report the demographic groups they reach, you need demographic information about *your* desired audience segments to cross-check against *media* audience profiles to find which media reach the audience segments you have targeted, and which do it most effectively.

If you know, for example, that the desired audience segment is female and between the ages of 26 and 35, analysis of mass media audience data is likely to reveal the media, or some program within a medium, that will reach the specified segment. Major mass media either commission and publish their own audience studies or purchase audience, circulation, and advertising research that is conducted and published by national firms such as Simmons Market Research Bureau, A. C. Nielsen Co., Arbitron Ratings Co. (ARB), Birch Radio, Verified Audit Circulation (VAC), and Mediamark Research, Inc. (MRI); additional information about advertising activity is provided by Leading National Advertisers (LNA), Broadcast Advertising Reports (BAR), Radio Expenditure Reports (RER), and Media Records (Wimmer & Dominick, 1987, pp. 306–340, 360–361).

Put Boundaries on Demographic Descriptors

The descriptors must be made as specific as possible by incorporating *boundaries*. It is not sufficient simply to specify "older people" because that is both imprecise and subjective; for example, to a 25-year-old planner, 40 years of age may be "older"; to a 40-year-old planner, 70 years of age may be "older." An age descriptor must be specified within clearly stated age boundaries, for example, "65 years of age or older."

Similarly, "affluent" is not a sufficient descriptor regarding income. It must be revised to specify what is meant by affluence—for example, an annual household income of $70,000 or more.

Specific descriptors are imperative because they enable cross-references to published mass media demographics to select those media that will reach each designated audience segment. Also, they enable cross-reference to publications of the U.S. Bureau of the Census, such as *Standard Metropolitan Statistical Area (SMSA)* reports. With a carefully defined set of demographic descriptors, you can enter reports and find census areas or tracts where persons with such characteristics reside. You can even match the descriptors to U.S. ZIP codes to facilitate mailings.

Examine the Need for Multiple Descriptors

More often than not, you will find that two or more demographic descriptors are necessary to describe a target audience.

Consider Life-Style and Psychographics Segmentation

Sometimes, audience segments might be defined in terms of behavioral patterns. *Life-style* characterizes predictable, overt behavioral patterns; *psychographics* is a term that describes predictable, psychological patterns, similar to what is found in personality research. A manager or planner who wishes to reach life-style or psychographic segments faces considerable problems because media audience statistics rarely are categorized by either variable. To be workable in media/channel planning, such analysis almost always requires the original collection of data in the proposed segments about demographics as well as either life-style or psychographics. Then, the behavioral variable can be correlated with demographic variables. Finally, the descriptors that produce statistically significant correlations can be cross-referenced to media reports or other documents to find the communication channels that are likely to reach the targeted segment.

Give Operational Definitions

You can describe an audience segment in terms that enable you to locate the individuals who make up the segment. For example, in a community campaign, one segment might be "opinion leaders." If you explain what constitutes an opinion leader—a process called *operational definition*—it is possible to locate those individuals, for example, "Individuals in the target area who have been mentioned by 20 persons or more in the community survey as being sought out for information or advice."

Specify Percentage of Effort for Each Segment

You must consider how much effort to direct to each audience segment when more than one is involved.

If only one segment is to be addressed, 100 percent of the campaign resources—media reach and frequency or budget—could be directed toward that segment. However, if two or more segments are targeted, some decision about the division of effort is required. For example, if there are two target segments, one of which originates 70 percent of a product's purchases and the other 30 percent, the media effort usually is apportioned similarly—70/30. This is important, in part, because resources are always finite and you usually cannot apportion equal effort to all target segments. Moreover, some segments are more prone to change or more important in the resolution of the problem. In such a case, you should place more effort where the payoff is likely to be the greatest.

Verify the Segmentation Strategy

Your strategy must be considered tentative until you obtain evidence through verification research to (1) confirm the choice of the segment or segments and (2) specify the percentage of effort that would be directed to each one.

Find How to Reach Targeted Segments

Chapter 7 will discuss the use of the segmentation plan to identify the channels that will reach the specified segments with the greatest efficiency and lowest cost. When a medium delivers a large audience but at the same time the desired segment is only a small proportion of the total, that medium would be an inefficient choice—particularly if another medium's audiences were found to deliver a larger proportion of the desired segment.

BEHAVIORAL ANALYSIS

Behavioral theory can help you better understand information processing, which is one of the main elements of problem analysis. The subsections that follow review aspects of communication theory that are especially useful for a manager or planner. I will demonstrate in later chapters how these are relevant to various parts of planning a campaign.

Cognitive Process: An Introduction

Cognitive process, the study of human information processing, deals with factors related to thinking—mainly information exposure and attention or perception, memory, analysis, and action orientation—that are antecedents to action (for seminal works, see Miller, 1967; Miller, Gallanter, & Pilbram, 1960; Bruner, Goodnow, & Austin, 1962; Schroder, Driver, & Streufert, 1967).

People develop *cognitive structures* both to organize the information they have acquired and to enable thinking. Cognitive structures usually are visualized in the form of diagrams that list concepts and illustrate their relationships and hierarchies (see Exhibit 2.1).

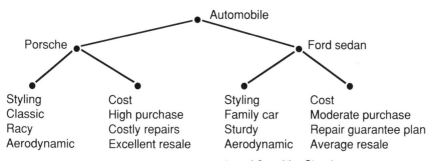

Porsche		Ford sedan	
Styling	Cost	Styling	Cost
Classic	High purchase	Family car	Moderate purchase
Racy	Costly repairs	Sturdy	Repair guarantee plan
Aerodynamic	Excellent resale	Aerodynamic	Average resale

EXHIBIT 2.1. Graphic Representation of Cognitive Structures

In effect, cognitive structures are a way of explaining how individuals organize information in order to evaluate stimuli (information and phenomena that they encounter), distinguish attributes that classify the information or phenomena (like the cost and styling attributes in Exhibit 2.1), and then integrate the information to improve future thinking or determine an appropriate response (Bruner, Goodnow, & Austin, 1962).

Individuals' thinking may be characterized by both *cognitive complexity* (how *much* information they have stored in cognitive structures) and *cognitive integration* (how well prepared they are to link information they already

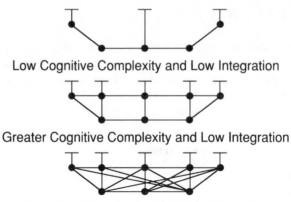

Low Cognitive Complexity and Low Integration

Greater Cognitive Complexity and Low Integration

Cognitive Complexity and High Integration

● = cognitive structures
connecting lines represent integration linkages

EXHIBIT 2.2. Cognition and Integration
Source: H. M. Schroder, M. J. Driver, and S. Steufert, *Human Information Processing.*
Copyright © 1967 by Holt, Rinehart and Winston. Reprinted by permission of Holt, Rinehart and Winston.

possess in order to evaluate new information or phenomena) (Schroder, Driver, & Streufert, 1967). See Exhibit 2.2.

Suppose that Exhibit 2.2 represents the knowledge of three individuals about a particular topic. The person represented in the first diagram has fewer cognitive structures than the second. You could say that the first individual knows less about the topic, which would affect interest in and interpretation of its aspects; messages would have to be planned to deal with that problem.

The difference between the persons represented in the second and third diagrams in Exhibit 2.2 is that whereas the number of cognitive structures is equal, the third person is better prepared to fit things together in different ways than the second; integrational linkages enable that person to discover more perspectives regarding relevance. This not only supports a more powerful thinking style but also increases the likelihood that more stimuli will be seen as relevant.

Learning Curve. Piaget (1967, pp. 143–162), a major cognitive theorist, characterized learning in cognitive and system terms, for example, system, development of structures, integration, and strategies. The very process implies that exposure to stimuli does not necessarily produce great results in the short run.

Evidence of this fact is found when learning over time is graphed (see Exhibit 2.3). The *S learning curve* is typical, although not universal; it shows

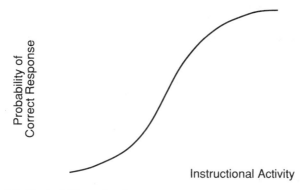

EXHIBIT 2.3. Typical *S* Learning Curve

Source: From *Learning: A Survey of Psychological Interpretations* by W. F. Hill. Copyright © 1985 by Harper & Row. Reprinted by permission of Harper & Row, Publishers, Inc.

that learning begins slowly, then for a time has a rather rapid gain, and in the last phase begins to diminish. The learning curve is duplicated in other learning-related fields, such as marketing and diffusion (for example, see Rogers with Shoemaker, 1971).

Experience with campaigns indicates that managers and planners usually must be satisfied with a maximum impact considerably less than 100 percent unless extensive message repetition over a long period of time can be afforded.

Cognitive Problem Solving. The concept of *cognitive plan* was introduced by Miller (1956, 1967) in relation to memory but was reintroduced in a larger context by Miller, Gallanter, and Pilbram (1960). As used by these authors, a plan is equivalent to a cognitive structure that provides a *process* for coping with stimuli—for example, storing information in memory and then retrieving it—or solving other problems. Miller's theory regarding memory is discussed later, but Miller, Gallanter, and Pilbram's illustration of a minimal problem-solving plan, which they called the TOTE unit, will be explained here (see Exhibit 2.4).

TOTE is an acronym for test-operation-test-exit. The paradigm indicates that an individual who is confronted with a stimulus (which, you will recall, means information or phenomena) tests initially to determine what attributes are involved. If that test indicates that a problem must be solved, the individual then selects and performs an operation to solve the perceived problem. Once that operation has been completed, the individual tests again to ascertain whether the operation solved the problem. If it did, the individual exits from the plan; if not, the individual reenters the loop to implement another operation. This procedure continues until a test criterion indicates that the problem has been solved; then the individual exits from the plan. The disso-

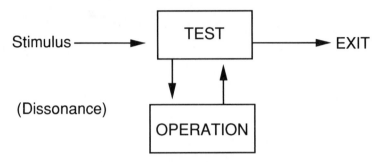

Exhibit 2.4. The Miller, Galanter, and Pilbram TOTE Unit
Source: G. A. Miller, E. Galanter, and K. Pilbram, *Plans and the Structure of Behavior.*
Copyright © 1969 by Holt, Rinehart and Winston. Reprinted by permission of G. A. Miller.

nance term in the TOTE unit indicates a situation in which an acceptable solution has not been attained.

The TOTE unit illustrates a specific cognitive structure that contains at least one general *procedure* for coping.

I find the TOTE unit suggests other related cognitive secondary plans that *must* exist to implement the overall plan, which I call a *procedure plan.* At least two other related families of cognitive structures are implicit in the TOTE unit; they are necessary to make such a procedural plan as the TOTE unit work: (1) a *test criteria plan* for particular classes of problems and (2) a *problem-solving activities plan* (see Exhibit 2.5).

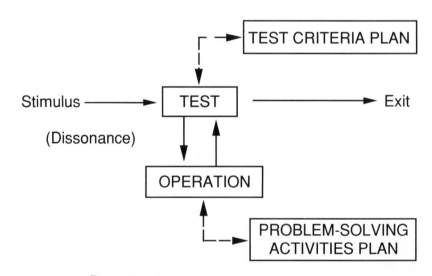

Exhibit 2.5. Modified TOTE Unit with Secondary Plans

A test criteria plan has two functions. First, it makes possible the initial assessment of new incoming stimuli—for example, whether a problem exists, what kind of problem it is, whether it needs to be solved, and what type of operation might solve it. Second, in cases in which some corrective activity is necessary, the test criteria plan provides criteria to help evaluate the result. The problem-solving activity plan offers an array of activities from which one or more might be selected.

The existence of test criteria plans is substantiated, for example, by what are essentially decisional criteria in the Rogers with Shoemaker (1971, p. 102) paradigm of the innovation-decision process. These criteria are relative advantage, compatibility, complexity, trialability, and observability.

Similarly, research findings concerning the critical dimensions of *source credibility* (Atkin, 1981, p. 275)—trustworthiness, expertise/competence, and dynamism/attractiveness—suggest other test criteria plans for the evaluation of communicators.

Work by Horn and Waingrow (1966) on a model of behavioral change in smoking suggests categories of test criteria plans for judging health risks: whether a threat exists, whether it is important enough to merit action, whether a personal risk is involved, and whether the individual can do anything to block it.

Furthermore, in the value-expectancy theory of motivation (Rotter, 1966, 1974; Weiner, 1980) and in Rokeach's (1972) conceptualization of the functions of values on behavior, the "instrumentality" concept is linked to evaluation of courses of action. Motivation theory is discussed in detail later.

Problem-solving activity plans relevant to communication campaigns are offered by a number of works: The *AIDA* (arousal, interest, desire, and action) persuasive copywriting formula is one example. The final *A* is designed to remind a writer to inform the reader, viewer, or listener what actions (or activities) are appropriate as a result of the conviction developed in the three earlier steps.

Kahneman's (1973) *capacity model of attention* indicates that when an individual confronts a stimulus that demands more than available attention capacity, and when arousal is great enough, the person will select appropriate "activities" to deal with the deficit. Kahneman's model implies that the individual probably has several problem-solving activity plans to address particular situations.

Fishbein and Ajzen (1975) use the term *intention* to describe what clearly seems to be problem-solving activity plans; their term is used to categorize specific actions that an individual has selected to implement a particular behavior within a specified time frame.

Similarly, McGuire (1980) concludes that many people do not implement improved health practices because they do not know what to do. The AIDA formula evolved from research findings on propaganda showing that even when persons apparently are convinced about the importance of an issue, they might not act because they do not know what actions are appropriate.

What does all this mean to you, as a manager or planner? Whether members of an audience segment act on the problem your campaign addresses depends on whether they have adequate or viable information about

1. Ways to assess whether a problem exists
2. Personal ability to solve the problem with some operation
3. Situation-appropriate problem-solving activities—that is, "how to solve it" steps
4. Ways to determine if a particular outcome is adequate.

The second category is often a problem when fatalism is involved or when individuals believe they do not have control over events in their lives, as in Rotter's (1966) discussion of externality in his locus of control personality theory. If deficiencies in procedure plans, test criteria plans, or test activity plans are detected, supplementary information might be vital to ensure the campaign's success.

Affect. Yet another class of cognitive structure concerns *affect*, which relates to feeling or emotion, either positive or negative, evoked by persons, phenomena, and information. The affect construct reminds us that information processing is not based entirely on rationality. Edelman (1964) uses the term *condensation symbols*, conceptually similar to affect symbols, to describe political communications that evoke strong feelings—like "commie" or "scab."

Affect is used extensively in communications, particularly advertising (sexually attractive models, cute children, and beautiful scenes) and political communication (former President Ronald Reagan is a notable example—strong, folksy, and warm).

Aversive messages such as appeals to fear are clearly based on affect. This particular cognitive structure produces less than predictable results when addressed to a general population; actually, negative messages that are not fear oriented and that offer solutions may be more effective (Fishbein & Ajzen, 1975, pp. 497–508). One plausible explanation is that individuals differ in their threshold tolerance levels for psychological discomfort; stimuli that exceed the individual's threshold would be enough to induce avoidance or flight. This may be explained in terms of cognitive plans that differ across individuals in regard to the testing of the affective meaning of particular fear stimuli, and identification of appropriate activities to guide overt behavior.

Memory. Vital to cognitive process, *memory* is necessary for individuals to keep new informational inputs in mind long enough to begin processing them. *Short-term memory* provides temporary storage while an individual cross-references attributes to existing cognitive structures.

If the new inputs are to be made relatively permanent, they must be incorporated in *long-term memory*, which in essence is equivalent to embedding the information in relevant cognitive structures to make remembering and future access possible.

Miller (1957) theorizes that after a brief exposure, people can remember an average of seven things (for which he uses the computer term *bits*), although some people will remember as few as five and others will remember as many as nine; he refers to this phenomenon as "the magical number seven, plus or minus two." To remember more information, Miller says, people group information (a process he calls *chunking*) into progressively larger units (which he calls *chunks* and *superchunks*). Additionally, Miller explains that to store and retrieve information, humans develop *memory plans* (see Lorayne & Lucas, 1974).

Plans, as explained, can be viewed as a specialized type of cognitive structure dealing with process, test criteria, and problem-solving activity. One plan for short-term memory is simple repetition, also called rehearsal; for example, you might repeat a phone number to hold it in memory until you can dial. Advertisements are also based on cognitive plans; individual facts and arguments are "chunked" under a slogan, and the slogan then becomes an activity plan to retrieve the information about an advertised product from memory. Lorayne and Lucas (1974) discuss various types of memory plans that might help to improve memory and recall.

Memory storage can take either *semantic* or *visual* (i.e., iconic) forms (Baddeley, 1976). Visual aspects of messages require careful consideration. Television reporter Lesley Stahl (1989) relates an experience that suggests the power of visual memory: The Reagan administration proposed cuts in funding for programs affecting both handicapped children and the elderly. At the time these proposals were reported in the media, President Reagan's advisors staged two "photo opportunities" in which he presented an award at a competition for handicapped youths and also was videotaped visiting a facility for the elderly. A TV program that reported the contradictions between policy actions and the photo opportunities was submitted to focus group analysis, that is, intensive interviews with small groups (a methodology discussed in Chapter 3); results indicated that Reagan was perceived as "pro" handicapped children and the elderly despite the oral content about the funding cuts.

This example also might be a testimonial to the strong affect attached to Reagan, which Stahl (1989) says was maintained by aides' careful orchestration of the content and symbolism of his public appearances.

Selectivity. People do not process all the information they encounter. This phenomenon is called *selectivity*, and it has been related to perception or exposure and attention processes as well as to memory. It has been suggested that individuals might tend to avoid information systematically when it conflicts with their attitudes, although education might predispose them to be more inclusive in seeking information (Freedman & Sears, 1965). *Uses and gratifications theory* suggests that individuals' beliefs that information or phenomena provide either utility or gratification may control selectivity (see Davison, Boylan, & Yu, 1976, pp. 131–158).

Cognitive structures and plans offer an explanation of selectivity by providing cues (test criteria plans) about beneficial or rewarding inputs. Exposure and attention to new information also is related to cognitive integration, which reveals linkages between cognitive structures or components within structures and suggests more relevant aspects. Exposure to and learning of new content may occur more readily when an individual recognizes or is led to consider that the content is "relevant"; that is, cognitive structures prove that the new content can be assimilated to stored information or linked to notions about what will produce rewards that an individual considers important. Connectionist theories of learning seem to support this position (Hill, 1963).

Other theories deal with cognitive behaviors that are relevant to selectivity:

1. Kahneman (1973) introduced *mental effort* as a cognitively based explanation of individuals' coping processes when exposed to complex stimuli, and he offered new insights on both selectivity and attention. In this theory, at any moment, an individual makes available a particular level of information-processing *capacity*, which is conceptually similar to energy. Incoming stimuli constitute a *demand* on capacity. If the *supplied capacity* exceeds or matches demand, there is no particular problem. However, if capacity is less than the demand of the information-processing task, coping behaviors occur. If the stimulus provides sufficient *arousal*, additional effort from *spare capacity* will be allocated. However if the stimulus does not create sufficient arousal, information processing is likely to be terminated—which may be an alternative explanation for selectivity. In Kahneman's theory, additional capacity allocation requires the utilization of *activities*, conceptually similar to cognitive plans, designed to deal with the processing task.

2. *Discount* is a cognitive process (Mortensen, 1972, pp. 137–138) that may be viewed as a form of selectivity. When an individual encounters information and thinks, "This cannot be true," "This cannot be *entirely* true," or "This is surely exaggerated," discount is involved; in essence, it appears to be a cognitive test criteria plan. Since cognitive structures such as plans provide an experiential context for evaluation, they can explain the decisional process not to take a situation, fact, proposition, or argument at face value. Note: Discount does not imply that an individual's assessment is correct; this may be one of the most crucial problems a manager or planner must address. For

example, in research on health behaviors, individuals frequently make seriously flawed or even fatal decisions—as in the case of the AIDS epidemic—based on their cognitions. A teenager might think, ''People like me are not at risk,'' despite the fact the person has encountered news reports that his or her age group is in a high-risk category.

3. *Knowledge gap* hypothesis deals with the proposition that some individuals predictably learn less than others although the same information is available to everyone through the mass media (Tichenor, Donohue, & Olien, 1970). If access to media is a given, what factors influence the effectiveness of information processing? The literature provides two: The individual may lack information-processing skills because of a lack of education, or the information may fail to demonstrate sufficient utility or other potential gratification to create arousal. Audience members' cognitive complexity and cognitive integration also may explain the knowledge gap; stimuli may not create arousal because there are no cognitive structures with relevant subordinate concepts and attributes to ''give meaning'' to the stimuli. For the same reason, even if arousal occurs, memory and learning may be impeded. Research supports the proposition that persons with low cognitive complexity and low cognitive integration—both identified by a measure of dogmatism—gain less from mass media content (Simmons & Garda, 1982).

Belief and Belief Structures.   Two more constructs regarded as essentially the same as cognitive structures are *belief* and *belief structures* (Rokeach, 1972; Fishbein & Ajzen, 1975); they also contribute to the analysis of complex communication behaviors, especially interpretive processes and motivation.

Fishbein and Ajzen (1975) define beliefs as subjective (intrapersonal) probability estimates about outcomes. Of great importance to communicators is the contention that individuals' beliefs are formed and modified through the intake and processing of information from *sources* (other people, mass media of communication, or other institutions) or from direct *experience* or observation; additional beliefs are *derived*—that is, generalized from existing beliefs, such as source and experiential beliefs.

Works providing perspectives on the applications of beliefs include the following:

1. A major model developed by Fishbein and Ajzen (1975) that deals with communication and behavior is based largely in beliefs. This work is discussed in more detail later.
2. In the health field, Hochbaum (1956, 1965) theorizes that behavior modification in response to health communication depends on four sets of beliefs: belief in susceptibility, belief in the severity of outcome, belief that

recommendations will lead to a desired outcome, and belief that someone can have a disease or problem and not know it. Moreover, Rodenstock (1966, 1969, 1974) initiated work on what is now known as the health belief model, and McGuire (1980) called attention to the importance of beliefs and expectancy theory to behavioral medicine, public health, and communication theories.

3. Beliefs also are instrumental to the explanation of modern motivational theory, particularly value-expectancy theory, as you will see. They yield influence over the individual.

4. Simmons, Hills, and Lee (1988) view humans as behavioral systems in which *rules* (a concept also used in a social interaction context by others, such as Shimanoff, 1981) govern an individual's behavior. They also view beliefs as being organized into cognitive structures, many of which establish rules essential to human functioning, regarding information seeking, exposure, and attention; information holding; information processes; motivational processes; preparation to perform overt behaviors; and behavior change. In particular, Simmons, Hills, and Lee contend that people's *belief rules* help them deal with

    a. The individual's knowledge about his or her world
    b. What attributes classify what phenomena—including ones that differentiate phenomena
    c. What things are called
    d. How things are related
    e. Assumptions about causality
    f. What things are "true" or not
    g. What things are important in one's own life (as opposed to important in a general sense)
    h. How things are accomplished or attained
    i. Whether one has personal control over, or personal responsibility for, his or her behaviors
    j. What information sources are useful and credible
    k. What factors external to the individual pose real limits or opportunities for behaviors the individual might pursue.

5. Rokeach (1972) conceptualizes beliefs, themselves, as being organized into systems, and he differentiates *belief and disbelief systems—* essentially cognitive structures, in my view. The ways in which an individual responds to information—drawing partly, mainly, or exclusively on beliefs, perhaps to the exclusion of disbeliefs—is something Rokeach has also investigated. He contends that a trait of dogmatism is the relative partitioning of belief and disbelief systems, the latter being discounted or ignored.

The Fishbein and Ajzen Model. Fishbein and Ajzen (1975) present a model that also makes extensive use of beliefs to explain behavior (see Exhibit 2.6).

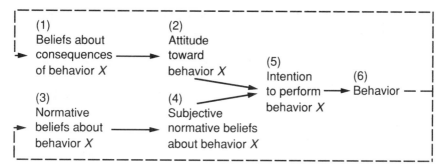

EXHIBIT 2.6. Fishbein and Ajzen Model
Source: Martin Fishbein and Icek Ajzen, *Belief, Attitude, Intention and Behavior* (Reading, MA: Addison-Wesley, 1975). Reprinted by permission.

Case Study. Suppose an individual unexpectedly inherits enough money to buy a Porsche—an automobile she has admired for years. In step 1, she would review her beliefs about the *consequences* that a purchase with the inherited money would imply—satisfaction, status, high insurance costs, possibilities of theft, etc. Her analysis of pros and cons would lead to step 2, attitude formation, which is a summative evaluational *assessment*; for example, is the considered purchase "good" or "bad"? Concurrently, she may be monitoring her social environment to observe other automobile owners, especially Porsche owners; her observations might be that Porsche owners appear to be higher-status individuals, Porsche drivers seem to have great fun, and many people express admiration for the car but that few persons who appear to be in her social group own Porsches. Moreover, she may get feedback from her parents and friends implying that buying a Porsche would seem "pretentious" or "snobbish." Her surveillance of norms contributes to step 4, which involves her decision about what is an appropriate personal *norm* for her own behavior in this case. If the attitudinal assessment is favorable and the subjective normative assessment is favorable, these factors would indicate whether she would move to step 5, which deals with intention, or specific plans for implementing the behavior. In this case, intention might involve knowledge about what to do next to claim the inheritance, shop for the car, close the deal, buy insurance, register the Porsche, and get the license. (McGuire, 1980, says that overt behaviors often do not occur because individuals simply do not know what action could be taken in a particular situation.) If intention is clear and explicit, she may move to step 6, the behavior, and buy the car. The behavior, itself, probably will have consequences that create feedback (the broken line in the figure) to reinforce or correct her belief system regarding automobile purchases.

The model suggests that a manager or planner who attempts to analyze behaviors in a target audience segment needs to examine how the members view these factors:

- Beliefs about the benefits and risks of a behavior that is being considered
- An attitude (a summation of beliefs) about whether the proposed behavior is "good" (acceptable)
- Beliefs about how other people view the behavior, essentially, an additional way of getting input about risks and benefits, in this case as perceived by others
- Beliefs about whether audience members consider the behavior appropriate in their own situation
- Beliefs about clear and reasonably feasible steps that will be taken in the foreseeable future to implement the behavior.

Motivation. Audience segments differ in regard to the variables that motivate their behaviors. These differences can be related to cognitive structures, and *motivation* can be viewed as another cognitive plan for coping.

Various major writers such as Sigmund Freud, Clark Hull, Kurt Lewin, John Atkinson, David McClelland, and Julian Rotter have contributed to the body of motivational theory that attempts to explain how, why, and under what conditions people deviate from a homeostatic (comfortable or steady) psychological state and react to stimuli they encounter in their environments (see Weiner, 1980).

It is not the introduction of a *stimulus*—a communication, for example—that *causes* motivation. A stimulus is only as significant as the individual makes it—which is where cognitive structures are involved since they organize the information, experience, and affect that assign significance.

Almost everyone in modern society has some motivation-related notions based on Freud's work, such as that individuals act from internal motivating states like *libido* (sexual), *id* (childlike, compulsive, and hedonistic), *ego* (mature, rational, and willing to delay gratification) and *superego* (authoritative and judgmental).

Furthermore, Maslow's (1954) *hierarchy of needs* suggests that individuals are motivated by stimuli in their environment that relate to internal need states, which are, beginning with the most basic, physiological (survival), safety, social affiliation, social recognition (ego gratification), and self-actualization (aesthetic or self-fulfillment). Whether an individual will respond to stimuli directed to any particular needs theoretically depends mainly on the need category from which the individual is operating currently and whether lower-level needs have been satisfied.

Lewin (1938) theorized that individuals engage in *purposive behavior* to attain goals. That is, individuals attach particular *valences*, indicators of the strength of desirability, to goals (Cartwright, 1951). However, Lewin also theorized that a goal that has a relatively strong valence will motivate an individual to attempt to attain it only if the person's *lifespace*, a personal base of experience and information, indicates that the goal is attainable. Lifespace can be related conceptually to an individual's beliefs about (1) the importance of goals and (2) whether the goals are attainable.

The *value-expectancy theory* of motivation, based largely on theoretical work by Rotter (1966, 1974), conceptually parallels Lewin's work with *lifespace* and *field theory* (Lewin, 1938; Cartwright, 1951). It can be expressed as a formula:

$$\text{Expectancy} = \text{Valence} \times \text{Instrumentality}$$

Expectancy is equivalent to drive force and is based on an individual's subjective (intrapersonal) probability estimates that a *valenced outcome* (desired outcome or reward) exists in a particular situation and that some behavior has *instrumentality* in leading to its attainment. In this context, belief is a term that can be substituted for subjectively estimated probability (Fishbein & Ajzen, 1975). Instrumentality deals with the individual's beliefs, too, in terms of judging whether particular behaviors lead to desired outcomes.

I regard value-expectancy theory as a major cognitive structure process plan, as already discussed; as such, it is more complex than the TOTE unit. Also, I infer that test criteria plans support evaluation of both valence and instrumentality. Furthermore, whether expectancy leads to action seems to depend on the individual's store of problem-solving activity plans.

Upper-level managers who are trained in statistics may find value-expectancy theory to be intuitively appealing since they often deal with statistical regression analysis and operational research as used in prediction and control. The $E = V \times I$ formula is conceptually similar to a statistical regression (prediction) formula, which implies that it is possible to determine which variables, each with a specific influence weight, contribute the most to an explanation of a particular process and eventually make efficient prediction possible (Fishbein & Ajzen, 1975).

Case Study. Suppose you first ask a person to rate on a scale of 0 to 10 (with 10 being most important) how important to him it would be to avoid getting AIDS. He replies, "10." That is valence: It characterizes an outcome and its personal importance. Second, you ask, "How certain are you—and please express this as a percentage—that utilizing safer sex procedures would make it possible for you to avoid getting AIDS?" He replies, "15 percent." That is instrumentality: It expresses the person's belief about whether a specified course of action will produce the desired outcome. Third, to calculate expectancy, you multiply V by I; in this case it would be $E = 10 \times .15 = 1.5$ (on the original scale of 0 to 10). The expectancy score here indicates weak drive. (This is a simplified example. The usual value-expectancy formula is summed across all relevant $V \times I$ dimensions that the individual would use in assessing a situation.)

The man's estimation that safer sex procedures were only slightly likely to affect the AIDS outcome would have been reached through a search of his belief structures (cognitive structures). He might have encountered beliefs or rules that say, "AIDS is not a disease of *my* group. No one in my group could possibly have AIDS, so I am not at risk. Condoms are not safe, based on what I have heard, since they sometimes break. If I *were* to get AIDS, they would have a vaccine by the time I got sick." Whenever instrumentality of some course of action is given a low rating, it is important to ask why. Individuals virtually always have a rule structure that explains their behaviors, and they usually can articulate it verbally if asked; these rules may seem illogical to you, but they must be addressed if they affect information processing related to the campaign's success.

The relation between beliefs and motivation is vital to the planning of messages that are intended to produce specific behaviors or behavioral changes. Information may be necessary to form beliefs. Information may be necessary to change beliefs. If you change beliefs, you change plans and plan rules affecting both test criteria plans and problem-solving activity plans.

Because different people form and act on different beliefs, general categories of motivational drive or need factors are less useful as motivational predictors in different audience segments than information about specific beliefs obtained through trustworthy research methods in specific audience segments.

Case Study. Beliefs related to valences do differ, both (1) in degree of strength and (2) across audience segments. A study was conducted among students at Boston University to ascertain what outcomes or rewards the subjects associated with smoking or with not smoking (Simmons, 1987). The basic methodology, tested in earlier studies (Hesketh, Simmons, & Marques, 1978; Simone, 1981), involved asking the individuals to rate how important they found various outcomes (i.e., rewards) related to smoking on a scale of 0 to 10, 10 being the highest value.[2] The results were submitted to a statistical procedure called factor analysis[3] to identify underlying outcome dimensions. The study identified 29, as presented in Exhibit 2.7. They may be considered audience-identified "rewards" for smoking or not smoking.

To determine the mean valence, or average strength of attractiveness, of

---

[2] This methodology is based on the value-expectancy theory of motivation. (See Weiner, 1980, pp. 141–178.)

[3] Explanation of factor analysis is beyond the scope of this book. However, you will find a highly readable exposition in F. N. Kerlinger, *Foundations of Behavioral Research,* 2nd ed. (New York: Holt, Rinehart and Winston, 1973), pp. 659ff.

Exhibit 2.7. Mean (Overall) Valences for Outcome Factors

Outcome Factor Content	Mean Valence	Standard Error	R
Assertiveness	8.729	.098	.85
Self-confidence	8.657	.113	.86
Independence	8.338	.106	.75
Self-control	8.266	.115	.79
Personal presentation	8.250	.139	.91
Behaving responsibly	8.177	.123	.80
Affiliation need	8.105	.111	.73
Affiliation need (II)	7.994	.117	.80
Feeling fresh, rested	7.839	.143	.88
Work efficiency	7.801	.140	.88
Personal rewards	7.800	.129	.77
Money management	7.793	.126	.60
Efficiency	7.757	.133	.83
Avoiding fire hazards	7.669	.197	.87
Odor-free environment	7.543	.182	.89
Group problem solving	7.507	.141	.91
Group acceptance	7.506	.133	.83
Organization	7.475	.139	.82
Environmental sensitivity	7.431	.162	.92
Positive health behavior	7.272	.158	.86
Environmental cleanliness	6.871	.165	.89
Money management (II)	6.842	.154	.82
Controlling stress	6.613	.179	.88
Organized life-style	6.193	.160	.67
Physical well-being	6.008	.195	.81
Social competence	5.935	.162	.66
Weight control	5.856	.218	.79
Substitute satisfactions	4.418	.167	.71
Pleasure enhancement	4.321	.158	.77

Note 1: Statements constituting the factors were rated by subjects on a scale from 0 (no importance) to 10. The grand mean constitutes the mean valence weight for each outcome factor.

Note 2: R indicates a split-half reliability test. The Horst formula is used when scales have odd numbers of items; in cases of scales with even numbers of items, results are comparable to the Spearman-Brown formula.

each outcome, arithmetic means of the importance ratings that were assigned by the individuals were calculated. The methodology establishes how important, in a comparative context, each outcome or reward is—in effect, suggesting how important each might be in audience motivation. A higher mean valence indicates relatively greater importance.

You do not need an understanding of statistics to see what has happened in Exhibit 2.7: Individuals rated some outcomes or rewards as being more important than others (a higher rating reflects more importance).

Exhibit 2.8 shows what happened when the data in the sample were

EXHIBIT 2.8. Valences (Strengths) of Motivational Outcomes (Rewards) Related to Smoking or Nonsmoking in Two Audience Segments

Outcome Factor	Male Valence ($n = 40$)	Female Valence ($n = 98$)	Two-tailed t ($df = 137$)
01 Feeling fresh, rested	7.5000	8.0170	−1.63
02 Self-confidence	8.2208	8.8690	−2.69**
03 Work efficiency	7.7250	7.8605	−0.44
04 Organization	7.0208	7.6327	−1.99*
05 Behaving responsibly	8.1792	8.2058	−0.10
06 Affiliation need	7.6500	8.3265	−2.87**
07 Positive health behavior	6.7300	7.4878	−2.17*
08 Assertiveness	8.6053	8.7908	−0.87
09 Self-control	8.0333	8.7908	−1.27
10 Independence	8.2143	8.4067	−0.84
11 Group acceptance	7.3708	7.5867	−0.74
12 Money management	6.4667	6.9745	−1.51
13 Group problem solving	6.9292	7.7959	−2.86**
14 Controlling stress	6.4607	6.6662	−0.51
15 Environmental sensitivity	7.1542	7.5272	−1.03
16 Weight control	4.3417	6.5017	−4.86**
17 Physical well-being	6.2300	5.8959	0.77
18 Personal rewards	7.5500	7.9133	−1.29
19 Pleasure enhancement	4.2375	4.2857	−0.14
20 Social competence	5.8400	5.9163	−0.21
21 Environmental cleanliness	6.6167	6.9711	−0.96
22 Substitute satisfactions	3.6900	4.7408	−2.78**
23 Organized life-style	5.8438	6.3240	−1.34
24 Avoiding fire hazards	7.8500	7.5694	−0.84
25 Odor-free environment	7.1563	7.6888	−1.33
26 Efficiency	7.1650	7.6888	−2.75**
27 Affiliation need (II)	7.4583	8.2585	−3.22**
28 Personal presentation	7.6900	8.4776	−2.58*
29 Money management (II)	7.2950	7.9918	−2.53*

Note 1: Statements constituting the factors were rated by subjects on a scale of 0 (no importance) to 10. The grand mean constitutes mean valence weight for each outcome factor.
Note 2: *$p \le .05$; **$p \le .01$.

segmented by gender. For example, males assigned the lowest valence, or lowest importance, to substitute satisfactions (like having a cigarette rather than eating or having sweets) and the highest to assertiveness. Meanwhile, women assigned the lowest valence to pleasure enhancement (smoking to make food or drink more pleasurable) and the highest to self-confidence. You can also see that males and females in the sample did not assign the same valences to particular outcomes in several cases; for example, women assigned a higher valence to subtitute satisfactions than did males.

Tests of differences between the pairs of mean valences were statistically significant for 11 of the outcomes or rewards; the differences that are greater than could be explained by chance are marked with asterisks in the right-hand column. In each case, women in the sample assigned higher valences: self-confidence, organization, affiliation need, positive health behaviors, substitute satisfactions, personal presentation, and money management. Where there are no statistical differences, it means that although the valence ratings may have differed slightly, they are not statistically different.

Again in Exhibit 2.8, even without knowledge of statistics, you can see that males and females rated rewards or outcomes differently. The statistical significance notation simply indicates that the difference between the way males and females rated the importance of a particular reward or outcome was so great that it could not have occurred by chance.

In summary, motivational valences differentiate audience segments classified by gender, as well as other segmentation criteria. In other words, any targeted audience segment can be expected to differ from others motivationally. A manager or planner must investigate those differences; otherwise, messages, and perhaps an entire campaign, might miss the intended motivational target and either be weakened or fail.

Attitude. In social psychology, which is distinct from cognitive psychology, *attitude* has been used as a principal explanatory structure for various aspects of information processing, behavior, and behavior change. There are various definitions of attitude, among them the following:

> A mental and neural state of readiness, organized through experience, exerting a directive or dynamic influence upon the individual's responses to all objects and situations with which it is related. (Allport, 1954, p. 45)

> An enduring system of positive or negative evaluations, emotional feelings and pro or con action tendencies with respect to a social object. (Krech, Crutchfield, & Ballachev, 1962, p. 177)

Fishbein and Ajzen (1975), who have a cognitive process orientation, also deal with attitude:

> Attitude is viewed as a *general* predisposition that does *not* [emphasis added] predispose the person to perform any specific behavior. Rather it leads to a set of intentions that indicate a certain amount of affect toward the object in question. Each of these intentions is related to a specific behavior, and thus the over-all affect as expressed by the pattern of a person's actions with respect to the object also corresponds to his attitude toward the subject. . . . Attitude scores are always obtained by a consideration of beliefs or intentions and their associated evaluations. (pp. 15, 53)

Unfortunately, as Fishbein and Ajzen (1975, p. 1) note, "Considering that attitude is probably 'the most distinctive and indispensible concept in con-

temporary American social psychology' [Allport, 1968, p. 59], it is characterized by an embarrassing degree of ambiguity and confusion.'' Not the least of
the problems is whether attitudes are reliable predictors of attitudes in a *large
percentage of cases* in any situation—an issue that is far from having reached
a satisfactory solution.

Another part of the problem is also conceptual in nature. Scholars who
deal with attitude tend to operationalize rather than clearly define the construct. Consequently, attitude often is treated as little more than a summation
of different components that usually are not explicitly identified; apparently
important components are not included systematically. One exception is
Daniel Katz (1970), who identified three components of attitude: *cognitive*
(knowledge), *affect* (emotion or feeling), and *conative* (policy orientation).
Katz also identified several functions of attitude: adjustment, ego defense,
value expression, and knowledge. His discussion of attitude components can
be viewed from a cognitive process perspective as differentiating types of
cognitive structures; his discussion of functions can be viewed as an attempt
to conceptualize how cognitive structures may serve thinking and behavior,
especially as related to cognitive problem analysis and coping test criteria and
activities. Another author who contributes to refinement of the attitude construct is Rokeach (1972), who differentiates between *attitude toward situation* and *attitude toward object*. Components and functions like those that
Katz suggests are not incorporated in widely used operationalizations of
attitude (i.e., telling how they will be measured).

Attitude change is another major concern of social psychologists (see
Severin with Tankard, 1988, pp. 144–196). Many of the major theories are
based on *cognitive consistency*, which implies that individuals attempt to
maintain a mental state that is relatively consistent over time, and therefore,
psychologically comfortable; when consistency is challenged or disrupted,
individuals try to restore it by changing either their attitudes or their behaviors, including seeking and processing more information. A common message
strategy is to introduce a stressful proposition (''You might not know it, but
you could have bad breath!'') that disturbs cognitive consistency, then introduce a solution to restore it (''But . . . you can solve the problem with Scope
mouthwash!''). In that sense, authors treat such theories as a class of motivational theory (Insko et al., 1975). Consistency is akin to the concept
of *homeostasis*, which is central to Freud's theorizing (Weiner, 1980,
pp. 10–11). Although authors have used different terms—Heider's (1946,
1958) *balance* theory, Newcomb's (1953, 1961; Newcomb, Turner, & Converse, 1965) *symmetry* theory, Osgood and Tannenbaum's (1955) *congruity*
theory, and Festinger's (1957) use of *consonance* in dissonance theory (Severin with Tankard, 1988, pp. 144–155)—the basic notion is virtually the
same. However, as with the basic construct of attitude, attitude-change
models tend to be problematic regarding reliable prediction in an acceptable
number of cases.

Insko et al. (1975) suggest that the failure of the individual to accept *personal responsibility* for the discrepancy between personal attitude or behavior and activity may void any tension toward cognitive consistency. An example helps clarify the point: Smokers should feel incongruity stress after confronting messages pointing out the conflict between smoking's cancer risks and the individual's desire for good health; smokers do not feel that stress because they think, in effect, "What can I do? I am habituated. Therefore, I am not responsible." I suggest that message elements relating to responsibility may be part of the solution; the introduction of "how-to" plans as part of messages may be another, to demonstrate a person can cope (become responsible and in control).

Rokeach (1972) suggests that failure to act may be traced to a conflict between attitude toward object and attitude toward situation: A person's attitude toward an object or objective (buying a Porsche, signing up for an aerobic exercise program, or joining a political protest demonstration) may be neutralized by a negative attitude toward the situation (lack of money, lack of energy or self-discipline, or fear of consequences). If we view these in the context of cognitive theory, we can equate them as part of a procedure plan for coping, particularly belief-based cognitions that are part of test criteria plans.

Rokeach (1972) also discusses *end-state values* and *instrumental values,* additional constructs that could help improve attitude-change theory's prediction potential. End-state or terminal values express what an individual wants to become or be in the long run; instrumental values express the individual's beliefs regarding behaviors that might lead to attainment of the end-state values. Rokeach's theorizing about those constructs and change processes conceptually parallels cognitive theorists' thinking about the value-expectancy theory of motivation. End-state values are somewhat like valenced outcomes, and instrumental values are somewhat like instrumentality. However, Rokeach holds that individuals have relatively few end-state values because these values are related to what people hope to have, become, or be in the long run, rather than being situation- or object-oriented; the latter, which is a main focus of value-expectance valences, presumably would produce a much greater array of valenced outcomes, as in Exhibit 2.7. Exhibit 2.9 presents a composite of men's and women's rankings of terminal values and instrumental values (Rokeach, 1973). Inasmuch as gender differences are found in the ratings, it is likely other differences would be found among other population segments, based on economics, age, occupation, or residence (especially urban versus rural).

Parenthetically, the juxtaposition of Rokeach's views and values and value-expectancy theory's valence and instrumentality concepts provides a context for an explanation of selectivity, in general, and salience and centrality, in particular. *Salience* describes things that are important to the individual currently—"in the front of the mind." Information that is perceived as serving either instrumental values or instrumentality analysis presumably would have, as selectivity theory calls it, utility; therefore, it would

EXHIBIT 2.9. American Men's and Women's Rankings of Values

Value	Men	Women
Terminal Values		
A comfortable life	4	13
An exciting life	18	18
A sense of accomplishment	7	10
A world at peace	1	1
A world of beauty	15	15
Equality	9	8
Family security	2	2
Freedom	3	3
Happiness	5	5
Inner harmony	13	12
Mature love	14	14
National security	10	11
Pleasure	17	16
Salvation	12	4
Self-respect	6	6
Social recognition	16	17
True friendship	11	9
Wisdom	8	7
Instrumental Values		
Ambitious	2	4
Broadminded	4	5
Capable	8	12
Cheerful	12	10
Clean	9	8
Courageous	5	6
Forgiving	6	2
Helpful	7	7
Honest	1	1
Imaginative	18	18
Independent	11	14
Intellectual	16	16
Logical	16	17
Loving	14	9
Obedient	17	15
Polite	13	13
Responsible	3	3
Self-controlled	10	11

Source: From *Theories of Human Communication,* First Ed., by Stephen W. Littlejohn. © 1983 by Wadsworth, Inc. Reprinted by Permission of Wadsworth, Inc. Compiled from Milton Rokeach, *The Nature of Human Values* (New York: Free Press, 1973).

be salient and, consequently, be given a relatively high exposure and attention priority.

Centrality describes things that have enduring or profound personal importance. Information that is perceived as serving either end-state values or valence analysis presumably would have centrality because those concepts relate to major, enduring cognitive system goals, and consequently, should gain high exposure and attention. It follows, then, that in a voluntary situation, information should gain exposure and attention if it evokes salience, centrality, or both; if those conditions are not met, it is likely to be disregarded—another cue to why behavioral analysis is essential to a successful campaign.

Societal Factors. Although many a manager or planner thinks mainly about the final audience segment or segments that must be reached and the mass media that will reach them, a broader perspective is vital because individuals and groups often assume very important *social influence* functions (Cohen, 1964; Lane & Sears, 1964, pp. 17–56, 83–93; Tedeschi, 1972; Severin with Tankard, 1988, pp. 134–142).

In many situations much information flows through *human networks*, as differentiated from diffusion through mass media. Elihu Katz (1960) explains a *two-step flow* of communication: Information from the mass media is diffused to persons who are called *opinion leaders* and they, in turn, retransmit it to others (see Exhibit 2.10).

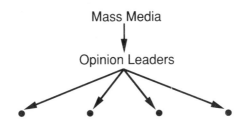

ExHIBIT 2.10. Two-Step Flow of Communication

A *multistep flow* of communication (illustrated in Exhibit 2.11) is an alternative formulation (Rogers with Shoemaker, 1971, pp. 202, 209–210). More individuals are involved; at any stage, some retransmit information, whereas others do not, becoming simply end users of the information.

Opinion leaders tend to be similar to the people who accept or seek information from them, but they are likely to have higher status, use media more frequently, and be *cosmopolite* in seeking information (using sources from outside the community) rather than *localite* (Rogers with Shoemaker, 1971, pp. 217–225). Like social or political elites, opinion leaders frequently are relatively specialized; they may emerge over time only in regard to issues or topics that they relate to their expertise or interests (Key, 1961).

The term opinion leader implies an intent to influence or persuade, but the validity of that assumption depends on the individual case. However, de facto influence may occur when individuals seek out another person to request information or an opinion or when a person who retransmits informa-

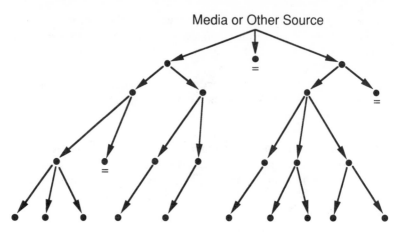

Media or Other Source

EXHIBIT 2.11. Multistep Flow of Communication

Note: The symbol = indicates that the individual does not retransmit the information.

tion does so either selectively or interpretively. Lewin introduced the terms *gatekeeping* for the process in which persons selectively filter and retransmit information and *gatekeepers* for persons who engage in these behaviors (Cartwright, 1951). *Change agents* (Rogers with Shoemaker, 1971, pp. 227–248) are conceptually similar to opinion leaders and gatekeepers, but their work combines elements of training, education, and persuasion. Change agents are specialists employed, for example, in programs for agricultural diffusion or in organizational training.

As the Fishbein and Ajzen (1975) model implies in regard to normative beliefs, individuals often reflect on the behavioral *norms* seen in the behaviors of others. This act may involve an elementary form of risk analysis. It also may reflect individuals' concerns regarding conformity and its benefits, as suggested by the importance of affiliation in Maslow's needs hierarchy. *Modeling* is another aspect of social influence in which an individual aspires, because of perceived benefits, to be like another person, who may be called a *role model*.

There is a hierarchy of *adopters of innovations*, and it indicates that segments of a population may delay implementation of new behaviors until they have been validated by others (Rogers with Shoemaker, 1971). The categories are

- True innovators, 2.5 percent of the total
- Early adopters, 13.5 percent
- Early majority, 34 percent
- Late majority, 34 percent
- Laggards, 16 percent

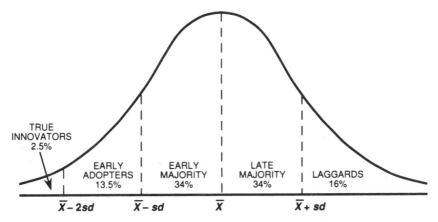

ExHIBIT 2.12. Adopter Categorization on the Basis of Innovativeness
Source: Reprinted with permission of the Free Press, a division of MacMillan Inc., from *The Communication of Innovations,* 2nd ed., by Everett Rogers with Fred Shoemaker. Copyright © 1971 by the Free Press.

The adopter categories (Exhibit 2.12) can be plotted against a learning curve (Rogers with Shoemaker, 1971), which relates the speed of adoption to both learning and problem analysis, as well as social communication and role modeling (Exhibit 2.13).

Some individuals intentionally attempt to persuade or control other individuals; there are also groups who try to mobilize individuals, control behaviors that are deviant from group norms, focus members' activities, and attain group goals and objectives. In this context, some individuals and groups have *resistance to change* as their main agenda. A manager or planner must be aware that not all propositions advanced by campaigns will be welcomed; in some cases the propositions actually may be harmful in one way or another (Klein, 1969; Watson, 1969). Individuals or groups who oppose activities and programs that they perceive as dysfunctional, and perhaps attempt to involve or enlist others in their "cause," exercise what Klein calls the *defender role.*

Behavioral Analysis Checklist. Based on these theories, you might develop a checklist for factors you should consider while doing exploratory research, for example, interviews with people in the desired audience segment, interviews with specialists or others who can speak with authority about people in the desired segment, or published sources like those reported in *Social Sciences Index.* Here are some factors you might want to consider:

1. What groups within a general population should be segmented not only for logical relevance to the problem but also for specific behav-

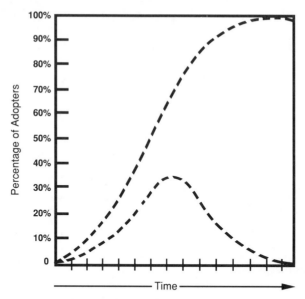

Both of these curves are for the same data, the adoption
of innovation overtime by members of a social system.
But the bell-shaped curve shows these data in terms of
the number of individuals adopting each year, whereas
the S-shaped curve shows these data on a cumulative
basis.

EXHIBIT 2.13. Adopter and Diffusion-Adoption Curves

Source: Reprinted with permission of the Free Press, a division of MacMillan Inc., from *The Communication of Innovations*, 2nd ed., by Everett Rogers with Fred Shoemaker. Copyright © 1971 by the Free Press.

ioral patterns? Some examples are previous involvement with the issue that the campaign addresses or similar issues (especially extensive involvement, as seen in activism or heavy consumption), knowledge about the issue or similar issues, beliefs or disbeliefs that could be used in messages to establish a common ground (like homophily), and the likelihood of being receptive to the proposition that a problem exists and that the campaign can help solve it.

2. What aspects of the problem are most likely to be salient or central when discussed in messages and lead to arousal in the target segment?

3. What similarities and differences exist between or among target segments in regard to the factors identified in the two previous questions?

4. Are there other differences between or among segments regarding language encoding and decoding (e.g., using cognitive attributes to decode) that might affect the campaign's communications? Some examples are language skills (literacy, which is indicative of lower cognitive complexity in the manipulation of written verbal symbols) and use (different vocabulary or jargon). For example, Strunin (1988) reports that while teenagers were being interviewed about sexual practices that contribute to the spread of AIDS, there was considerable confusion about the "standard" language used for certain body parts; also, when subjects were asked whether AIDS is spread by semen, respondents often interpreted that term as "sea men" (sailors).

5. What is the evidence that individuals in the desired target segment or segments understand what to do or how to do it once they are convinced by some persuasive communication? As noted, some portion of any population will lack appropriate cognitive plans, procedural plans (a general problem-solving strategy), activity plans (specific intrapersonal how-to-do-it instructions), and test criteria plans. If research discovers a deficiency among substantial numbers of people in the desired segment or segments, messages may have to be designed to compensate; otherwise, as Fishbein and Ajzen (1975) suggest about lack of intention (a type of activity plan), overt behavior probably will not result.

6. What rewards (valence) and means of attainment (instrumentality) are considered meaningful by those in the target segment? In general, experience indicates that messages that position products, services, or ideas as being relevant to existing needs or desires are more likely to be effective than those that attempt to create altogether new needs or desires. Moreover, if the messages you might consider do not evoke perceptions of instrumentality, it is essential to probe or search for reasons, because these reasons will need to be addressed in messages to make the issue *salient* or *central* and enhance arousal potential.

7. Do large numbers of persons in the desired segment psychologically view themselves as not responsible personally for behaviors that the campaign addresses? In many cases, incorporation of advice in messages about how to cope might help alleviate this problem.

8. Do values play a part in the problem and can they be used in formulating a message strategy?

9. How might affect be used to create arousal, utilizing the gratifications element of selectivity theory to gain leverage? If anyone in the campaign team suggests using affective fear appeals, you should consider whether negative messages with proposed solutions might be less threatening and produce better results.

10. What mass media or other channels are used by the persons whom you must reach? Out of this array, you must verify which are considered most informative and also most authoritative or trustworthy.

11. If information channels are vital to the problem, what are the pat-

terns (two-step or multistep flow, for example) and who serves as influentials or gatekeepers? These questions are especially important for managers and planners who work with pubic relations, communication, and nonprofit organizations and programs such as community development and education, social service delivery, health communication, and agricultural diffusion.

12. What reference groups affect large numbers of individuals in the desired segment because they either provide cues about appropriate behaviors and risks or actually engage in activities designed to influence behaviors?

13. Will individuals or groups who believe that they have a stake in the issue addressed by the campaign engage in active opposition because they cast themselves in defender roles? Whether or how such resistance can be addressed can be a vital matter for discussion, especially in crisis management campaigns.

14. Are your *expectations* or those of your client or upper-level managers about observable or measurable campaign impacts within a stated time frame realistic in the light of experiences summarized in learning, diffusion-adoption, and marketing curves? Reflections on this question should take into account evidence that the moderate effects model of impact is more appropriate than the large effects model, also called the powerful effects model (Atkin, 1981; Severin with Tankard, 1988, pp. 311–330).

15. What enabling factors affect the likelihood that behaviors recommended by the campaign will be implemented? In many cases, communication to a target audience cannot overcome the problem, but communication directed to the client or upper-level managers might bring about policy changes that reduce or eliminate it. For example, during economic slumps, messages cannot sell automobiles because potential buyers are worried about money; feedback about that problem leads automakers to offer rebates, lower or even zero financing rates, or other incentives. Failure to address enabling factors can weaken or defeat campaigns. During the Reagan presidency, health communications designed to attack drug abuse were undermined by funding cutbacks in treatment programs; this reduction extended waiting periods for vacancies in treatment centers to the point that many drug users lost motivation to enter the program.

CAUSAL REASONING AS A MANAGEMENT INFORMATION FILTER

Inevitably, problem analysis introduces so many variables that the overall view is lost. Force field analysis is a technique that helps reduce the volume of variables presumed to influence the behaviors that a campaign is expected to affect. However, a manager or planner might first consider using *causal analysis* to help filter out extraneous information; one of the first steps in analysis is determining how to reduce the volume of information by setting aside that which logically cannot affect the issue. The following are some useful criteria for such an analysis:

1. *Contributory conditions* are factors or variables that in some way affect the phenomenon that you are trying to explain. Although this filter is not particularly discriminating, it may help rule out certain propositions as implausible.
2. *Sufficient conditions* are those that, by themselves, can lead to the occurrence of a specified phenomenon.
3. *Necessary conditions* are those that must be present in order for a specified phenomenon to occur.
4. *Sufficient but not necessary conditions* are those that may, by themselves, lead to the occurrence of a specific phenomenon; however, the phenomenon can occur as a result of other conditions as well.
5. *Necessary but not sufficient conditions* are those that must be present for a specified phenomenon to occur; however, such a condition will not, in itself, lead to the occurrence of the specified phenomenon.
6. A *necessary and sufficient condition* is some condition that must be present in order for a specified phenomenon to occur and can lead to the occurrence in the absence of other conditions.
7. A *contingent condition* is one that coexists with others; often a relationship or effect will not result unless the contingent condition is present.

Case Study. The following clarifies these distinctions. Suppose a manager or planner is working with a campaign to gain adoption of a chemical fertilizer by a group of economically marginal farmers who own their own land in a less developed nation. The question is whether a campaign's introduction of knowledge about the practice is likely to bring about the desired adoption. The analysis might develop in this way:

1. Knowledge produced by the campaign regarding the practice passes the test of being a likely contributory condition since adoption clearly implies at least awareness and comprehension of the process (although comprehension could be learned by trial and error) as well as of risks and advantages. Moreover, adoption is unlikely to occur in the absence of any information about the practice.
2. Knowledge produced by the campaign regarding the practice is not a sufficient condition in itself because many of the farmers cannot implement the behavior with knowledge alone.
3. Unless certain contributory conditions are present, no adoption is likely to occur in this case as a result of the campaign. Most obvious

are financing and equipment. (Examining contributory conditions often leads a manager or planner to recognize that unless some *enabling factors* are provided, as well as information, nothing will occur. In this case, it might involve planning for credit and perhaps an equipment loan program.)
4. Knowledge from the campaign regarding the practice seems to be a necessary condition because knowledge is necessary. However, an unanswered question is whether knowledge produced by the campaign will be a necessary condition for adoption to occur or whether it might result otherwise; for example, farmers might become aware of the practice by observing other farmers who use chemical fertilizers and become convinced by talking with the early adopters. (This last observation also might lead to a reassessment of whether the early adopters might be brought into the campaign as opinion leaders, providing both interpersonal communication channels and influence.)

FORCE FIELD ANALYSIS

By the time you have completed the ideal state and real state analyses, a group of facts or assumptions will have emerged about why the audience segment might behave in a particular way. Force field analysis provides a managerial technique for reducing the complexity of the information and crystallizing the trends in order to focus on the critical variables.

Without this technique, you might group the facts or assumptions into two columns: the first listing variables favoring the desired behavior, and the second listing variables opposing the desired behavior. This can be a useful first step in structuring the available information. However, force field analysis (see Hersey & Blanchard, 1986, pp. 122–24 and 277–80) is a more powerful heuristic technique that can help to conceptualize and explain which variables are critical and how strong their effects are.

Force field analysis is based on the work of Lewin regarding lifespace and change processes (Lewin, 1938; Cartwright, 1951). The scheme assumes that any behavioral situation can be described as a quasi-stationary equilibrium, controlled by opposing sets of variables. One group, called *driving forces,* favors the behavior named in the situation. The other, called *restraining forces*, opposes the specified behavior. Not all variables in the situation are of equal importance. Each has a valence, which is an expression of its relative strength.

Force field analysis lends itself to graphic presentation, as in Exhibit 2.14. You should note that this particular analysis deals with a specific target audience, that is, nonsmoking workers in a particular firm. It also deals with a particular behavioral domain—getting them to encourage fellow workers not to smoke.

EXHIBIT 2.14. Force Field Analysis Diagram

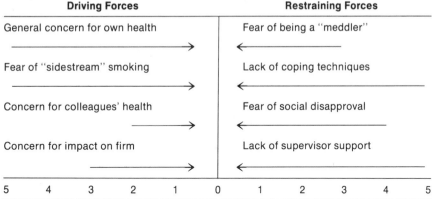

Target Audience: *Nonsmokers* in Company *X* Office Behavior: Opposing Smoking in the Workplace

Driving Forces	**Restraining Forces**
General concern for own health	Fear of being a "meddler"
Fear of "sidestream" smoking	Lack of coping techniques
Concern for colleagues' health	Fear of social disapproval
Concern for impact on firm	Lack of supervisor support

5   4   3   2   1   0   1   2   3   4   5

Note: "Sidestream" smoking refers to a situation in which an individual inhales and is affected by smoke produced by another person; also known as passive smoking.

The variables listed in the driving forces column are, presumably, those that would favor activation of the nonsmokers. The variables in the restraining column are, presumably, those that would discourage nonsmokers from taking action. The variables in a force field analysis do not constitute an exhaustive inventory. Only those considered most likely to control the behavior are considered. This is, in effect, part of the weeding process.

Arrow lengths in the force field analysis indicate the relative valence or strength of each variable.[4] Smaller valences can constitute grounds for eliminating variables from the analysis, unless they are held purposively in the analysis pending validation research.

The vertical center line symbolizes graphically the *present state of equilibrium*. The sum of the valences on each side presumably are in balance.

The fact that the arrows seem to be opposed—for example, "concern about health" and "fear of being a meddler"—has no particular significance. It is the cumulative weight of the driving forces and the cumulative weight of the restraining forces that bring about the equilibrium. Your change strategy, therefore, must concentrate on the selective weakening or strengthening of valences for specific variables.

---

[4] Valences can be measured methodologically. One approach is to utilize the factor-analytic technique developed and tested by Hesketh, Simmons, and Marques (1978); Simone (1981), or Simmons (1987). A second approach is to use rating scale results. A third approach is to record the percentage of subjects in a target audience subscribing to a particular belief as a proxy measure of its valence. For example, we might find in the data that 80 percent of those in the segment are concerned about their personal health. That finding could be recorded in the force field analysis, the scale at the bottom of the graphic being converted to percentages instead of valence numbers of 0 to 10.

At the outset, the force field analysis is a tentative conceptual device. It helps you to give order to the variables, eliminate some, and give reasoned evaluation about which ones seem to be crucial.

Each audience segment requires its own force field analysis because the behavioral tendencies of different audience segments are usually controlled by different sets of variables; even when the same variables are involved, the valences may be different. Moreover, quite often it is found that analyses of variables that affect other audiences' behaviors will incorporate new variables. For example, compare the similarities and differences in Exhibits 2.14, 2.15, and 2.16 regarding their own involvement of nonsmokers, smokers and supervisors in the implementation of a new policy against smoking in a workplace.

EXHIBIT 2.15. Second Example of Force Field Analysis

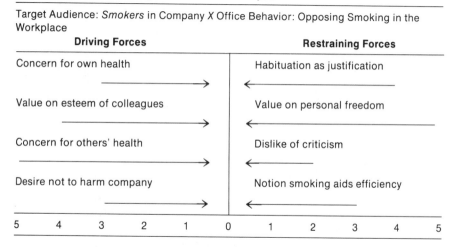

Target Audience: *Smokers* in Company *X* Office Behavior: Opposing Smoking in the Workplace

Driving Forces	Restraining Forces
Concern for own health	Habituation as justification
Value on esteem of colleagues	Value on personal freedom
Concern for others' health	Dislike of criticism
Desire not to harm company	Notion smoking aids efficiency

5   4   3   2   1   0   1   2   3   4   5

You should regard the results of the force field analysis as speculative until some form of validation research is conducted and confirmatory evidence is obtained.

Force Field Analysis and Strategy. You can utilize force field analysis to develop specific basic strategies for behavioral change once the analysis of variables in the force field has been confirmed. The basic choices are to use messages to

- Weaken the restraining forces
- Strengthen the driving forces (However, if you do this without addressing the restraining forces, a disproportionately large increase in resistance might result.)

Exhibit 2.16. Third Example of Force Field Analysis

Target Audience: *Supervisors* in Company *X* Office Behavior: Opposing Smoking in the Workplace

Driving Forces		Restraining Forces
Concern for own health		Habituation as justification
$\longrightarrow$		$\longleftarrow$
Value on leadership role		Value on personal freedom
$\longrightarrow$		$\longleftarrow$
Concern for others' health		Dislike of conflict'
$\longrightarrow$		$\longleftarrow$
Desire to conform to policy		Notion smoking aids efficiency
$\longrightarrow$		$\longleftarrow$

```
5     4     3     2     1     0     1     2     3     4     5
```

- Selectively strengthen driving forces, and at the same time, weaken selected restraining forces
- Recognize that simply reinforcing certain variables identified as driving forces might be desirable or necessary.

In the example in Exhibit 2.14, a workable strategy might be the following:

1. *Reinforce or strengthen the driving forces.* Specifically, reinforce beliefs about subjects' health and the potential danger of sidestream smoking. Elaborate on beliefs about the negative impact of smoking in the work environment; for example, explain research documenting increased sick days, lessened efficiency, costs of cleaning and of replacing burn-damaged furniture and carpeting, etc. Reinforce the belief that it is proper to be assertive about concerns for fellow workers' health.

2. *Weaken the restraining forces.* Specifically, reinforce or build on supervisors' beliefs that they have a leadership role; for example, explain that leadership involves encouraging positive health behaviors, especially when such changed behaviors are also beneficial to the firm. Reinterpret nonsmokers' beliefs about "meddling" as a "sign of caring." Build beliefs among nonsmokers about the availability of strategies to deal with "stop smoking" requests to smokers without being offensive—that is, teach coping strategies. And reinterpret beliefs about social disapproval; for example, explain that the intervention campaign is a matter of group concern.

SUMMARY

This chapter introduces systems-based managerial analysis techniques used in strategic planning of campaigns—notably real state/ideal state analyses, segmentation, and force field analysis.

The real state/ideal state analyses provide answers to these questions: What goal or goals must the campaign address? What can we learn from the client's, the organization's, or others' experiences? What are realistic goals, and what strategy can make possible their satisfactory attainment?

The analysis procedures focus attention on

1. The selection of an audience segment
2. Variables that might control behaviors in the situation
3. An appropriate message strategy, including positioning
4. A strategy for the use of media and other channels to distribute the message efficiently.

Behavioral theory provides analytical frameworks that are exceptionally important in problem analysis. As the section on behavioral analysis explains, an understanding of cognitive theory and the procedures and rules individuals use in processing information is vital because they shed light on how people deal with information and how these processes affect learning and motivation in a campaign. This chapter also discusses social and enabling factors. A checklist is provided to help you focus on factors that may be especially important.

Beliefs and basic notions of motivation theory provide an indispensible foundation for force field analysis, which is a valuable management analysis technique that helps sort out the crucial variables and their relative strengths of influence on the behaviors of individual audience segments. The theory perspectives section illustrates how such variables and their importance vary across audience segments.

Causal analysis is designed to help you filter assumptions that go into the force field analysis process, to prevent the analysis from losing its focus because of excessive, and perhaps irrelevant, information.

You should consider the assumptions emerging from any force field analysis to be tentative and subject to verification research. Once each tentative analysis has been confirmed or modified, you can use the results to generate a change strategy. That strategy, in turn, provides the rationale for management by objectives (MBO) specifications. (MBO is discussed in Chapter 5.)

The next two chapters discuss three basic methodologies for verification research.

REFERENCES

G. W. Allport, "The Historical Background of Modern Social Psychology," in G. Lindzey (ed.), *Handbook of Social Psychology,* Vol. 1 (Reading, MA: Addison-Wesley, 1954), pp. 3–56.

G. W. Allport, "The Historical Background of Modern Social Psychology," in G. Lindzey and E. Aronson (eds.), *Handbook of Social Psychology,* 2nd ed., Vol. 1 (Reading, MA: Addison-Wesley, 1968), p. 1–80.

C. K. Atkin, "Mass Media Information Campaign Effectiveness," in R. E. Rice and W. J. Paisley (eds.), *Public Communication Campaigns* (Beverly Hills, CA: Sage, 1981).

A. D. Baddeley, *The Psychology of Memory* (New York: Basic Books, 1976).

R. A. Bauer, "The Obstinate Audience," in W. Schramm and D. F. Roberts (eds.), *The Process and Effects of Mass Communication* (Urbana: University of Illinois Press, 1971).

Jerome Bruner, J. J. Goodnow, and G. A. Austin, *A Study of Thinking* (New York: Wiley, 1962).

Walter Buckley, *Sociology and Modern Systems Theory* (Englewood Cliffs, NJ: Prentice-Hall, 1967).

D. Cartwright, *Field Theory in Social Science: Selected Theoretical Papers of Kurt Lewin* (New York: Harper Torchbooks, 1951).

A. R. Cohen, *Attitude Change and Social Influence* (New York: Basic Books, 1964).

W. P. Davison, J. Boylan, and F. T. C. Yu, *Mass Media Systems and Effects* (New York: Holt, Rinehart and Winston, 1976).

Murray Edelman, *The Symbolic Uses of Politics* (Urbana: University of Illinois Press, 1964).

Leon Festinger, *A Theory of Cognitive Dissonance* (Stanford, CA: Stanford University Press, 1957).

Martin Fishbein and Icek Ajzen, *Belief, Attitude, Intention and Behavior* (Reading, MA: Addison-Wesley, 1975).

J. L. Freedman and D. O. Sears, "Selective Exposure," in L. Berkowitz (ed.), *Advances in Experimental Social Psychology,* Vol. 2 (New York: Academic Press, 1965).

Fritz Heider, "Attitudes and Cognitive Organization," *Journal of Psychology,* 21 (1946): 107–112.

Fritz Heider, *The Psychology of Interpersonal Relations* (New York: Wiley, 1958).

Paul Hersey and K. H. Blanchard, *Management of Organizational Behavior,* 5th ed. (Englewood Cliffs, NJ: Prentice-Hall, 1986).

J. Hesketh, R. E. Simmons, and S. Marques, "Determining Outcomes and Valences for Teaching: A Factor Analysis Approach," paper presented to the Interamerican Psychological Assn., Lima, Peru, 1978.

W. F. Hill, *Learning: A Survey of Psychological Interpretations,* rev. ed. (Scranton, PA: Chandler, 1963).

G. M. Hochbaum, "Public Participation in Medical Screening Programs: A Socio-Psychological Study" (Washington, DC: U.S. Government Printing Office, Public Health Service Publication 572, 19, 1956).

G. M. Hochbaum, "Modern Theories of Communication," in R. E. Hartley and E. L. Hartley (eds.), *Readings in Psychology,* 3rd ed. (New York: Crowell, 1965).

Daniel Horn and S. Waingrow, "Some Dimensions for a Model for Smoking Behavior Change," *American Journal of Public Health*, 56–12 (1966): 21–26.

Chester Insko, S. Worchel, R. Folger, and A. Kutkus, "A Balance Theory Interpretation of Dissonance," *Psychological Review*, 82 (1975): 169–183.

Daniel Kahneman, *Attention and Effort* (Englewood Cliffs, NJ: Prentice-Hall, 1973).

Daniel Katz, "The Functional Approach to the Study of Attitudes," in K. K. Sereno and C. D. Mortensen (eds.), *Foundations of Communication Theory* (New York: Harper & Row, 1970), pp. 234–259.

Elihu Katz, "The Two-Step Flow of Communication: An Up-to-Date Report on an Hypothesis," *Public Opinion Quarterly*, 21 (1960): 61–78.

V. O. Key, Jr., *Public Opinion and American Democracy* (New York: Knopf, 1961).

Donald Klein, "Some Notes on the Dynamics of Resistance to Change: The Defender Role," in W. G. Bennis, K. D. Benne, and R. Chin (eds.), *The Planning of Change*, 2nd ed. (New York: Holt, Rinehart and Winston, 1969), pp. 498–507.

D. Krech, R. S. Crutchfield, and E. L. Ballachev, *Individual in Society: A Textbook of Social Psychology* (New York: McGraw-Hill, 1962).

R. E. Lane and D. O. Sears, *Public Opinion* (Englewood Cliffs, NJ: Prentice-Hall, 1964).

Kurt Lewin, *The Conceptual Representation and the Measurement of Psychological Forces* (Durham, NC: Duke University Press, 1938).

Harry Lorayne and J. Lucas, *The Memory Book* (New York: Ballantine Books, 1974).

W. J. McGuire, "Behavioral Medicine, Public Health and Communication Theories," *National Forum*, Winter 1980, pp. 18–24.

Abraham Maslow, *Motivation and Personality* (New York: Harper & Row, 1954).

G. A. Miller, "The Magical Number Seven, Plus or Minus Two. Some Limits on Our Capacity for Processing Information," *Psychological Review*, 63 (1956): 81–97.

G. A. Miller, *The Psychology of Communication* (New York: Basic Books, 1967).

G. A. Miller, E. Galanter, and K. Pilbram, *Plans and the Structure of Behavior* (New York: Holt, Rinehart and Winston, 1960).

C. D. Mortensen, *Communication* (New York: McGraw-Hill, 1972).

Theodore Newcomb, "An Approach to the Study of Communicative Acts," *Psychological Review*, 60 (1953): 393–404.

Theodore Newcomb, *The Acquaintance Process* (New York: Holt, Rinehart and Winston, 1961).

Theodore Newcomb, R. Turner, and P. Converse, *Social Psychology: The Study of Human Interaction* (New York: Holt, Rinehart and Winston, 1965).

Charles Osgood and P. H. Tannenbaum, "The Principle of Congruity in the Prediction of Attitude Change," *Psychological Review*, 62 (1955): 42–55.

Jean Piaget, *Six Psychological Studies* (New York: Vintage Books, 1967).

Rosser Reeves, *Reality in Advertising* (New York: Knopf, 1961).

Al Ries and Jack Trout, *Positioning: The Battle for Your Mind,* rev. ed. (New York: McGraw-Hill, 1986).

I. M. Rodenstock, "Why People Use Health Services," *Milbank Memorial Fund Quarterly*, 44 (1966): 94ff.

I. M. Rodenstock, "Prevention of Illness and Maintenance of Health," in J. Kosa, A. Antonovsky & I. K. Zola. (eds.), *Poverty and Health: A Sociological Analysis* (Cambridge, MA: Harvard University Press, 1969), pp. 168–170.

I. M. Rodenstock, "The Health Belief Model and Preventive Health Behavior," in M. H. Becker (ed.), *The Health Belief Model and Personal Health Behavior* (Thorofare, NJ: Slack, 1974), pp. 42–50.

E. M. Rogers with F. Shoemaker, *The Communication of Innovations*, 2nd ed. (New York: Free Press, 1971).

Milton Rokeach, *Beliefs, Attitudes and Values* (San Francisco: Jossey-Bass, 1972).

Milton Rokeach, *The Nature of Human Values* (New York: Free Press, 1973).

Julian Rotter, "Generalized Expectancies for Internal Versus External Control of Reinforcement," *Psychological Monographs*, 80 (1966): Whole No. 609.

Julian Rotter, *Social Learning and Clinical Psychology* (Englewood Cliffs, NJ: Prentice-Hall, 1974).

H. M. Schroder, M. J. Driver, and S. Streufert, *Human Information Processing* (New York: Holt, Rinehart and Winston, 1967).

W. J. Severin with J. W. Tankard, Jr., *Communication Theories*, 2nd ed. (White Plains, NY: Longman, 1988). A valuable reference, especially for novices, concerning communication behaviors.

S. Shimanoff, *Communication Rules* (Beverly Hills, CA: Sage, 1981).

R. E. Simmons, "Measurement of Motivational Rewards in Smoking: Assessing Valenced Outcomes That Differentiate Audience Segments," presented to the Health Communication Division, International Communication Assn., Montreal, May 1987.

R. E. Simmons and E. C. Garda, "Dogmatism and the 'Knowledge Gap' Among Users of the Mass Media: A Study in Brasilia, Brazil," *Gazette*, Fall 1982.

R. E. Simmons, C. L. Hills, and J.-S. Lee, "Behavioral and Managerial Models That Can Help Improve AIDS Campaign Planning," presented to the Health Communication Division, International Communication Assn., New Orleans, May 1988.

M. Simone, "A Methodological Approach to the Identification of Communication-Related Work Outcomes and Measurement of Their Valences," unpublished master's thesis, College of Communication, Boston University, 1981.

Lesley Stahl, interview on "All Things Considered," National Public Radio, April 12, 1989.

Lee Strunin, address to health communication class, College of Communication, Boston University, April 12, 1988.

J. T. Tedeschi (ed.), *The Social Influence Processes* (Chicago: Aldine-Atherton, 1972).

P. J. Tichenor, G. A. Donohue, and C. N. Olien, "Mass Media Flow and Differential Growth in Knowledge," *Public Opinion Quarterly*, 34–2 (1970): 159–170.

Goodwin Watson, "Resistance to Change," in W. G. Bennis, K. D. Benne, and R. Chin (eds.), *The Planning of Change*, 2nd ed. (New York: Holt, Rinehart and Winston, 1969), pp. 498–507.

Bernard Weiner, *Human Motivation* (New York: Holt, Rinehart and Winston, 1980). Highly readable explanation of the evolution of motivational theory.

R. D. Wimmer and J. R. Dominick, *Mass Media Research*, 2nd ed. (Belmont, CA: Wadsworth, 1987).

FURTHER READINGS

D. A. Aaker and J. G. Meyers, *Advertising Management* (Englewood Cliffs, NJ: Prentice-Hall, 1975).

Icek Ajzen and Martin Fishbein, *Understanding Attitudes and Predicting Social*

Behavior (Englewood Cliffs, NJ: Prentice-Hall, 1980).

L. F. Alwitt and A. A. Mitchell (eds.), *Psychological Processes and Advertising Effects* (Hillsdale, NJ: L. Erlbaum, 1985).

J. A. Anderson and T. P. Meyer, *Mediated Communication: A Social Action Perspective* (Newbury Park, CA: Sage, 1988).

E. W. Brody, *Public Relations Programming and Production* (New York: Praeger, 1988).

M. S. Clark and S. T. Fiske (eds.), *Affect and Cognition: The Seventeenth Annual Carnegie Symposium on Cognition* (Hillsdale, NJ: L. Erlbaum, 1972).

D. R. Cox, "Cues for Advertising Strategists," in L. A. Dexter and D. M. White (eds.), *People, Society and Mass Communication* (New York: Free Press, 1964).

Lewis Donohew, H. E. Sypher, and E. T. Higgins (eds.), *Communication, Social Cognition and Affect* (Hillsdale, NJ: L. Erlbaum, 1987).

Leon Festinger and E. Aronson, "The Arousal and Reduction of Dissonance in Social Contexts," in Dorwin Cartwright and A. Zander (eds.), *Group Dynamics* (New York: Harper & Row, 1960), pp. 214–231.

J. E. Grunig and Todd Hunt, *Managing Public Relations* (New York: Holt, Rinehart and Winston, 1984).

R. I. Haley, *Developing Effective Communications Strategy: A Benefit Segmentation Approach* (New York: Wiley, 1985).

M. J. Houston and R. J. Lutz, *Marketing Communications* (Chicago: American Marketing Assn., 1985).

Philip Kotler, *Marketing Management: Analysis, Planning and Control*, 4th ed. (Englewood Cliffs, NJ: Prentice-Hall, 1980).

———, *Marketing for Nonprofit Organizations*, 2nd ed. (Englewood Cliffs, NJ: Prentice-Hall, 1982).

———, *Strategic Marketing for Educational Institutions* (Englewood Cliffs, NJ: Prentice-Hall, 1985).

G. L. Kreps and B. C. Thornton, *Health Communication* (White Plains, NY: Longman, 1984).

Otto Lerbinger, *Designs for Persuasive Communication* (Englewood Cliffs, NJ: Prentice-Hall, 1972).

———, *Managing Corporate Crises: Strategies for Executives* (Boston: Barrington Press, 1986).

Otto Lerbinger and A. J. Sullivan (eds.), *Manager's Public Relations Handbook* (New York: Basic Books, 1965).

S. W. Littlejohn, *Theories of Human Communication*, 2nd ed. (Belmont, CA: Wadsworth, 1983).

N. R. Nager and T. H. Allen, *Public Relations: Management by Objectives* (White Plains, NY: Longman, 1984).

M. L. Ray, *Advertising and Communication Management* (Englewood Cliffs, NJ: Prentice-Hall, 1982).

R. E. Rice and W. J. Paisley (eds.), *Public Communication Campaigns* (Beverly Hills, CA: Sage, 1981).

E. M. Rogers, *Communication Strategies for Family Planning* (New York: Free Press, 1973).

D. E. Schultz, D. Martin, and W. P. Brown, *Strategic Advertising Campaigns* (Chicago: Crain, 1984).

D. O. Sears and J. L. Freedman, "Selective Exposure to Information," *Public Opinion Quarterly*, 31 (1964): 194–213.

N. H. Sperber and Otto Lerbinger, *Manager's Public Relations Handbook* (Reading, MA: Addison-Wesley, 1982).

J. W. Weiss, *The Management of Change* (New York: Praeger, 1986).

CHAPTER 3

Basic Validation Research Methods

After following the steps discussed in the previous chapter, as a manager or planner you must next determine whether you should trust your segmentation and force field analysis as a basis for action. This chapter will deal with three research methodologies that meet verification needs but also could be used for exploratory purposes.

1. *Survey research* uses questionnaires to interview large numbers of persons who usually are selected through scientific probability sampling methods and who represent the characteristics specified for the target audience or audiences.
2. *Focus group research* entails small-group interviewing among persons who presumably represent characteristics of the target audience segment or segments.
3. *In-depth interviewing*, like focus group research, deals with small numbers of persons but involves interviewing them at length as individuals. This methodology may be considered a subset of focus group interviewing and sometimes is called individual focus sessions.

COMPARISON OF THREE RESEARCH METHODOLOGIES

This section provides an overview of the three methodologies. In the case of survey research, only an introduction is presented because Chapter 4 contains extensive information about the design and implementation of surveys.

Survey Research

A highly structured methodology, *survey research* involves data collection among large numbers of persons who are selected by scientific sampling procedures from a large grouping called a population. Interviewing in survey research almost always is accomplished with, and controlled by, questionnaires.

Probability sampling in survey research makes it possible to calculate how many persons would be needed in a specific study. The sampling methodology underlying the procedures also ensures the representativeness of the sample that is obtained. Large numbers alone will not make a sample representative. However, when probability sampling methodology is used, the number of persons interviewed does become a factor; this controls the precision of the estimate from sample data to the group being studied. Survey research makes it possible to

1. Obtain statistical summaries of trends—for example, "15 percent of a probability sample of adults in the lower 48 states are not aware that Alaska is a U.S. state."
2. Specify the precision with which the summary can be projected—for example, "Between 10 and 20 percent of the target population does not know that Alaska is a state."
3. Tell how confident you are about that projection—for example, "We are 95 percent confident concerning those bounds on the estimation."

Survey research can help you obtain superior data for managerial needs, although the execution of a survey and the analysis of results require more time and produce higher costs.

Focus Group Research

An informal and less structured approach to data collection and analysis, *focus group research* often is attractive because projects can be executed quickly at relatively little cost. The methodology involves interviewing one group or more, each group consisting of 10 to 14 individuals. When a campaign has different target audiences, each must be represented by an individual focus group. How the individuals are picked for focus groups is not scientific; persons who share the characteristics specified for a particular target audience are located and invited to participate. This process is likely to result in nonrepresentative samples. Persons who agree to participate are invited to a central interviewing site, where they usually find a coffee-klatsch setting. A trained specialist conducts each focus group session, using *nondirective interviewing* techniques: No formal questionnaire is utilized, but the interviewer uses informal questions or cues to encourage the group members to talk openly about the interview themes—for example, those linked to segmentation and force field analysis assumptions—and to interact and elaborate on the discussion.

Because several focus group meetings can be held sequentially in one day or conducted concurrently by different persons, you might be able to obtain results for analysis in as little as one working day.

However, there are some drawbacks to focus group research, from a managerial point of view. First, it provides "soft," or impressionistic, results. Second, you cannot be absolutely certain that the persons who are selected or who agree to participate are actually representative; thus, the obtained results might not be truly generalizable to an intended audience segment. Third, with small groups of individuals, it is virtually useless to try to interpret the results in statistical terms—for example, "60 percent are uncertain how Acquired Immunodeficiency Syndrome (AIDS) is spread." Finally, focus group research does not enable you to make projections with any stated degree of either precision or certainty.

When you face stringent time and budget restrictions as you develop a campaign problem analysis, focus group research can be an attractive, utilitarian alternative to survey research. However, the need for representative, generalizable results and stated levels of precision or confidence—which frequently are demanded by clients or upper-level managers—might cause you to turn to survey research. This often is the case when major risks such as win-or-lose situations in marketing, advertising, public relations, political campaigns, and public health epidemics or other types of crisis management depend on the quality of the data obtained by research.

In-Depth Interviewing

Assembling 10 to 14 persons in one location at one time for a focus group can be difficult. *In-depth interviewing* or *intensive interviewing* (Williamson, Karp, & Dalphin, 1977, pp. 164–197) may provide an attractive alternative; it is conceptually similar to focus group interviewing but is conducted with individuals one at a time in sessions that typically last about 45 minutes.

A variation of this research methodology, called *individual focus sessions* (IFS) (Wimmer & Dominick, 1987, p. 155), is similar in methodology to focus group research in preparation, empathic nondirective interviewing, and probing. Moreover, as Wimmer and Dominick observe, it also totally rules out the chance, encountered in focus groups, that some individual or individuals may attempt to dominate. A relative weakness, as compared with focus groups, is that IFS offers no interviewee interactions to serve as catalysts. Other weaknesses are that lengthy, intensive interviewing sessions may cause fatigue and also increase the total interviewing time and expense.

The remainder of this chapter discusses focus group research in greater detail. The methodology is rather simple, and the information that follows is sufficient to get you started quickly if you need to begin exploratory research soon. Focus groups also can be used for verification research in problem analysis.

IMPLEMENTING FOCUS GROUP RESEARCH

Focus group research requires mastery of only a few basics. However, successful implementation is more an art than a science. Satisfactory results depend to a considerable degree on the practitioner's intuition and good sense.

At the outset, you must have a clear idea of your target audience segment or segments. The key purpose of intensive interviewing with persons representing each segment is to produce information that supports or rejects key operating assumptions for the campaign as defined in the real state and ideal state analyses, segmentation strategy, and force field analysis. In addition, such small-group interviewing sometimes turns up new insights that would be unlikely to emerge in survey research, where the structure of the questionnaire generally discourages general exploration because it is not cost effective.

Constituting Focus Groups

The quality and representativeness of any focus group depends in large part on how well you can identify each target segment and get the cooperation of persons who are presumed to be typical of that segment. In most cases, the selection is purposive: Individuals are picked ''on purpose'' because they are presumed to match the characteristics of an audience segment. However, although the individuals might match adequately on some characteristics, they might be atypical in others that are important. The fact that some individuals volunteer readily to participate in focus group research whereas others decline might skew the representation of some characteristics. What often results is a hidden bias—over- or underrepresentation in the focus group of certain critical attributes that exist in the target segment. When a list of members of each target segment exists or can be constructed, such selection biases can be countered or cancelled through random selection. (Procedures for random or probability selection are discussed in Chapter 4.)

The selection of focus group participants commonly involves screening procedures. Wimmer and Dominick (1987, pp. 488–489) suggest the following:

1. Individuals should not be drawn from one organization only. Sometimes there is a temptation to cut corners, but then the members of the focus group would tend to be highly homogeneous in characteristics and, therefore, possibly nonrepresentative.

2. Persons who have participated in related focus group interviews during the last year should be omitted.
3. Relatives of participants should not be allowed to participate in the same focus group or other focus groups being conducted for the same project.
4. Because some persons may not show up, overrecruitment is necessary.
5. Persons who agree to be interviewed must be informed that if they arrive late, they will not be permitted to participate. Often, focus group sessions start with background explanations; persons who arrive late will be unable to participate fully without such information.
6. Arrangements for payment should be made clear, especially in regard to the policy about individuals who arrive late and the possibility that not enough people will be obtained to constitute a group.

The number of individuals selected for each group is not uniform in all cases. However, having too few might limit the types of experiences represented, and having too many might inhibit participation. As a general rule, 10 to 14 participants should be adequate.

Number of Groups

Each target audience segment should be represented by a separate group; mixing subjects is inadvisable. The logic of segmentation and force field analysis is that each segment operates on the basis of some distinctive or unique pattern of behavioral factors, so combining persons from different segments in a single focus group yields less information about individual segments and blurs distinctions.

Additionally, a campaign manager or planner might insist on the replication of focus groups. With one focus group per audience segment, findings might be unique to that particular focus group; if two or even three focus groups are formed for each segment, comparisons can be made across comparable groups to see whether certain important results are repeated. When they are, you can be more certain that real trends exist and the focus groups are representative.

Preparing for the Interviews

Focus group interviewing requires a special psychological orientation, as well as empathy skills (Katz, 1963; Howell, 1982) and thorough preparation. The interviewer—or, better, *moderator*—does not work from a structured questionnaire but may rely on memory or notes to keep the inquiry on track.

A potential moderator should spend extensive time before the interviews to obtain, organize, and synthesize information about the problem. Familiarity with the content makes quick and relevant action possible. Notes for a session should be concise, rather than copious, to provide rapid, unobtrusive prompts for memory.

Nondirective Interviewing

The moderator must be sensitive to what the participants are saying, instill confidence, and be ready to detect cues that indicate a need for tactful and timely efforts to extract needed information, for example, when interviewees are hesitant or shy. An understanding of group dynamics is vital; one person's viewpoint can be used as a catalyst to open up discussion by other members of the group.

Case Study. Here is a sample focus group dialogue that illustrates some of the principles just discussed:

MODERATOR: We're here today to talk about why people practice preventive health maintenance—that is, why they do or don't learn about how to protect their own health and avoid putting off problems till they become major ones. Particularly, we want to talk about why males who are professionals and in the same age group as your husbands seem ambivalent about health maintenance. Anyone have any ideas?

MRS. CUNNINGHAM: I don't know, but it seems some men "want to be taken care of." My husband's mother worried over his ailments and scheduled his medical appointments. Now he expects me to do it for him.

MODERATOR: Anyone else here encounter this problem? [Three persons are seen to nod their heads in agreement.]

MRS. ALDER: I certainly do. But lately, I've tried to get my husband to take more responsibility. We set up a calendar for regular appointments. We also note on the kitchen calendar special programs at the health maintenance organization that will deal with our special problems—when the meetings will be held, and where to call to sign up.

MODERATOR: Mrs. Franklin, you seemed to be on the verge of saying something. What was it?

MRS. FRANKLIN: I think women have been brainwashed into thinking that health is women's business and men have been brainwashed into a macho mentality that contends that a man is a wimp if he doesn't keep his pains to himself and just keep plodding along—even if it leads to stress and a heart attack.

MRS. ADLER: Uh-huh. That's the reason I think women have to begin to reeducate their mates—and themselves, as well, about preventive health maintenance.

MODERATOR: Could I see a show of hands here: How many of you would say you were brought up to think health was "women's business" and that males in the family were supposed to "tough it out"? (Ten of 12 participants raise their hands.)

MRS. THURMAN: My husband equates my handling his health appointments and such as a sign of my "caring."

MODERATOR: From what we've found out, that's not unusual. The question is: Is that the best thing for him? What happens when you can't anticipate his problems?

MRS. ADLER: He probably gets her up in the middle of the night and . . .

MRS. THURMAN: He suffers . . . and not quietly. And I suffer. There ought to be some ways to break the chain.

MODERATOR: Mrs. Alder gave one suggestion about agreeing on regular checkup dates and posting notices of health information programs. What other ways can you see?

This interview segment confirms several characteristic patterns:

1. The moderator has a clear theme but is not highly directive in terms of controlling the discussion.
2. The moderator encourages individuals to elaborate on others' statements when they seem to provide useful information or insights.
3. The moderator is quick to recognize nonverbal cues—eye contact, throat clearing, hand movements—that indicate a reticent person might be ready to contribute. Asking for some behavior such as a show of hands may be used to draw the individual into the dialogue.
4. The moderator often restates what might be trends to verify them.
5. The moderator sometimes cites trends from sources outside the group, such as research reports, to reassure participants when they seem to be concerned that they are out of the mainstream.

Nonverbal Cues

The sample interview embodies suggestions of *nonverbal cues* (Mortensen, 1972, pp. 209–253, & 289–310), for example, when the moderator first noticed that Mrs. Franklin seemed to want to talk. She may have gestured, leaned forward in anticipation, or momentarily displayed concern. If various nonverbal cues are understood by the moderator, he or she should be able to take appropriate steps to ensure successful interviewing.

Situational geography cues deal with aspects of layout that indicate what relationships are expected or permitted (see Mortensen, 1972, pp. 289–319). A seating arrangement that makes it possible for all members of an interviewing session to have eye contact is important; persons who are excluded tend to think that they are not expected to enter into the conversation. Circular seating arrangements facilitate eye contact and also suggest equality. A horseshoe-shaped seating arrangement, with the moderator in the opening of the U, makes eye contact possible and provides a cue that interaction among interviewees is expected to be generally democratic; however, the fact that the moderator is seated somewhat apart and where everyone's gaze is focused suggests an element of control.

Body language cues include body and head positions and use of hands. People lean forward when interested, and slouching may indicate disengagement or disinterest. (Although it might also indicate a very relaxed state.) Eye contact usually suggests involvement, whereas averting the eyes may indicate disinterest, nervousness, or evasion. Individuals often tilt their heads to one side or the other while listening carefully. Nodding of the head may be a signal of agreement, though it could indicate fatigue. When body language cues are checked against other observations, the interpretation of cues is likely to be more accurate.

Microfacial cues are expressions that flash across a person's face in a fraction of a second but are often perceived by others (Mortensen, 1972, p. 322). As with body language cues, microfacial expressions suggest particular frames of mind; for example, an extremely rapid raising of one eyebrow suggests skepticism, of both eyebrows suggests surprise, or a flickering sneer suggests disdain.

Facilitating and blocking cues can be used by a moderator to encourage or discourage participation, usually when dealing with particular situations. Mortensen (1972, pp. 229–237) refers to these as communication *regulators*. Sustained eye contact, smiles, affirmative nods, and pointing are examples of *facilitating cues*. Avoidance of eye contact, shaking the head from side to side (as when saying no), and disapproving facial cues can serve as *blocking cues* that inhibit individuals from participating. Blocking cues must be used selectively; otherwise, individuals who receive them may become discouraged and withdraw.

Game-playing cues are often present in focus groups. Some individuals may have both a goal and a game plan—both of which tend to be evident in many social situations (Berne, 1964, 1976). Part of the game involves the ability of a moderator to recognize that a game is in progress. Another part of the game involves the moderator's improvision of a counter strategy. Cues can suggest that an individual might be involved in one or more of the following games, although it is possible to encounter shifts in games as well as strategies during a single session:

- The Leader ("*I* am the one *really* in charge here!")
- The Expert ("I know more about this than *anyone!*")
- The Bully ("*You* do not understand the problem! That is a *dumb* suggestion!")
- The Parent ("I suggest we do it *this* way [*my* way]")
- The Leader ("Come on! Let's get our act together. We can make a breakthrough if we *try*! Assault the objective now!")
- The Cynic/Pessimist ("There's no way of solving this problem. It's not worth our time, anyhow")

- The Victim ("Now don't hit me for saying this . . .")
- The Child ("I don't understand complex topics. This thinking hurts my head. I want my teddy bear!")

Transactional Analysis

Another vantage point a moderator might consider in the conduct of focus group research is *transactional analysis*, which is based on the work of Eric Berne (see Berne, 1964, 1976; Harris, 1969; James, 1975; Wagner, 1981). The conceptual scheme contends that each individual engaged in interpersonal dialogue speaks from one of three *ego states*—though not necessarily consistently—Parent, Adult, and Child (usually abbreviated as *P-A-C*). The Parent may be authoritarian or paternalistic, that is, controlling, judgmental, and willing to rebuke or punish. The Child tends to be lacking in self-confidence; seeks approval; is eager to evade confrontation; is overly deferential; is sometimes petulant and self-pitying; and is often vacillating, even to the point of completely reversing position when encountering opposition. The Adult is frank, open, and nonthreatening in expressing and receiving information, points of view, and even criticism; this person's demeanor suggests self-worth, competence, and well-being and a belief that the other person in the dialogue has equivalent, admirable characteristics.

In a democratic situation, communication is easiest, and perhaps most effective, when all individuals speak from their Adult ego states. Communication becomes crossed when people speak from different ego states as in Exhibit 3.1; then a blockage occurs.

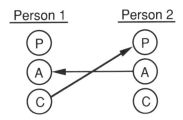

ExHIBIT 3.1. Example of Blocked Communication Transaction
Source: Muriel James, *The OK Boss* (Reading, MA: Addison-Wesley, 1975). Reprinted by permission from Muriel James.

Once an individual senses a blocked transaction, awareness of the difference in ego-state positions tends to become obvious. This may suggest a strategy to "uncross" the communication and remove the blockage. Often, it is possible to maneuver an individual into another, more salutary ego state. For example, consider this dialogue as a possible solution for the problem expressed in Exhibit 3.1:

PERSON 1: I really feel dumb! I don't understand this at all. Well . . . my opinions probably don't count for much here anyhow.

PERSON 2: You've been doing just fine so far. Tell me what you understand, and perhaps some of us can help clear up what's puzzling you. Everyone has something that "throws" them at one time or another.

Setting Up for Focus Group Interviews

Focus group settings should be comfortable and facilitate interaction— a kind of living room, perhaps, or a conference room with a large, round table. The main idea is to establish a friendly environment that puts individuals at ease.

Recording the Sessions

Since the moderator must expend considerable psychological effort to keep the discussion on track and moving efficiently, it would not be realistic to expect the same individual to take detailed notes. Some moderators make notes after the sessions, attempting to reconstruct the main points. However, both detail and context may be lost when that is done.

A widely used alternative is a conference recording system, in which tapes can be transcribed for analysis. Videotape recordings also can be useful; they have the advantage of capturing nonverbal cues that may be essential to the interpretation of what has been recorded. However, videotaping has disadvantages as well: It is usually intrusive and relatively costly.

Analysis of Session Results

There are no hard rules for analyzing session results, other than that the information should be written down. However, here are some things you might consider:

If focus groups are used for exploratory purposes, rather than verification of segmentation strategy and force field analyses, you should be alert initially to indications of the level of participants' concern with the problem; if the level is low, it might pose challenges to your segmentation assumptions. If participants do offer views, you should look for patterns in agreement because repetition often suggests something about the degree of concern.

The 11 inventory categories suggested in Chapter 2 for the ideal state/ real state analyses might serve as a framework for clustering observations. You should also be alert to contrasts because points of view other than those you consider likely may emerge, offering fresh perspectives on your problem. Usually, it is helpful to synthesize the findings in written summaries. Additionally, you can speed up the analysis by dividing the work into two sequential activities: (1) organization of facts and (2) evaluation. If you attempt to organize and evaluate at the same time, you are almost certain to vacillate between one activity and the other.

If the results are used for verification, the problem is simpler because the ideal state/real state analyses, segmentation strategy, and force field analysis provide the structure. The main concerns are whether the assumptions or facts that were stated actually are supported by the findings. You need to be alert to repetition or elaboration that might suggest intensity of concerns for evaluating different factors in the summary diagrams. Additionally, although most of the emphasis is on verification, it is important to look for points of view that challenge or contradict assumptions stated in the problem analysis or indicate it needs to be substantially reassessed.

The problem analysis must always be considered tentative until research leads to either confirmation or revision, and work then begins on the managerial objectives that will shape and control the campaign. Additionally, as in the analysis of exploratory results, you should plan the work here in two steps—organization, then evaluation.

Selecting a Research Firm

In even relatively small organizations, a manager or planner may prefer to delegate the work to a focus group research firm. Wimmer and Dominick (1987, pp. 486–488) suggest factors that should be considered:

1. Do not select a firm based on its membership in some reputable organization alone; the firm may have bought a membership in order to gain credibility.
2. Call colleagues who work in management, planning, or research to ask for recommendations.
3. If you are not familiar with a research firm, ask for a list of its clients and contact them to verify their satisfaction.
4. Inspect the interviewing setup of the firm you are considering. The location should be easy to reach, be safe, and have adequate parking. The quarters should be comfortable and agreeable and should provide space for about 14 persons. The equipment should be adequate and probably should be tested, for example, to be sure that microphones are sufficiently sensitive to pick up voices anywhere in the room and that they produce clear sound quality.
5. You should consider meeting and discussing procedures and operations with key personnel, especially the person who will conduct the research. Moreover, you should verify policies about payment to interviewees and the firm, for example, what laypersons and professionals who are interviewed will be paid (usually payments are higher for the latter group) and what will occur if the firm does not attract a sufficient number of interviewees for any particular session.

SUMMARY

This chapter discusses the advantages and disadvantages of survey research, focus groups, and in-depth interviewing. Such methodologies are extremely useful, particularly in verification research.

Structured, systematic research methodologies are vital to verify stratification and force field analysis assumptions. Unstructured or improvised research leaves a manager or planner vulnerable because subjects may be nonrepresentative and findings may be skewed or biased in ways not easily detected. You must take every step to be certain that the data, facts, or opinions you collect are representative and correctly relate the essence of the situation. Improvised research leads to poor results that are managerially unacceptable. Worse, bad information leads to bad managerial decisions.

Systematic implementation of survey research, focus groups, or in-depth interviewing will determine the quality of your information and the trust you can place in it.

Survey research is superior to either focus groups or in-depth interviewing: The methodology ensures representative samples, offers formulas to determine how many persons must be interviewed, and makes possible specified levels of precision in the projection of findings. The next chapter will discuss survey research methodology in considerable detail.

Focus group research is a simple, relatively quick, and inexpensive method that may be an alternative to the more complex, time-consuming, and costly survey research. Limitations of focus groups concern representativeness and a virtual exclusion of possibilities for statistical analysis and statistical projection of apparent trends. Replication of focus groups is a way to improve confidence in detected trends, but it does not resolve the statistical problems. However, when you must confront a choice between no verification and focus group research, the latter is always preferable. In-depth interviewing is conceptually similar to focus group research in exploration and probing, although it is conducted with individuals rather than groups.

If you or your subordinates must conduct focus group research, the awareness of behaviors relating to small group processes as well as mastery of managerial planning and execution procedures are vital. This chapter gives specific suggestions.

If you decide it is more efficient to use a research firm for focus group or in-depth interviewing, criteria for selection are presented.

A manager or planner must be seriously concerned with research because if misleading results are obtained as a result of planning without verification, all subsequent decisions based on those early assumptions are likely to be in error.

REFERENCES

Eric Berne, *The Games People Play* (New York: Grove Press, 1964).

Eric Berne, *Beyond Games and Scripts* (New York: Grove Press, 1976).

Thomas Harris, *I'm Okay—You're OK: A Practical Guide to Transactional Analysis* (New York: Harper & Row, 1969).

W. S. Howell, *The Empathic Communicator* (Belmont, CA: Wadsworth, 1982).

Muriel James, *The OK Boss* (Reading, MA: Addison-Wesley, 1975).

Robert L. Katz, *Empathy: Its Nature and Uses* (New York: Free Press, 1963).

C. D. Mortensen, *Communication* (New York: McGraw-Hill, 1972).

Abe Wagner, *The Transactional Manager: How to Solve Your People Problem with T.A.* (Englewood Cliffs, NJ: Prentice-Hall, 1981).

J. B. Williamson, D. A. Karp, and J. R. Dalphin, *The Research Craft* (Boston: Little, Brown, 1977).

R. D. Wimmer and J. R. Dominick, *Mass Media Research*, 2nd ed. (Belmont, CA: Wadsworth, 1987).

FURTHER READINGS

F. N. Kerlinger, *Foundations of Behavioral Research*, 2nd ed. (New York: Holt, Rinehart and Winston, 1973).

L. H. Kidder, *Selltiz, Wrightsman and Cook's Research Methods in Social Relations*, 4th ed. (New York: Holt, Rinehart and Winston, 1980).

Leslie Kish, *Survey Sampling* (New York: Wiley, 1965).

R. W. Pace and D. F. Faules, *Organizational Communication*, 2nd ed. (Englewood Cliffs, NJ: Prentice-Hall, 1989).

R. S. Ross, *Small Groups in Organizational Settings* (Englewood Cliffs, NJ: Prentice-Hall, 1989).

CHAPTER 4

Survey Research Methodology

Managers and planners often must deal with campaigns in which the risk attached to "soft" research, such as focus groups or in-depth interviewing, is unacceptable. Usually, such situations do not allow for more than a minimal margin of measurement error—as in a competitive market. These situations also may demand precise measurement of the *KAMP variables*, knowledge, affect, motivation, and practice, and others at the outset to establish benchmark or baseline data against which end-of-campaign evaluation results can be compared.

The *survey research* methodology presented here serves not only exploratory and verification needs but also media strategy formulation and end-of-project evaluation. Survey research, also called "questionnaire research," enables you to obtain managerially defensible data that are (1) representative, (2) generalizable to a specific audience segment, and (3) precise estimators of audience characteristics.

This chapter provides substantial detail about survey research because the information serves two goals: (1) improving your efficiency as a manager or planner and (2) aiding your training of subordinates to whom you might delegate research tasks.

The following pages explain how to plan survey research relatively quickly, implement sampling, collect data efficiently, and analyze and interpret data simply. You need not worry about "math shock"; this chapter introduces you to two easy-to-master statistical techniques.

1. *Frequency and percentage analysis* involves counting the number of persons who give particular responses and calculating their percentages.

2. *Cross-tabulation analysis* deals with an elementary form of relational or correlational analysis that can also be interpreted in terms of frequencies and percentages. The logic of cross-tabulation analysis is explained in terms of sorting and subsorting responses and then counting. Also, this chapter explains elementary rules for the interpretation of the resulting data tables.

USING DUMMY DATA TABLES TO PLAN SURVEY RESEARCH

Planning a questionnaire, which usually is your first step in survey research, is easy if you use (1) *dummy data tables* to specify the formats and the variables essential to the final data analysis and (2) *operationalization* to explain how you intend to measure these variables, which also might be called factors or concepts.

Dummy data tables include all the characteristics of a final report's tables, *except the actual figures*. Research fieldwork provides the data later.

At this point, you must learn the standard components of data tables:

1. A heading, with a table number, and a summary description of the table's contents

2. The exact wording of the question or questions used in the table (although some investigators prefer to give that information in an appendix): The wording or structure of a question sometimes can affect the nature of the response; persons who evaluate the research results usually want to know the wording in order to have a context for data interpretation.

3. A label for the variable, factor, or concept: In tables that involve more than one variable (which alternatively may be called a factor or concept), each must be labeled.

4. Labels for each level of measurement, or response category, of each variable in a table.

5. Frequencies of response for each level of each variable: As explained, a frequency is simply the number of persons giving a particular response.

6. Each frequency count transformed into a percentage: This makes possible the comparison of answers on a common base of 100 percentage points. When the total number of responses in a category is small, for example, fewer than 30, this step is not necessary because when there are few cases, even small changes in frequency counts produce disproportionately large percentage changes.

7. The N, or total number of responses, for a table or for totals of response groupings in a table: Column and row frequency totals in a table are important; for example, anyone reading a table can verify quickly the totals used to calculate percentages.

8. An accounting for nonresponse: Persons who read a table need to know when a question is not answered, to determine N as a base for percentages.

9. Finally, explanatory footnotes: Not all tables require explanatory footnotes, but sometimes you may need them to give statistical significance criteria or identify sources of data from other research.

Univariate Dummy Data Tables

A univariate format deals with one question at a time and mainly serves to report how many respondents selected each response category and what percentage responded to each. The format resembles Exhibit 4.1.

EXHIBIT 4.1. Example of Univariate Table
Table X: Exposure to Information About Relationship Between Cigarette Smoking and Cancer

	%	**Frequency**
Exposed to information	_____ %	( )
Not exposed to information	_____ %	( )
Totals	100%	( )
Nonresponse = _____		

Note: Response frequencies are given in parentheses.

In this example, you can see that to get the needed information, you would have to ask only one question, whether respondents have been exposed to information about cigarette smoking and cancer. You can also see that the question would have two answer categories or response levels: exposed or not exposed.

More often, you may be interested in relationships involving two or three variables. By using cross-tabulation of the responses to two or more questions, you can be more specific in determining the conditions under which an answer or behavior results. For example, you might wonder whether an answer pattern would be the same if it were broken down according to smoking behavior (smokers versus nonsmokers). Such a question can be answered by a bivariate (two-variable) cross-tabulation table.

Bivariate Dummy Data Tables

A manager or planner makes extensive use of bivariate tables in campaign planning. First, these tables are a way to test whether behaviors that seem to control the problem correlate statistically with specific demographic characteristics. Second, they can be used to determine whether demographic segments that distinguish target audience segments correlate statistically with mass media or other communication channels. In the latter case, the information supports the development of media and channel strategy and plans (discussed in Chapter 7).

A bivariate cross-tabulation dummy data table has the format in Exhibit 4.2. This example shows that two questions must be written for a questionnaire. One deals with exposure to information and has two response categories: exposed or not exposed. The other deals with whether the respondent smokes and has two response levels: smoker or nonsmoker.

Exhibit 4.2. Example of Bivariate Table

Table *X*: Relationship Between Whether Subject Smokes and Exposure to Information About Cancer

Exposure to Information	Whether Subject Smokes	
	Smoker	*Nonsmoker*
Exposed	_____ %	_____ %
	( )	( )
Not Exposed	_____ %	_____ %
	( )	( )
Totals	100%	100%
	( )	( )
Nonresponse = _____		

Note: Response frequencies are given in parentheses.

Multivariate Dummy Data Tables

Sometimes you must examine effects of a third variable on the relationship between two other variables—for example, the two in Exhibit 4.2. Suppose you want to determine whether gender affects the initial relationship between smoking status and information exposure. Here, you would introduce gender as a *test factor* or *control variable*.

The resulting multivariate (in this case, three-variable) table resembles the format in Exhibit 4.3. Notice what happens to the table format if you introduce a third variable to test for its effect on the original two-variable relationship. It causes the original table to be reproduced a number of times equal to the levels of measurement or response categories in the third variable. Since the third variable, gender, has two levels of measurement—male and female—the bivariate table is reproduced two times: One subtable reports responses of male subjects only; the other subtable reports responses of female subjects only.

Three questions are necessary to obtain the data for this multivariate table. One question deals with exposure to information about cigarette smoking and cancer, and it has two levels of measurement or response: exposed or

Exhibit 4.3. Example of Multivariate Table
Table *X*: Relationship Between Smoking and Exposure to Information, Controlled for Gender

Exposure	Males		Females	
	Smoker	Nonsmoker	Smoker	Nonsmoker
Exposed	_____%	_____%	_____%	_____%
	( )	( )	( )	( )
Not exposed	_____%	_____%	_____%	_____%
	( )	( )	( )	( )
Totals	100%	100%	100%	100%
	( )	( )	( )	( )
Nonresponse = _____				

Note: Response frequencies are given in parentheses.

not exposed. The second concerns whether the subjects smoke, and it has two levels of measurement: smokers or nonsmokers. The third ascertains the gender of the subjects, and it has two levels of measurement: male or female.

Conventions for Bivariate Table Organization

Two conventions determine which is the row variable and which is the column variable in cross-tabulation tables:

1. If you put the independent, or predictor, variable at the top of a table (on the columns), you would place the dependent, or outcome, variable at the side of the table (on the rows).
2. If you put the independent or predictor, variable at the side of a table (on the rows), you would place the dependent, or outcome, variable at the top of the table (on the columns).

Usually, it is reasonably easy to identify the independent, or predictor, variable. You usually treat demographic variables such as age, gender, education, or income as independent, or predictor, variables. Additionally, there is a simple logic test to determine what variables fall into what classes. When you think in terms of the phrases "If I know X, can I predict Y?" or "Is X correlated with Y?" the odds are strong that whatever variable you substitute for the abstract symbol X is the independent, or predictor, variable, and whatever variable you substitute for Y is the dependent, or outcome, variable.

Picking the convention for the table setup is not a matter of choosing the correct way. Both conventions are acceptable. The first probably is easier for a novice to master and use efficiently. It tends to simplify basic data analysis. However, you might use the second format when results from several tables must be condensed and compiled in a single, large table.

To further simplify the discussion of two- and three-variable tables, this chapter uses the first convention hereafter: Predictor, or independent, variables will be put at the top, and outcome, or dependent, variables will be put at the side.

OPERATIONALIZATION

Operationalization requires that whatever you measure—you may call it a variable, a concept, or a factor—must be explained in terms of how it should be measured. Here are some examples:

1. *Education:* Education of the individual will be measured by asking the last grade of formal education that the person fully completed.
2. *Age:* Age will be determined by asking the individual's age on the last previous birthday. Ages will be grouped into the following intervals: up to 18, 18–34, 34–44, 45–54, 55–64, and 65 or older.
3. *Adoption rate:* The adoption rate (adoption of new practices or techniques) will be measured by asking the individual to cite new practices or techniques used now but not used before the training session. The number of practices cited will be the rate for that individual.
4. *Attitude toward X.* The individual's attitude toward X (some concept that would be specified) will be measured by asking ten questions with content clearly related to the topic—that is, with *face validity*. Each response that shows a favorable attitude toward X will be given a value of one (1) in coding; other answers will be given a value of zero (0). The degree of the individual's attitudinal favorability toward X will be ascertained by summing the values assigned to the ten answers in each questionnaire.

Operationalization helps focus your attention on what will be measured and how. Additionally, it implies that you should begin to think about the number of levels of measurement or response categories you want for each variable. This decision is easiest when you use nominal categories (ones classified by name)—for example, in the operationalization of "party preference," Democrat, Republican, and Independent. Although you usually have an idea about the number of answers that must be considered and can list them, occasionally you will be aware that some answers cannot be envisioned while planning is under way. Here, you can incorporate the category "other." When you use such a catchall category, interviewers ask respondents for explanations during interviews. The details can be recorded, categorized, and coded later, if that proves to be desirable. Sometimes you may find the category "other" useful in a pretest of your questionnaire; this pretest may yield unanticipated but valuable new categories that should be added to the questionnaire before full-scale interviewing in the field gets under way.

In summary, dummy data tables and operationalization structure the planning of research by requiring you to specify

1. *What* you must measure
2. *How* you intend to measure each variable
3. *What or how many levels* of each variable you must measure
4. What *relationships, associations, or correlations* you intend to examine
5. How you expect to *tabulate* or *analyze* the data your research obtains
6. How you plan to report the data—that is, in what format

The economy you gain in planning is substantial.

Once you have determined what data are necessary, you need to design a questionnaire. The next section discusses the formulation of questions.

DESIGNING AN EFFECTIVE QUESTIONNAIRE

The Format of Questions and Declarations

Most of the time, you use questions and declarations to obtain information. Questions are interrogatory forms, such as "Did you read a daily newspaper yesterday?" Declarations are statements to which a questionnaire asks a respondent to react, such as "Now, I'd like you to use one of these five categories to tell me how you feel about the statement I am about to read: agree strongly, agree, disagree, or disagree strongly. The statement: The United States should elect a president for six-year terms instead of four-year terms."

Both questions and declarations share a basic format in questionnaires: They contain a stem and a response section. The *stem* is the main text of the question or the declaration. The *response section* is the part of the question or declaration where an interviewee's response will be recorded. The response section may be made up of lines on which answers can be recorded verbatim or summarized or of answers that can be checked off.

There are four rules for the basic format of a question or declaration:

1. The question stem (the part beginning, "Do you have a radio . . ." in Exhibit 4.4) should be double-spaced.

EXHIBIT 4.4. Question Stem and Response Section

5. Do you have a radio in working order in your car?

1 ( ) Yes   2 ( ) No   3 ( ) No response

2. The response section (the part with the check-off boxes in this example) should be indented at least three spaces. The indentation creates a finger of white that points to the question stem, making it stand out visually. This format reduces the likelihood that an interviewer or interviewee might miss the stem of any question or declaration inadvertently.

3. When a question or declaration has prestructured response categories (as in Exhibit 4.4), they should be single-spaced. The usual layout is vertical, except when there are a limited number of short response categories—for example, "Yes," "No," and "Don't know"; in this case, the categories may be placed horizontally, provided there is sufficient space to separate them visually.

4. If the question requires an interviewer or interviewee to record an answer verbatim or to summarize it, at least two double-spaced lines should be provided.

Six Standard Question and Declaration Formats

There are six basic question and declaration formats in survey research with which you should be familiar: (1) the open-ended question, (2) the check-the-answer or prestructured question, (3) the forced-choice question, (4) the Likert-type declaration, (5) the continuum-type response, and (6) the filter question.

Open-Ended Question. The open-ended question looks like Exhibit 4.5.

EXHIBIT 4.5. The Open-Ended Question

---

6. If you became the manager of your section, what would be the first three things you would do?

    (INTERVIEWER: PROBE FOR SPECIFICS) _____

    _____

    _____

Open-ended questions are useful, particularly to gain information in pretests about what prestructured response categories might be developed and in exploratory studies where responses might provide insights about your problem.

Open-ended questions in a final questionnaire tend to create problems. During an interview, only a skillful interviewer obtains adequate responses, and it requires more time to record answers, which may interrupt the rapport between an interviewer and an interviewee. In self-administered questionnaires, individuals may give cryptic answers. Furthermore, deciphering respondents' or interviewers' handwriting while editing the questionnaires before data coding can be exceptionally difficult; time may be lost while verification goes on. Finally, if you intend to quantify responses for analysis and presentation, you must sample questionnaires, tabulate the sampled answers to establish representative categories for coding, and then code all the responses into appropriate categories for data processing. Overall, open-ended questions are very time-consuming.

When a manager or planner wants quantifiable information, but also wants some explanation from the interviewees, an alternative is to use a structured question (as in Exhibit 4.6) and then to follow with an open-ended question, such as "What are your reasons for saying that?" The initial question could be used for quantitative analysis, and an open-ended question could be used to obtain quotations to enhance and "humanize" your report.

Check-the-Answer Question. The check-the-answer format has prestructured or preestablished response categories. When an interviewee responds, the individual (or the interviewer) simply checks the appropriate response category (see Exhibit 4.6). In this example, if you worry about answers that might have been overlooked in the formulation of response categories, the category "other" can be inserted.

EXHIBIT 4.6. Check-the-Answer Question

15. How did the length of time between your on-campus interview with our company and the next contact compare to other companies' practies you have experienced?

    1 ( ) Shorter
    2 ( ) About the same
    3 ( ) Longer

Forced-Choice Question. When you are interested in specific information to the exclusion of other responses, you should use this format (see Exhibit 4.7). If you do not generalize the interpretation of the resulting data to other situations the question does not cover, this format is both defensible and useful.

EXHIBIT 4.7. Forced-Choice Question

34. Would you prefer to attend the proposed research seminar on Monday afternoon or Friday afternoon?

    1 ( ) Monday afternoon
    2 ( ) Friday afternoon

The forced-choice format looks very much like the check-the-answer format, but the answer categories are not necessarily exhaustive and do not include the category "other" to cover unanticipated answers.

Likert-Type Declaration. The Likert-type declaration derives from a technique developed by Rensis Likert, a pioneer in the elaboration of attitude scales. However, it also serves as a basis for single declarations to which interviewees respond. An advantage of the Likert-type declaration is that it measures both direction (pro or con) and intensity (degree of strength), which makes it particularly suitable for the measurement of beliefs, opinions, attitudes, or values that have both of these characteristics (see Exhibit 4.8).

EXHIBIT 4.8. Likert-Type Declaration

---

23. You felt that you were understood by the interviewer during the interview.

      1 ( ) Agree strongly
      2 ( ) Agree
      3 ( ) Don't know
      4 ( ) Disagree
      5 ( ) Disagree strongly

Five standard response categories follow the stem, always the same ones. You might decide to develop a declaration that uses other response categories, for example, "Frequently," Occasionally," "Rarely," and "Never." This is quite acceptable but technically is not a Likert-type declaration.

Continuum-Type Response. Exhibit 4.9 illustrates this format, in which respondents are instructed either to state or to check with an X where their evaluation falls on a particular continuum. The middle position (3) is equivalent to "neutral" or "don't know"; responses toward either end of the continuum indicate greater intensity—2 signifies "somewhat or relatively high," and 4 "somewhat or relatively low"; 1 signifies "high," and 5 "low."

EXHIBIT 4.9. Continuum-Type Response

---

13. In relation to your on-campus interview, please rate
    1 The professionalism of the interviewer.
      HIGH : : : : : : LOW

         1 2 3 4 5

    2 The placement official's opinion of his company.
      HIGH : : : : : : LOW

         1 2 3 4 5

Like the Likert-type declaration, a continuum measures both direction and intensity.

Filter Question. The filter question detects persons who should not answer one or more questions that follow and routes them to the next appropriate item or section. In Exhibit 4.10, a manager or planner intends to check the readership of the November issue of a newsletter. Therefore, persons who did not read that issue must be "filtered out"; question 13 serves as the filter: It sends persons who should not answer question 14 directly to question 15, the next appropriate item.

These formats are not difficult to master, and they enable you to deal with many different research problems. The basic formats discussed here can be modified, and most managers or planners develop their own style, eventually. The next section explains how to develop scales.

EXHIBIT 4.10. Filter Question

13. Did you read the November edition of the employee
    newsletter?
         1 ( ) Yes   2 ( ) No → (Skip to Question 15)

14. Did you read the newsletter:
         1 ( ) The same day you received it?
         2 ( ) Within a week after you received it?
         3 ( ) More than a week after you received it?

15. Did you receive the employee newsletter at your
    home?
         1 ( ) Yes   2 ( ) No   3 ( ) Don't know

Simple, Summated Measurement Scales

On many occasions, a manager or planner needs a more complex measure of knowledge, beliefs, opinions, attitudes, and values—one that combines several submeasures—in order to create a more reliable indicator than simple questions or declarations.

Under such conditions, you might consider the elaboration and use of a measurement *scale*. Scales offer certain advantages.

First, beliefs, opinions, attitudes, and values represent complex cognitive structures. For example, think about how you evaluate your trust in your own doctor. It is difficult to find a single characteristic that would explain why you trust a physician. Your attitude is likely to be a reflection of several components, such as whether the doctor listens sympathetically; how friends who go to the same doctor regard this person; the doctor's medical training, empathy, appearance, and conduct during your past illnesses; and so on. Thus, a measure that is a composite of these attitudes generally gives a better characterization than one question alone.

Also, an attitude scale may be a more valid measure and predictor if it incorporates subscales relating to knowledge, affect, and policy, as suggested by Daniel Katz, and those designed to test attitude toward the object and attitude toward the situation, as suggested by Milton Rokeach. Chapter 2 discusses these perspectives.

Second, scales comprising several subscales are more reliable in measurement. As a general rule, increasing the number of subscales in a scale improves reliability. *Reliability* is the ability of an instrument (such as a scale) or item (such as a question) to measure consistently across individuals in repeated applications.

A simple, summated scale is one highly useful approach to the development of belief, attitude, or value measurement scales. It presents to an interviewee seven or more questions or statements (subscales) about a topic, and numerical values are assigned to each answer category. Then, to obtain any individual's scale position, the numerical values are simply summed.

Case Study. Suppose that it is necessary to evaluate how clients perceive the communicative behaviors of workers in a service unit of a social welfare agency. All six subscales, or statements, in Exhibit 4.11 are related to the topic of the treatment of clients. This clear relationship signifies that the scale should have *semantic* or *face validity*, the most basic form of validity. In the

---

EXHIBIT 4.11. Format of a Simple, Summated Scale

(INTERVIEWER: READ ALOUD) I'm going to read several statements to you about how people in the client service unit at the agency deal with clients. I'd like you to tell me how you feel about the things I mention. I will ask you to respond in terms of the categories on this card (HAND CARD "B"): Strongly agree, Agree, Don't know, Disagree, or Strongly disagree. Now, here is the first one:
(REPEAT THIS STEM EACH TIME:) The workers in the client service unit:

(a) Do not seem to care about people like me.
      1 ( )SA   2 ( )A   3 ( )DK   4 ( )D   5 ( )SD
(b) Seem to solve problems as quickly as possible.
      5 ( )SA   4 ( )A   3 ( )DK   2 ( )D   1 ( )SD
(c) Attempt to understand what I try to explain.
      5 ( )AS   4 ( )A   3 ( )DK   2 ( )D   1 ( )SD
(d) Are generally unpleasant.
      1 ( )SA   2 ( )A   3 ( )DK   4 ( )D   5 ( )SD
(e) Attempt to explain policies in a clear manner.
      5 ( )SA   4 ( )A   3 ( )DK   2 ( )D   1 ( )SD
(f) Give clear instructions on how to solve problems.
      5 ( )SA   4 ( )A   3 ( )DK   2 ( )D   1 ( )SD

Note: SA = Strongly agree, A = Agree, DK = Don't know, D = Disagree, and SD = Strongly disagree.

development of a scale, you may want to ask colleagues to judge whether all the items logically relate to what the scale proposes to measure. If the items are semantically irrelevant, they must be revised or replaced.

When you assign numerical values to the answer categories for data processing, you always give the highest number to whatever category signifies "the most." Even for declarations in negative form, the answer that represents the greatest favorability toward the unit workers still gets the highest numerical value. The reason underlying the scoring scheme is that it is consistent. Also, some declarations are reversed in direction—that is, negative instead of affirmative—to reduce the likelihood of *response set*, a tendency to respond automatically, without discriminating. Reversal of the declarations tends to discourage automatic response with the same answer.

Each subject's score for the total scale can be determined by adding the numerical scores for all the responses. Some researchers include a box at the bottom of the scale and instruct the interviewers to calculate the total. Others code the individual responses and then instruct a computer to sum the scores and record the scale total for each individual.

Writing Effective Questions and Declarations

The writing of questions or declarations for questionnaires is principally an exercise in *functional* communication; whatever conveys the sense of the idea to a subject with fidelity and to all subjects with consistency passes the effectiveness test.

To fulfill these objectives, you should use the following guidelines:

Frame Questions or Declarations in Simple Sentences. Twenty-one words should be the goal for the length of an average question or declaration, although it might be shorter. Consider whether longer questions can be simplified by dividing them or reducing the number of words. People unfortunately tend to be more pretentious when writing than when speaking. Consequently, it helps to read the text aloud, then ask, Is that how it would be said in natural conversation? If the answer is no, the text should be simplified.

Employ Commonly Used Language. Questionnaires should communicate, not impress interviewees with the writer's education or literacy.

Eliminate Ambiguous Phrasing. If a typical interviewee needs an explanation to clarify the meaning of a question or declaration, it is not explicit enough. One goal in editing a questionnaire should be to modify text whose meaning is unclear. You may detect and eliminate other ambiguities after a questionnaire pretest. However, it is always wise to do your best work at the outset.

Revise Questions That "Lead" the Subject. Questions that contain either blatant or subtle cues about "acceptable" answers bias results. Often you recognize these because they begin with cues such as "Don't you think . . ." or "Wouldn't you say. . . ."

Divide "Double-Barreled" Questions. These questions are ones that actually contain two questions in one, for example, "Do you like Candidate X and his position on pollution control?" If you get a yes answer, you cannot tell whether the individual is referring to the first part, the second part, or both. This uncertainty contributes to measurement error.

Measure Actual Rather Than Hypothetical Behaviors. Hypothetical questions, such as those that begin "Would you. . . ." sometimes evoke the "halo effect"—that is, the person feels pressed to give a socially acceptable or desirable answer. One way to avoid this problem is to measure actual behaviors that are comparable to the ones of interest. For example, asking interviewees whether they would like to see more cultural programs on television probably would get a positive response among a substantial portion of those interviewed, although many would not watch such programs. A better predictor would involve asking whether interviewees have attended concerts or plays recently, bought certain types of records or books, and so on. With a little polishing, such questions can obtain baseline data that prove the interviewees' actual involvement—which is a better estimator of the real level of interest.

Deal with Recent Behaviors. Unfortunately, memory becomes less dependable as the length of time a question covers increases. Subjects do answer, but they use "reconstructed logic"; that is, they mentally reconstruct the past according to what they think should have happened, and the results might not reflect reality. Ask about activities "yesterday" or "during the past week." Also, all interviewees will then be responding to a constant frame of reference, reducing the likelihood of measurement error.

List Choices in Writing When Interviewees Must Pick or Rank a Topic or Item from Among Several. Choices should be made clear in self-administered questionnaires and provided on cards in face-to-face interviews. Relying on memory is risky; people usually remember five to nine items, seven being the average. Forcing people to do a task they cannot accommodate will contribute to measurement error.

Additionally, people recall the first and last items more readily in orally presented lists. These are examples of order effects in learning; the former is *primacy effect* and the latter *recency effect*. It is easier for interviewees to remember other than first or last items in written lists. If you believe position in the list could influence the outcome, you could produce sets of question-naire pages or cards with a rotated order. Coding of rotated answer categories can accommodate different orders, so that data processing need not become confused.

Make Answer or Response Categories in Prestructured Questions or Declara-tions Mutually Exclusive. For example, it is not acceptable to write age categories that overlap, such as 19–25, 25–35, and 35–45 because some interviewees are classified inconsistently in either of two categories, contrib-uting to measurement error. Mutually exclusive categories would be 18–24, 25–34, and so on.

Underline Words If They Must Be Emphasized When the Question or Decla-ration Is Read. Underlining calls attention to the important aspects of the text and ensures that interviewers will stress them uniformly across all inter-views.

Write Special Questionnaire Instructions In Capital Letters or Italics and Underline. An interviewer, for example, often must read instructions such as "READ ALOUD," "IF ANSWER IS NO, SKIP TO QUESTION 8," or "HAND CARD C TO SUBJECT." The convention of capitalizing and under-lining makes the instructions stand out, thus making it less likely that they might be missed or misread.

Checking for Missing Information

If you write each question on a separate half-sheet of paper in standard format, you will be able to sort the items to determine whether there are accidental omissions. Most questionnaires deal with what we call the D.M. KAMP variables, so you might use these as sorting categories:

- *D*emographic variables
- *M*edia or channel variables
- *K*nowledge variables
- *A*ffect variables
- *M*otivational variables
- *P*ractice variables

An additional advantage to this technique is that later you can re-sort and paste the questions and declarations to assemble a draft questionnaire quickly. This can be photocopied to provide questionnaires for editing. If changes must be made, the pasteup can be separated and revisions inserted.

Questionnaire Format

Now it is time to consider how to set up a *questionnaire format*—what to include and in what sequence. The following is a typical standardized sequence:

- Administrative information
- Introduction section
- Question section
- Final administrative section

Administrative Information. Begin the questionnaire by putting in the upper right-hand corner of the first page two important administrative items:

- Interview number: _____
- Time interview begins: _____ A.M./P.M.

Each interview must have its own unique identifier number to (1) help in verifying completion, (2) coordinate documents later in coding and tabulation, (3) link the interview questionnaire with the resulting data cards if you plan to use computer data processing, and (4) keep the data in correct order.

Also, in a pretest you should verify when interviews begin and end, which allows you to calculate actual and average interviewing times and determine how many interviews can be completed per day or per hour.

Introduction Section. Following the administrative items, the questionnaire should include a simple, standardized introduction for the interviewer to read aloud or for the interviewee to read if the interview is self-administered. The introduction precedes the first question and might be stated like this:

> INTERVIEWER (READ ALOUD OR PARAPHRASE): I am (*NAME*) of Health Communication Associates, Boston. We are conducting a study of knowledge about AIDS—Acquired Immunodeficiency Syndrome—among members of the public. Your answers will help public health planners understand where information campaigns are working well and where they can be improved. Your participation is very important. We hope you'll help us by answering a few questions that will take only about ten minutes to complete. May I go on?

Question Section. In opening the question section of the questionnaire, you can build the trust of, and rapport with, interviewees by using simple questions. In this example, you should consider questions about demographics, media use, or opinions about current issues as "warm-up" for your questionnaire.

Assume that by this time you have draft questions prepared in format. You should sort them into a logical sequence. Sometimes you might insert "filler" questions when you want to separate related questions to prevent a line of questioning from becoming too obvious. You may use existing questions for this purpose since inclusion of "dummy" or throwaway questions, for which answers will not be processed, increases interviewing time and constitutes waste.

If demographic questions do not serve warm-up purposes in the opening of a questionnaire, they should make up the final section.

Final Administrative Section. To complete a questionnaire, you should include four final administrative items: (1) an address or phone number, (2) demographics, (3) ending time, and (4) interviewer's comment.

An address or phone number should be obtained for each person interviewed—although not a name since interviewees usually are assured of anonymity. Some method of locating each interviewee is essential because you should verify about 10 to 15 percent of the completed interviews. Callbacks should be made independently to ascertain that interviews are not fabricated and are correct. In phone surveys, the numbers called should be recorded for verification callbacks.

Demographics should be supplied to identify each interviewee. Demographic data serve as verification, as well as in checking data, life-style analysis, and media or channel selection. Particularly in verification callbacks a verifier's job is easier when it is possible to ask for respondents in specific terms, for example, "Is there someone living here who is 35 years old, male, and who was interviewed in a marketing study one night last week?"

The ending time for each interview is useful. The beginning and ending time questions may be dropped after a pretest is completed unless you think you will need the information to manage interviewers. Some organizations pay interviewers for time worked rather than on a per-interview basis, so the information might continue to be important in actual field interviewing.

A section where interviewers can record comments should be provided. Usually, comments about difficulties with the questions in a pretest are valuable in the editing of a final questionnaire. You must examine comments about noncompletion of individual questionnaires to make decisions about whether to order additional callbacks to complete interviews, send another interviewer if "difficult" cases arise, or pay for an interviewer's unsuccessful field calls.

Editing a Questionnaire

After these steps, a questionnaire must be edited. It may be necessary to "smooth out" continuity or flow or to redesign some questions or layouts to save space or prevent a particular question stem and its response categories from being split over two pages. Additionally, you should verify the numbering of questions and the instructions to the interviewers—especially the "skip to" messages associated with filter questions; you must verify and check off each one individually.

For face-to-face interviewing, you must prepare $8 \times 5\frac{1}{2}$-inch cue cards for each question that requires cards as handouts. Each card should be differentiated by letter or number and the identification written into related questions in the questionnaire.

The edited questionnaire can be photocopied and circulated among your colleagues for criticism and suggestions. These photocopies also can be used to conduct one or more in-house test interviews with research or planning staff members. This step may enable you to detect obvious problems and produce a reasonably final, functional questionnaire. After these steps, you should arrange production of about 30 copies for a field pretest.

Field Pretesting a Questionnaire

Besides in-house test interviews, it is customary to execute a field pretest of a questionnaire. Test interviews should be conducted with persons like those who must be interviewed in the project, under conditions similar to those of the actual field research.

You should take care to draw pretest subjects who are not in the sampling area to prevent possible sensitization of your study group. The sampling plan usually is complete by this time, which makes it possible to select areas where interviewing will not be done in the main study. Pretests may be conducted in these nonsampled areas.

We next deal with a crucial part of the research project: the selection of the sample. If the planning of the sample is inadequate, the resulting data will not be trustworthy.

BASIC CONCEPTS UNDERLYING
SCIENTIFIC SAMPLING

Rarely is it feasible to interview all persons in a population (often called an audience in communication research and planning) or even all persons in a segment of the population (often called a target audience) because of the time or costs involved.

Scientific sampling reduces the interviewing time and cost and the volume of data to be analyzed. But more important, it produces data that you can generalize to a specified group with a stated level of confidence and use to make projections within stated precision.

People use sampling subjectively whenever they need to investigate something big or complex or when there is not enough time or money to examine all elements needed to make a decision. For example, if you plan to buy a new Ford, you would not test-drive every Ford in the world to estimate its quality.

Basic Terminology of Sampling

To begin to appreciate scientific sampling, as opposed to commonsense sampling, you must comprehend the following:

Universe is a collection of elements, all with some characteristics in common. For example, the following illustrates the nature of a universe of voters in a particular area:

RRNNRDDDRRRRRIIIDDDDDDDDDDDRRRRRRRRRRIIRRRRRDDDDDDDIIII
IRRRRRRRNNODDDDDDDDDDDDDDIIIIRRRRRRRNNNNNNNDDDDDDDDD

In this list *R* represents Republicans, *D* Democrats, *I* Independents, and *N* adults not registered to vote. All have voting status in common.

A universe usually is so immense or geographically diffuse that it is of little interest to a campaign manager or planner. Most likely, you would deal with a population.

Population is an identifiable segment or subset of a universe. In the preceding universe, if you are trying to predict how actual voters might respond to political issues, the entire universe would not be of interest since persons who are not registered cannot vote. Thus, the population of interest is registered voters who are Republicans, Democrats, or Independents.

You do not have to sample all registered voters in the United States to have a valid sample if your research interest is to predict voting, say, in Maryland. You could sample the population of registered voters in Maryland, who are a subset of the universe of U.S. registered voters. In any universe of adult citizens, you can segment the total into populations by using location, age, gender, income, education, or other variables as criteria.

In communication, these analogies might help you: (1) *Universe* is broad, as is *total audience*; (2) *population* is narrower—a segment—as is *target audience*.

Sampling frame specifically defines how you intend to pick members of the population for study or interviewing.

Consider a universe consisting of college and university professors in greater Boston. A population drawn from the universe could be those teaching or conducting research at Boston University.

A sampling frame might be operationalized in this way: "teaching and research professors who are (1) listed by the Boston University personnel office, (2) above the rank of instructor, and (3) full-time teachers or researchers." A sampling frame operationalizes—or gives specific instructions—to determine what units in the population legitimately should be selected. As a result, you can be explicit about to whom you can generalize the findings from a study.

Failure to state a sampling frame concisely may cause you to interview persons who are not part of a population that you need to study, which can render your data worthless. Moreover, this failure can make it impossible to explain to whom your sampling results can be generalized.

Sampling unit is the smallest unit of analysis with which you intend to work or to use in generalizing the data. Examples are

- Individual—the person, alone
- Conjugal pair—husband and wife, together
- Nuclear family unit—husband, wife, and children, together.

Sample is a collection of elements (people or other) classified by a sampling unit (individual, conjugal pair, etc.) that is drawn from a universe or population, but usually the latter. A sample must represent a clearly defined group of elements.

Factors That Affect Sample Quality

Major factors that dictate the quality of the sample are (1) sampling bias, (2) sampling method, (3) sample size, (4) sampling error, (5) precision, and (6) check-data.

Sampling bias is the systematic overrepresentation or underrepresentation of some characteristic in a population. Suppose women constitute 50 percent of an organization's employees, but a sample in this organization obtains 20 percent women and 80 percent men. This sample is biased because it systematically underrepresents females and overrepresents males.

Sampling bias occurs predictably when the sampling procedures (1) allow people to enter the sample by self-selection, (2) give interviewers opportunities to introduce their own predispositions in the choice of sample elements, or generally (3) do not enable the investigator to be sure of the probability that an element in the population will be selected for the sample.

The principal solution to the problem of sampling bias is the use of scientific sampling methods, which ensures that each population element will have either an *equal* or a *known* chance of becoming part of the sample. For example, if you use a random numbers table to pick subjects in a population of 30 individuals, each person's chance of selection is 1 in 30.

Sampling methods are procedures used to select a sample from a population. Several basic and effective sampling methods will be presented shortly.

Sample size is the number of elements selected from the population for study. In scientific probability sampling, the optimum sample size can be determined through formulas or tables based on mathematical laws of probability. Furthermore, a sample of 350 should yield results that are equally valid in a population of 100,000 as in a population of 10,000. In other words, the commonsense notion that sample size must somehow increase in proportion to the size of the population is not valid.

Sampling error refers to the variability in estimation of some population characteristic from sample data, as compared with what you would find if it were possible to study 100 percent of the population.

Findings obtained by sampling are only estimates of the phenomenon in the population. For example, suppose a survey finds that 45 percent of a population supports an issue. If it were possible to interview everyone in that population, it might be found that the real support percentage is 48, not 45. Sampling error is the difference between the real value in the population and the percentage obtained through sampling.

Precision deals with how small the sampling error is. The magnitude of sampling error depends mainly on two things: (1) the sampling method used to draw the sample and (2) the sample size. However, as stated, the size of the parent population does not control either the sampling error or the precision of estimation.

There is an inverse relationship between sampling error and precision: The smaller the sampling error, the greater the precision of estimation.

Sampling error and precision are stated in points "plus or minus" in relation to the estimate obtained through sampling. To return to the previous example, suppose 45 percent of a sample agrees with a proposition, and you use a formula or table that reveals the sampling error, as related to the sampling method and sample size, to be 3 points. This means that the actual value in the population is likely to be between 45 percent + 3 (48 percent) and 45 percent − 3 (42 percent).

If the sample size were smaller, the sampling error would be greater. For example, suppose that a formula or table for sample size/sampling error relationships (discussed later in this chapter) reveals that a smaller sample size yields a sampling error of 5 points. Thus if the sample data show 45 percent support, the value in the population is likely to fall between 50 percent (45 percent + 5) and 40 percent (45 percent − 5). It is evident that the "spread" in estimation would be greater—that is, as the sampling error increases, the precision of estimation decreases.

Check-data are external data that serve as benchmarks against which data from a sample can be compared to determine whether the sample is representative. Usually, demographic information from the sample data—age, gender, education, income, race—can be compared to similar information from trustworthy sources such as the U.S. Bureau of the Census reports. Check-data are especially important if you must use sampling methods that do not support the calculation of sampling error or when you are not overly confident about sampling methods used by someone else and need to estimate the probable sampling error, for example, if a survey research project draws a presumably representative sample of students from each class level in a particular university and obtains 28 percent second-year students. The registrar's office provides check-data that show that the real percentage of second-year students in this population is 25 percent. The discrepancy between the sample estimate and the external, reliable check-data is only three points. This suggests that the sampling effort yielded an acceptable difference between the obtained sample data and the population data. (However, using more than one check-data indicator might make you feel even more secure in that belief.)

There are two major families of sampling methods—*probability* and *nonprobability*. The first, which is based on mathematical laws of probability, is superior because it produces results that are much more likely to be representative and make possible precise estimation. However, a nonprobability method is explained as a possible ''compromise,'' when time or cost pressures must be addressed. We will examine each in considerable detail.

PROBABILITY SAMPLING METHODS

This section discusses the basic *probability sampling methods* you are most likely to use: (1) interval sampling, (2) simple random sampling with a table of random numbers, (3) random phone dialing, (4) cluster sampling, and (5) multistage random sampling.

Interval Sampling

In interval sampling, subjects are selected from a printed list by determining a consistent interval between names. When a population is a listed one—for example, an organization that has all its employees listed on a central roster or telephone subscribers in a phone book—interval sampling may be particularly attractive. The same may be true if you are able to compile a list of the elements forming the population of interest.

Consider a hypothetical application in a community. Suppose you have determined that telephone subscribers are not different from nonsubscribers in relation to the principal variables of the study, and you decide to draw a sample size of 300 from a newly published phone book with 60,000 names.

The first problem is to determine the skip interval for the sample. To obtain this, you simply divide the number of units in the population by the number of sample units needed. Here, 60,000 is divided by 300. The skip interval therefore is 200 (i.e., 60,000/300 = 200). You then would sample every 200th household with a telephone.

You should take an additional step before you begin the actual selection. The starting point should be randomized to prevent bias linked to a particular starting point and reduce the likelihood that the same households have been sampled in another study with a similar skip interval. You might write numbers 1 through 5 on slips of paper, put them into a container, mix them thoroughly, and then have someone draw one out by chance to pick the first unit in the sample. Suppose the number is 3. Then the third household on the list becomes the first sample unit. Thereafter, you would add the skip interval to the last unit recorded to determine the next sample unit. The number of each sample unit is compared with the name or address that corresponds, and that information is recorded. The interval sampling calculations look like this:

$$3 + 200 = 203 + 200 = 403 + 200 = 603 \ldots$$

The italicized numbers are the units that would be sampled from the list in the phone book.

We advocate using a random numbers table (see the next section) rather than slips of paper to pick the first sample unit; the latter might not be truly randomized despite mixing, creating a chance that some units would have a greater likelihood of selection than others. Moreover, random phone-number generation (also discussed later) is preferable over sampling from phone books because the published lists are neither up to date nor complete—which may create sampling bias.

If a population list used in interval sampling has no particular order, the resulting sample is equivalent to one obtained by simple random sampling. However, if the list is ordered—for example, with members of a company listed within departments—the results of the interval sampling is self-stratifying; that is, the strata in the population (such as the percentages of people in different departments) are represented in terms of their presence in the total population. For example, if Department A has 35 percent of the total employees, an interval sample from a department-by-department list of employees results in about 35 percent of all sample units being from Department A.

Simple Random Sampling

We have all seen names on slips of paper being mixed in an urn, hat, or other container and then drawn by a person who does not look at them. This is a rudimentary—but nonscientific—form of random sampling. However, the slips might not be mixed thoroughly or static electricity might cause some slips to cling to others and have an unequal chance of being picked. For these reasons, you should insist on a scientific method of selection based on a *random numbers table*.

The last pages of almost any standard statistics textbook (e.g., Roscoe, 1975) contain random numbers tables. Some computers provide software, or procedures, to produce random numbers, and some hand-held electronic calculators generate them. The use of a table from a statistics book will be discussed here.

Numbers in a random numbers table occur purely by chance. That is, any number in the table has the same likelihood, or chance, of occurrence as any other number. That being true, any population unit drawn for a sample with a random numbers table has a chance equal to that of any other unit in the population of being picked. Thus a sample obtained through simple random sampling is representative of the population from which it was drawn.

A random numbers table has a series of columns of random digits like those in Exhibit 4.12.

Exhibit 4.12. Section of a Random Numbers Table

	(1)	(2)	(3)	(4)	(5)	(6)
(1)	32405	47901	01073	13924	30711	00341
(2)	13221	16503	44762	86302	05639	96742
(3)	02865	85672	11076	10001	07320	04769
(4)	17153	49201	12304	19999	06308	56082
(5)	39305	90909	11042	19228	40176	42001

Note: This is an abridged table and is not adequate for actual sampling. For a complete table, consult Roscoe (1975) or any other statistics text.

You need to understand certain conventions, or rules, about procedures for entering and reading a random numbers table.

Picking an Entry Point. There are more complex ways to enter a random numbers table, but a simple and workable procedure is the "uninformed bettor" method: Hold a pencil in one hand, point it at the table, close your eyes, move the pencil around, and then drop the point onto the table. Whatever number is closest to the pencil point serves as your entry.

Another procedure is to pick two numbers and use them to designate the intersection of the row and column. Suppose that the number of the current month will be used to determine the column and the date of the day will determine the row: If today's date were March 2, the table would be entered at the intersection of column 3 and row 2.

Reading the Table. To begin, you should determine the number of digits in the highest-numbered population unit in your population. A unit of 432, say, has three digits; you would thus prepare to read columns of three digits in the table—for example, the first three digits of each number in each column. Then you must decide about the direction in which the table should be read. You could read down a column from the entry point to the bottom of the table, then begin again at the top of the next column to the right.

Next, you need to decide what numbers to record. The hypothetical population has 432 units. Therefore, you look for numbers from 001 to 432.

(Treat all numbers as though they are right-justified; when a population unit has a number with fewer digits than the highest-numbered unit in the population, add one zero or more at the left. For example, 1 in this case becomes 001, 35 becomes 035, and 78 becomes 078.)

To show how it all fits together, suppose you have decided to enter the table at the intersection of column 3 and row 2 (find that point in Exhibit 4.12; the number is 44762). You read the left-most three digits, 447, which is greater than the highest number in the population (it is 432), so you disregard it. The next number down the column is 110; it falls within the limits of 001 and 432, so you would record it to identify the first sample unit. The next number is 123 and also falls within the limits of 001 and 432, and you would record it to identify the second sample unit. The next number down the column is 110. Since that number already is on your list, you would disregard it. Continuing to the top of the next column to the right, you encounter 139; you record it to identify the third sample unit. The next number in the table is 863, which is outside the numbered units in the population, and therefore you disregard it. And so it goes until you have the needed list of identifiers. Finally, you compare the list of numbers obtained against the numbered population list to determine what number corresponds with what listed population unit.

Random Phone-Number Generation

A telephone survey introduces a need for a special case of random selection. Sampling from phone books yields biased samples because the newest numbers are not listed and some persons pay to obtain unlisted numbers, which amounts to systematic exclusion. In major U.S. cities, up to about 48 percent of the home telephones are unpublished and unlisted by directory assistance. The problem can be addressed through random phone-number generation. This system produces numbers by chance that are equivalent to both listed and unlisted phone numbers in specified telephone exchange areas.

One variation requires a listing of the prefixes—the first three digits—for the telephone exchanges in each area where the sample must be drawn.

For example, assume that there are six exchanges in a specified area. (In the United States, exchanges are often listed in the Yellow Pages. Otherwise, they can be obtained from the phone companies.) You give each exchange an identifier number—in this case, 1 through 6 (see Exhibit 4.13). Next, you use a random numbers table to create a list of randomly selected prefixes that is equal to the number of units wanted in the sample. For example, you state

EXHIBIT 4.13. Listing of Phone Exchange Numbers

(1) 373-	(2) 891-	(3) 362-
(4) 277-	(5) 292-	(6) 876-

your conventions for entering and reading the table—this time, columns of one digit. Suppose the first random numbers you encounter are 5, 1, 0, 3, and 3. If you match these with the identifier numbers in parentheses in Exhibit 4.12, you get 292- (corresponding to 5), 373- (corresponding to 1)—skipping 0 (since there is no identifier 0 in the list)—362-, and 362- (the latter two corresponding to the random numbers 3 and 3). The last two are the same, presenting no problem because they occur purely by chance, and when the last four digits are filled in, the randomly generated phone numbers will be different anyway.

Usually you must create more than the number of exchange units needed in the event that some calls are not answered or some randomly generated numbers are not in use. About 30 percent might fall into that latter category. Finally, you return to each prefix designated randomly and use the random numbers table to obtain the last four digits to complete each number. One convention is to enter the table at any point, then read and record four digits of each random number in the table, proceeding from the starting point to the bottom of the column and then continuing to the top of the next column. For example, if you refer to Exhibit 4.12, the random numbers table segment, and make a convention to enter column 1 and row 1, then read the left-most four digits, 3240 would be added to the first prefix 292-, to form the first randomly generated telephone number 292-3240. The next would be 373-1322. In the end, you have a list in which each randomly picked exchange prefix is matched with four random digits from the numbers table.

You may need to modify your questionnaire to select specified types of interviewees within the households reached. For example, any household reached by a randomly generated phone number is randomly selected. However, not every household reached by this system has someone with the personal characteristics the sampling frame demands. Filter questions, illustrated earlier, can be used at the beginning of a questionnaire to select individuals who correspond to the specified sampling frame.

Cluster Sampling

Generally, interval and simple random sampling give very good results because they result in a dispersion of the sampling units in the population. Where the population is heterogeneous (having characteristics that vary widely), such dispersion is more likely to enhance representativeness of the sample. However, sometimes you encounter a homogeneous population (i.e., one in which similarities are relatively great) or a situation in which both interval and simple random sampling would create a problem because they disperse sampling units, and you do not have the time or resources to deal with widely dispersed sampling units. In either case, cluster sampling might be an attractive alternative.

Clustering involves the sampling of units that are grouped—for example, names that occur together on a list or adjacent houses in a residential block. A considerable economy in sampling results. Suppose that a simple random sample results in the selection of one household per block in a city; a desired sample size of 300 dictates that you must sample 300 blocks, then a house in each block. Most likely, the sampling units or households are dispersed widely across the city, increasing the time for initial interviews and the callbacks that are usually necessary. However, if you decide that it is satisfactory to sample clusters of three households in each sampled residential block, only 100 blocks would be sampled, a cluster of three households being sampled within each of the 100 blocks. To calculate the number of clusters, you divide the number of sampling units needed (the sample size) by the proposed cluster size, which in the preceding example is 300/3 = 100 clusters. Use of this sampling technique requires the statement of a convention or rule to identify the cluster.

Case Study. Suppose, for example, that you are dealing with an organization that has 2,100 employees and you decide that a sample size of 300 suffices. To determine the number of clusters, you first decide how large each cluster should be. Grouped elements often are more alike; therefore clustering has the effect of reducing the sampling of varied characteristics in the population. To limit homogeneity problems, smaller sampling clusters are preferred; you might specify clusters of only three units each. Next, to calculate the number of clusters, you divide the desired sample size by the cluster size. In this example, 100 clusters (300/3 = 100) are needed. Sampling from a list, you might think of combining clustering with the interval sampling technique: To obtain a skip interval, you divide the population size (2,100) by the number of clusters needed (100 here). The skip interval is 21 (2,100/100 = 21). Then, every 21st unit in the list becomes a starting point for a cluster. As explained earlier, you select the first from of a random numbers table, then progressively add the skip interval and record the results. Suppose the first cluster begins with unit 5. The plan would resemble the one in Exhibit 4.14.

EXHIBIT 4.14. Example of Cluster Sampling

Sample Cluster Starting Point	Population Units in Sample Cluster
5	5, 6, 7
+ 21 (skip interval)	
= 26	26, 27, 28
+ 21 (skip interval)	
= 47	47, 48, 49
+ 21 (skip interval)	
= 68	68, 69, 70
(etc.)	

Case Study. It might be helpful to work through another example. This time, we will combine cluster sampling and simple random sampling. Suppose there are 900 residential blocks in a small town and that 100 clusters of 3 households each are to be drawn. The solution could be worked out as follows:

You would enumerate the blocks on a town map, numbering them from 001 to 900 so that each possible block has a three-digit identifier number. This constitutes a listing of the population of blocks. Next, you use a random numbers table and the procedures explained earlier to pick 100 blocks randomly. Eventually, interviewers can be trained to complete the selection of clusters. They would be instructed in the use of the random numbers table and would be told to go to each block you specify and do the following: Walk around the block and carefully locate and make a map of every living unit (house, apartment in houses, garage apartments, apartments in apartment buildings, etc.). Given each its own individual identifier number for sampling. Pick one living unit from the list, using the random numbers table, which serves as the starting point for a cluster. (For example, if 20 living units were found and numbered 01 through 20, and 15 were the number obtained from the random numbers table, housing units 15, 16, and 17 would make up the cluster.)

Multistage Probability Sampling

In multistage probability sampling, the selection is accomplished in several stages, each based on probabilistic sampling methods. The two previous sampling designs use the logic of *chaining* probability sampling methods to solve a problem, but multistage random sampling usually involves three or more stages.

If you reread the case study of residential block clusters, you may realize that in the first stage, either interval or simple random sampling could have been used to identify the blocks for the sample. In the second stage, simple random sampling was used to pick the starting point for the clusters. If the illustration were extended to a third stage, such as the selection of a subject within a household, simple random sampling could be used again; for example, you could list the adults in the household, give each an identifier number, and then use the random numbers table to pick an identifier number by chance and match it with the identifier number of some household member to pick an interviewee. This constitutes multistage probability sampling.

NONPROBABILITY QUOTA SAMPLING

At times, you might elect to use a comparatively well-controlled form of *nonprobability sampling* known as *quota sampling* to get data more quickly at a lower cost. This sampling method uses stratification in an attempt to guarantee representativeness, but since the final selection of subjects is in the hands of interviewers—rather than being controlled by probability methods—the actual representativeness can be doubtful. Until the 1940s, quota sampling was used extensively for various types of research with relatively good results. Check-data, explained earlier, provide a way of testing sample data for representativeness or freedom from bias and also precision. However, the quality of the data and the degree of confidence in data obtained through quota sampling usually cannot equal that of data obtained through any probability sampling method.

Cost and time savings that result from quota sampling might be enough to counterbalance its weaknesses. A manager or planner often evaluates a sampling design in terms of getting (1) the best possible data for representativeness and precision, (2) at the lowest possible cost or within the budget specified, and (3) within the work deadline specified.

Quota sampling has a reasonable chance of being representative because it involves stratification. Characteristics in a population are represented in the sample in the same proportions in which they exist in the sampled population. For example, if the population has 45 percent males and 55 percent females, the quota sample ensures that 45 percent of the interviews are completed with males and 55 percent with females. However, since the ultimate selection of the persons who will be interviewed is left to interviewers, there is a chance that they might somehow introduce selection biases. Worse yet, because these biases might not be immediately evident, there often is no way to adjust the sample data statistically to offset them.

Case Study. Suppose you must draw a quota sample of members of an organization that is divided into departments. You list departments and numbers of members, then calculate the percentage of the total staff in each department. See Exhibit 4.15 for hypothetical data.

EXHIBIT 4.15. Determination of Substratum Percentages

Department	Employees	Percentage of Total
A	200	20% (200/1000 × 100)
B	500	50% (500/1000 × 100)
C	100	10% (100/1000 × 100)
D	200	20% (200/1000 × 100)
Totals	1000	100%

Next you decide you need a sample size of 300. The quota of sample units allocated to each substratum, or department, is calculated from the preceding information. For Department A, the sample quota is 60 (300 × 20 percent = 60); for Department B, 150 (300 × 50 percent = 150); for Department C, 30 (300 × 10 percent = 30); and for Department D, 60 (300 × 20 percent = 60).

Interviewers are assigned to the different departments, and the quota for interviews in each is specified. The interviews can be completed with any individual in the specified department, at the discretion of the interviewer. However, an interview assigned to be completed in one department cannot be completed in another department. The same rules hold true in a sample of residential blocks, where interviewers must work within the specified area and complete the quota of types of interviews assigned to them. Again, the provision would be that any person in a block who matched the specified quota characteristics can be substituted if another is not available or refuses to participate.

The advantage of being able to substitute is substantial. Remember that probability sampling requires that a specific unit be picked: After a probability method makes the selection, there can be no substitution, as a general rule. Therefore, in probability sampling, interviewers might have to return as many as five times to complete one interview. However, in quota sampling, since persons who are substituted may differ on characteristics that are not part of the sampling criteria, the sample may be biased.

To improve representativeness, quota sample stratification can be based on more than one criterion, such as both gender and education level or gender and income level. However, stratification criteria are meaningless unless they are correlated statistically with the important variables in a study; for example, gender differences affect life-style, buying patterns, and roles; education affects information processing, life-style and roles; and income affects life-style, buying patterns, and roles, among other things.

Even under the best of conditions, this sampling method produces a larger sampling error than any probability sampling method (there will be less precision in projections based on the obtained data). As a rule of thumb, data obtained through this nonprobabilistic sampling method produces a sampling error about 1.5 times greater than data obtained through simple random sampling.

DETERMINING SAMPLE SIZES
IN LARGE POPULATIONS

Data obtained through sampling are simply estimates of data or characteristics that one would find if it were possible to study or interview every unit in the population. The difference between sample data and population data is sampling error, and the larger the sampling error, the smaller the precision of estimation.

Sampling error is affected by (1) the sample size, (2) the probability of occurrence of the event or phenomenon that is being studied, and (3) the sampling method that is selected. The relationship can be expressed in a formula, as in Exhibit 4.16.

EXHIBIT 4.16. Determination of Sample Size

$$\text{sample size needed} = \frac{\genfrac{}{}{0pt}{}{\text{probability}}{\text{of occurrence}} \times \genfrac{}{}{0pt}{}{100 - \text{probability}}{\text{of occurrence}}}{[\text{sampling error desired}/1.96]^2}$$

Suppose you know from a previous study that 20 percent of a population favors a particular issue. This serves as a reasonable estimate of the *probability of occurrence*, a basis for the determination of sample size. The percentage sign is dropped and the number treated as an integer, or whole number. The other term in the numerator is solved by subtracting from 100 the estimate of probability of occurrence (100 − 20 = 80).

Next, suppose you decide that a sampling error of 5 points is acceptable. That is, if the new study finds that 20 percent of the interviewees still favor the issue, the situation in the entire population from which the sample was drawn is not likely to vary more than plus or minus 5 points (or between 20% + 5 = 25% and 20% − 5 = 15%).

To obtain the denominator of the equation, you divide 5 by 1.96, which would produce 2.25. (The 1.96 is a statistical correction factor that makes possible a statement of 95 percent confidence about the projection within specified limits. This factor is explained further.) Next, 2.25 would be squared, producing 6.51.

To complete the calculations, you multiply the two terms in the numerator (20 × 80) and get 1,600. Next, you divide by 6.51, the denominator figure obtained in the previous paragraph. This results in 246 (rounded off), which would be the needed sample size. (Results in Exhibit 4.17 vary from those obtained through the formula because the table is calculated with a factor of 2 rather than the usual 1.96 to correct for a 95 percent confidence level, as in Exhibit 4.16.)

This formula is based on what is called the 95 percent confidence level—which signifies that if samples are drawn repeatedly from the same population, in 95 of every 100 tries the value being measured would not be likely to vary from the one estimate obtained through one sample more than the number of points specified by the sampling error. You or any reader can be 95 percent confident that the true population value is unlikely to be either greater than 25 percent or less than 15 percent.

More precisely, it would mean that if it were found that 20 percent favored the issue, only rarely—only 5 times in 100 cases—would cases fall beyond the estimated limits of 25 and 15 percent. These upper and lower bounds are called the *confidence limits* for estimation at the 95 percent

Exhibit 4.17. Sampling Errors for Specified Sample Sizes

Survey Result is:	5% or 95%	10% or 90%	15% or 85%	20% or 80%	25% or 75%	30% or 70%	35% or 65%	40% or 60%	45% or 55%	50% or 50%
Sample Size: 25	8.7	12.0	14.3	16.0	17.3	18.3	19.1	19.6	19.8	20.0
50	6.2	8.5	10.1	11.4	12.3	13.0	13.5	13.9	14.1	14.2
75	5.0	6.9	8.2	9.2	10.0	10.5	11.0	11.3	11.4	11.5
100	4.4	6.0	7.1	8.0	8.7	9.2	9.5	9.8	9.9	10.0
150	3.6	4.9	5.9	6.6	7.1	7.5	7.8	8.0	8.1	8.2
200	3.1	4.3	5.1	5.7	6.1	6.5	6.8	7.0	7.0	7.0
250	2.7	3.7	4.5	5.0	5.5	5.8	6.0	6.2	6.2	6.3
300	2.5	3.5	4.1	4.6	5.0	5.3	5.5	5.7	5.8	5.8
400	2.2	3.0	3.6	4.0	4.3	4.6	4.8	4.9	5.0	5.0
500	2.0	2.7	3.2	3.6	3.9	4.1	4.3	4.4	4.5	4.5
600	1.8	2.5	2.9	3.3	3.6	3.8	3.9	4.0	4.1	4.1
800	1.5	2.1	2.5	2.8	3.0	3.2	3.3	3.4	3.5	3.5
1,000	1.4	1.9	2.3	2.6	2.8	2.9	3.1	3.1	3.2	3.2
2,000	.96	1.3	1.6	1.8	1.9	2.0	2.1	2.2	2.2	2.2
3,000	.79	1.1	1.3	1.5	1.6	1.7	1.7	1.8	1.8	1.8
4,000	.69	.95	1.1	1.3	1.4	1.4	1.5	1.5	1.6	1.6
5,000	.62	.85	1.0	1.1	1.2	1.3	1.4	1.4	1.4	1.4
10,000	.44	.60	.71	.80	.87	.92	.95	.98	.99	1.0
50,000	.17	.24	.29	.32	.35	.37	.38	.39	.40	.40

Probable deviation (plus or minus) of results due to sample size only (calculated for 95 percent confidence level)

Source: Joe Belden, *A Broadcasting Research Primer* (Washington, DC: National Association of Broadcasters, 1966), p. 19. Reprinted by permission.

confidence level. Thus, probability sampling makes possible precise estimation, whereas with nonprobability sampling a little or a lot of guesswork is involved. This is one of the most powerful advantages probability sampling offers to effective management.

If you prefer to avoid the sampling error/sample size formula, Exhibit 4.17 presents a summary table that corresponds to sample sizes for commonly estimated or real survey results or occurrences.

If the probability of occurrence is estimated as 20 percent, you go to the column heading "20% or 80%," then read down to the desired sampling error, that is, 5. Then you read to the left to encounter the sample size that gives you that sampling error: 250. (The difference in the correction factor given in the previous formula accounts for the small discrepancy between the sample size of 246 obtained from the formula and the 250 sample size obtained from the table.)

Use of either the table or the formula gives you a satisfactory guide, although both are related primarily to simple random samples. Exact calculation of the sample size to obtain a given sampling error, or exact calculation of sampling error resulting from a given sample size, requires different formulas in different situations (see Kish, 1965).

The formula or the table can serve to estimate sample size and sampling error outcomes for sampling procedures other than simple random sampling. However, other procedures will produce different outcomes. For example, stratified probability sampling inevitably produces smaller sampling error, given the same sample size as in simple random sampling. Quota sampling yields a sampling error approximately 1.5 times whatever value would be estimated from the simple random sampling model.

If exact calculation of sampling error is necessary, you should consult a statistician who is expert in sampling. Formulas for sampling error tend to be rather difficult for novices in situations involving more complex sampling procedures, such as stratified probability sampling. If you have even a modest grasp of inferential statistics, Kish (1965) provides relatively readable explanations about advanced sampling techniques.

TABULATING SURVEY RESULTS

Managers and planners as well as researchers need to understand the basic steps in data tabulation, even if the individual intends to use a computer. When you understand the steps, you will find it much easier to comprehend computer frequency-and-percentage or cross-tabulation programs. Also, when a computer is not available, it makes it possible for you to do tabulation by hand or instruct others how to do it.

Tabulating Responses for a Univariate Table

First, you need to understand the tabulation of responses for a one-variable, or univariate, table, such as the one in Exhibit 4.1. The question there was whether interviewees have been exposed to information about the relationship between cigarette smoking and cancer.

Imagine you have 500 questionnaires. You must ascertain how many people answer that they were exposed to the information and how many said they were not. This task is equivalent to turning to that question in the completed questionnaires, looking at each response, and putting each questionnaire into one of two sorting piles, such as those in Exhibit 4.18. Then you would count the number in each pile. The result is equivalent to the frequency for each answer category. The data should be noted in an appropriate place in your table.

ExHIBIT 4.18. Tabulation Piles for Univariate Table

Exposed to information
Not exposed to information

If you want to calculate the percentage of responses for each category, you first add the frequencies in the two piles to obtain the total. Next, you divide the frequency for the first pile by the total (which gives you a proportion), then multiply by 100 to obtain the percentage. To obtain the percentage for the second category, you repeat the operation with the second pile.

Tabulating Data for a Bivariate Table

Similar logic explains tabulation operations for a bivariate table, often used in correlational analysis (see Exhibit 4.1). The main difference operationally is that a bivariate table requires more sorting piles. First, you sort the questionnaires to determine how many individuals responded to each answer category in the first variable—which is what was done for Exhibit 4.18. Second, you subsort the questionnaires from each of those two piles according to the response categories for the second variable. Third, you count and note the frequencies for each resulting pile. Fourth, you calculate the percentages for each pile in relation to the total for the particular column in which the sorting pile lies.

In Exhibit 4.2, you see that the second variable determines whether the subject is a smoker or a nonsmoker. This indicates that the original two sorting piles must be subsorted into "smoker" and "nonsmoker" piles, like the ones in Exhibit 4.19.

EXHIBIT 4.19. Tabulation Piles for Bivariate Table

Smoker/exposed	Nonsmoker/exposed
Smoker/not exposed	Nonsmoker/not exposed

Once you have obtained the frequency of each response for each pile—it may be better to begin thinking of them as "data cells" in the table—it is possible to calculate the percentages.

When the independent, or predictor, variable is at the top of the table, as in Exhibit 4.2, the percentages will be calculated from the columns.

Tabulating Multivariate Table Responses

When you are confronted with a multivariate table, such as Exhibit 4.3, the tabulation process once again involves the same logic of sorting into piles: (1) You sort on the first variable; (2) then you subsort on the second variable; and finally, (3) you subsort on the third variable. Procedures for obtaining percentages for table cells are the same as in the previous example. For Exhibit 4.3, you obtain the sorting piles in Exhibit 4.20. Remember that the third variable is the gender of the subject.

EXHIBIT 4.20. Tabulation Piles for a Multivariate Table

Males/ Smokers/ Exposed	Males/ Nonsmokers/ Exposed	Females/ Smokers/ Exposed	Females/ Nonsmokers/ Exposed
Males/ Smokers/ Not exposed	Males/ Nonsmokers/ Not exposed	Females/ Smokers/ Not exposed	Females/ Nonsmokers/ Not exposed

CALCULATING AND COMPARING PERCENTAGES

Earlier, we specified two basic conventions for setting up cross-tabulation tables:

1. When you place the independent, or predictor, variable at the top of the table, or "on the columns," the dependent or outcome variable should be at the side, or "on the rows."

EXHIBIT 4.21. Example of Table with Independent
Variable Situated on the Columns

	Read Newspaper Yesterday	
Knows Fact *X*	*No*	*Yes*
Yes	40%	55%
	(400)	(550)
No	60%	45%
	(600)	(450)
TOTALS	100%	100%
	(1,000)	(1,000)

2. When you place the independent, or predictor, variable at the side of the table, or "on the rows,," the dependent or outcome variable should be at the top of the table, or "on the columns."

Recognizing the difference is important, because the convention controls how the percentages are calculated in the tables and how the primary comparison of percentages in cells is made.

Under the first convention, as in Exhibit 4.21, the percentages are calculated down the columns, or column-wise, and the primary comparison of percentages is across the columns. You would compare the cells in the top row. To determine if newspaper reading seems to predict whether subjects know fact X, you would compare 40 percent and 55 percent.

Because the percentage of subjects knowing fact X is greater among those who read a newspaper yesterday (55 percent) than among those who did not (40 percent), you can infer that newspaper reading is a predictor of knowledge.

When the percentage difference between the compared cells is 11 points or more, there is likely to be a statistical difference. With tables that have more than two columns or more than two rows, differences of as little as 7 points can produce a statistical difference. One of the advantages of statistics is that you can use formulas to analyze data and reduce your risk of an erroneous decision. For example, you can specify a test level: "If I say there is a difference [or a relationship], I do not want to risk being wrong more than 5 times out of 100 cases." This is an example of the so-called .05 statistical test level.

Visual inspection of data makes possible trustworthy inferences in about 70 to 80 percent of the cases. However, you can gain higher levels of certainty—such as 95 times out of 100, with the .05 test level—only by using an appropriate statistical test. A *z-test* can be used to compare two independent percentages or proportions from a "two by two" table—one with two columns and two rows. The *chi-square* and *median tests*, both nonparametric statistical tests, are used with cross-tabulation tables, the first to test for statistical relationships and the latter for differences. For details about the tests, consult statistical texts listed at the end of this chapter, especially Brown, Amos, and Mink (1975) if you are a beginner, but also McNemar (1962), Guilford (1973), or Roscoe (1975).

Under the second convention for setting up tables, the percentages are calculated across the columns, or row-wise, and the primary comparison of percentages is down the columns. If you look at Exhibit 4.22, which uses the same information and data as Exhibit 4.21, you compare 55 percent and 40 percent—the same as in the previous table. However, the primary comparison is down the column.

EXHIBIT 4.22. Example of Table with Independent Variable Situated on the Rows

	Knows Fact X		
Read Newspaper Yesterday	*No*	*Yes*	**Totals**
Yes	45%	55%	100
	(450)	(550)	(1,000)
No	60%	40%	100%
	(600)	(400)	(1,000)

Another important practice deals with the presentation of the levels of measurement, or response categories, in cross-tabulation tables. Many times, you will work with levels of measurement that represent ordinal data—data that arrange responses from high score to low score, or vice versa. When you use such ordinal categories, and the independent, or predictor, variable is "on the columns," as in Exhibit 4.21, the response categories for the independent, or predictor, variable should be listed in ascending order (low to high) from left to right, and the response categories for the dependent, or outcome, variable should be listed in descending order (high to low) from the top of the table to the bottom. (Some statistical packages for computers have "recode" commands or other commends that enable you to reverse a questionnaire's ordering of categories in variables to accomplish the objective discussed here with a minimum of trouble.) This convention offers certain advantages, especially in the interpretation of cross-tabulation tables that deal with possible correlations between variables. When the convention is followed, and both the variables are ordinal in nature,

- A positive correlation produces large percentages in the upper-right and lower-left cells of a cross-tabulation table.

- A negative correlation produces large percentages in the upper-left and lower-right cells of a table.
- No correlation would be suggested if there is little difference between the percentages in the row cells of a table.

These generalizations correspond roughly to what would occur in a correlational scatter plot, which is one way of depicting correlational data (see Brown, Amos, & Mink, 1975, for an elementary discussion of correlational procedures, scatter plots, and chi-square analysis).

SUMMARY

Survey research produces markedly superior results as compared with those obtained through "softer" research methods such as focus group or intensive interviewing:

1. Obtained data are representative because of widely accepted sampling methods applied in objectively identified populations.
2. Reliability of measurement is ensured by using questionnaires constructed with widely accepted methods or techniques, such as question or statement formats and attitude scales.
3. Interviewer-introduced bias is largely controlled because sampling procedures prevent personal choices from influencing the results and the questionnaire restricts personal variations in the way questions are presented.
4. Formulas or tables make it possible to select sample size as it relates to sampling error, or vice versa. Consequently, you can implement decisions about the degree of precision—including confidence limits and confidence level—you need, and you can be sure that you neither waste funds collecting too many interviews nor undermine the intended precision level of your data projections by interviewing too few subjects.

Dummy data tables are a means of defining both (1) data-collection measurement needs, including the determination of what questions and response categories are needed, and (2) the eventual data analysis plan. This plan helps control both omissions and excess data collection, either of which can prove wasteful. This chapter also provides guidelines for developing and checking questionnaires.

Both probability and nonprobability sampling methods are explained here. Probability sampling methods are superior, but quota sampling, which is a form of nonprobability sampling, may be useful under some circumstances to deal with time or cost pressures.

Conventions for organizing and interpreting basic data tables, such as for cross-tabulation, are presented in this chapter. The main emphasis regarding analysis is on comparison of percentages, but appropriate statistical tests are suggested for cases in which certainty about decisions is essential.

REFERENCES

F. L. Brown, J. R. Amos, and O. G. Mink, *Statistical Concepts: A Basic Program*, 2nd ed. (New York: Harper & Row, 1975). An easy, excellent programmed, or self-instruction, text for persons who border on math shock yet must understand the basic concepts of statistics.

J. P. Guilford, *Fundamental Statistics in Psychology and Education*, 5th ed. (New York: McGraw-Hill, 1973). An authoritative and extensive treatment of statistics; may prove daunting to novices, however.

Leslie Kish, *Survey Sampling* (New York: Wiley, 1965).

Quinn McNemar, *Psychological Statistics*, 3rd ed. (New York: Wiley, 1962). A source of much little-known but useful information on cross-tabulation analysis.

J. T. Roscoe, *Fundamental Research Statistics for the Behavioral Sciences*, 2nd ed. (New York: Holt, Rinehart and Winston, 1975). A statistical "cookbook"—easy to follow, step by step, with extensive information about "do's" and "don'ts" that benefit persons with less experience in statistics.

FURTHER READINGS

F. N. Kerlinger, *Foundations of Behavioral Research*, 2nd ed. (New York: Holt, Rinehart and Winston, 1973). A superb general reference with the most important aspects of research design and analysis; applicable to behavioral and managerial research.

L. H. Kidder, *Selltiz, Wrightsman & Cook's Research Methods in Social Relations*, 4th ed. (New York: Holt, Rinehart and Winston, 1980). Another "classic" general reference on research.

Morris Rosenberg, *The Logic of Survey Analysis* (New York: Basic Books, 1968). An unusually good resource concerning the reading and interpretation of cross-tabulation tables without resource to statistical tests.

CHAPTER 5

Objectives: Planning for Testable Results

By this time, you have identified the target audience segment for your campaign and verified the force field analysis assumptions. You now need to use that information to develop the goals and objectives for your campaign. A major management technique to help you conceptualize and state goals and objectives is *management by objectives (MBO)*.

Organizational resources are almost always finite. Consequently, a manager or planner must identify the most time- and cost-effective ways to utilize human resources, materials, and capital to fulfill goals and objectives. Management by objectives helps you develop a system that

1. Is capable of being presented to all concerned persons in writing—so no one should have any doubt about what must be accomplished
2. Requires the statement of specific observable or measurable outcomes that your campaign must accomplish at its conclusion
3. Ensures that the messages you include in your campaign are clearly related to objectives, increasing the probability they can bring about the desired end-of-campaign results
4. Facilitates *work delegation* by expressing in unambiguous terms what tasks you expect subordinates to complete (Subordinates also benefit from clear statements about what they must produce and the criteria that should be used to judge whether the outcomes they produce are satisfactory.)
5. Allows you to determine whether outcomes produced by subordinates meet stated objectives
6. Enables you to ascertain (1) whether the communication campaign produces the intended outcomes and (2) whether the outcomes can be

attributed to the campaign rather than to other forces in the environment

Peter Drucker (1954) is the originator of the MBO concept, but George Odiorne (1965) is recognized as the person who, as early as 1955, pioneered the management training that led to MBO's wider adoption (Kondrasuk, 1982). Others who made early contributions to the diffusion of MBO are Colley (1964), with his DAGMAR system (Defining Advertising Goals for Measured Advertising Results), and McConkey (1965, 1975), who began with corporate applications and later showed how MBO could serve nonprofit organizations. More recently, other authors have elaborated on the use of objectives in public relations (Ross, 1977; Grunig & Hunt, 1984; Nager & Allen, 1984; Brody, 1988), advertising (Weilbacher, 1979), and nonprofit organizations (Mali, 1978). Although communication organizations lag in the application of MBO, the general management community embraces the technique. A 1982 study reports that about 60 percent of the respondents in a study of 320 industries and government organizations used MBO, and 90 percent of these found the technique valuable (Ruth & Brooks, 1982).

Planning that is not based on a system like MBO is very likely to cause problems. Communication campaign managers or planners often cannot tell a superior or a client what specific outcomes their efforts should produce because they never make explicit or commit to writing the outcomes they intend to attain. Moreover, when they do attempt to state "goals," the form is often inexplicit or abstract. Too often, their goals include phrases like "improve understanding," "produce favorable attitudes," "improve our PR position," or "develop a new image." All of these statements are too vague because they do not permit meaningful evaluation. For example, how can a manager or planner know: (1) If a target audience "understands" since understanding is an internal process and no criteria are stated for measuring it? (2) Whether attitudes are affected at all or which ones are affected since, once again, specific measurement criteria are not given? (3) If the "PR position" is improved since the goal does not define what factors are to be changed, in what ways they are to be changed, or how change will be measured? (4) If the desired "new image" is instituted since the stated goal does not define what elements—for example, ideas or a symbol system configuration—are to be addressed, and again, criteria are not given for testing what is an internal process in the target audience segment or segments?

Similar problems exist concerning campaign work assignments. If a manager or planner delegates work and expresses intentions orally or only in general terms, there is a risk that (1) some tasks that are not identified will not be undertaken or (2) some or many tasks may be completed in a way that will not contribute to the attainment of the desired outcomes. Waste is more likely to occur in expenditures of time, money, and effort. This efficiency can also affect worker morale and confidence in a manager's or planner's leadership.

GUIDELINES FOR WRITING
MANAGEMENT BY OBJECTIVES (MBO)

Management by objectives enables you to prevent problems like these by having you state in writing

1. *Global objectives,* which are the general outcomes that must be produced by a campaign
2. *Intermediate objectives,* which are the task outcomes or end points of activities that must be completed by workers in order to execute a campaign
3. *Terminal objectives,* which are specific, measurable, or observable end results that a campaign must attain

Global Objectives

Similar to the notion of a goal, a global objective states in a few words the intended *general impact* of a campaign. Global objectives evolve from a needs assessment, such as a real state/ideal state problem analysis (see Chapter 2). This analysis should suggest a limited number—usually one to five—of statements of broad outcomes that must be realized in order to attain the ideal state.

You should be able to express a single global objective clearly in no more than one sentence, and global objectives for a communication campaign should incorporate essential boundaries—that is, specific audience segments, a particular topic or focus, and a specific time period.

Global objectives do not identify all the particulars of the outcomes to be attained since these will be stated later in terminal objectives. You must think of a global objective as a *summation* of these specific impacts.

For example, a global objective in a nutrition communication project might be expressed in this way:

- By December 31 of this year, teach mothers of recently born infants in three villages [which would be named here] to prepare correctly a powdered food supplement and administer the resulting liquid formula in conformity with specified sanitary procedures.

This global objective states specific boundaries: (1) the target audience—women with new babies in specified villages, (2) a deadline for completion—December 31 of this year, and (3) a specific domain of activity—teaching how to prepare a food supplement correctly and how to administer it properly.

However, this global objective does not give details about the specific operations that the women in the target audience must learn to demonstrate. Also, it does not deal with the activities that are necessary to mount the project or carry out the teaching. These details should be expressed in terminal and intermediate objectives.

Intermediate Objectives

Intermediate objectives state *tasks* that must be completed during the actual execution of the project in order to implement and attain the terminal and global objectives.

Intermediate objectives specify the *outcomes* (end results) of specific work, and they must be developed as part of the work-planning system, which will be discussed in Chapter 8. At this point, it is sufficient to explain that intermediate objectives deal with the end points of *"doing" activities,* such as implementing the media strategy, ordering the production of video-tapes, getting bids on contract work, obtaining legal releases, distributing materials, or conducting evaluation research.

Examples of intermediate objectives for the implementation of a communication campaign are

   • Advertising copy for the blood donor posters *completed.*

or

   • Cost estimates for printing of posters *obtained* from printer.

Intermediate objectives enable a manager to delegate work successfully and inform subordinates what tasks must be done and what constitutes closure. With the aid of Program Evaluation and Review Technique-Critical Path Method (PERT-CPM), you can define campaign activities and their relationships and incorporate a deadline for each intermediate objective.

Intermediate objectives must be specific and written, so there is absolutely no ambiguity about what constitutes satisfactory completion.

Subordinates tend to respond positively to MBO-based planning of work. First, it is flexible because it permits workers to choose how they will accomplish the outcomes specified in the intermediate objectives. Second, it is humane because it reduces uncertainty about performance and evaluation.

You, too, should find the MBO system flexible; although intermediate objectives should be written after a reasonably thorough analysis and deadlines should be as realistic as possible, you can still make revisions. Even during the execution of the campaign, an alert manager or planner can use feedback to monitor the project and decide whether intermediate objectives require modification.

Terminal Objectives

Terminal objectives state the specific standards that must be met by the end of a campaign to prove its success. At a minimum, these standards must be stated in *observable* or *measurable terms*. They may deal with either quantitative or qualitative characteristics. If you are confronted with terminal objectives that are not observable, your task as a manager or planner is to transform them so they are either observable or measurable.

Fortunately, many communication campaigns are designed to produce objectively demonstrable outcomes such as buying, utilizing, producing, or consuming. Consequently, they lend themselves to fairly easy formulation of terminal objectives. However, some campaigns deal with subjective outcomes, such as knowledge, attitude, affect (feeling), opinion, or belief. How can you make these outcomes observable or measurable? Here are some widely used approaches.

Specification of Overt Behavior. You usually will want to write or rewrite the objective with an active verb that requires an overt behavior. For example, an unacceptable terminal objective might be transformed in this way:

- Members of the target audience *shall state correctly* that AIDS (Acquired Immunodeficiency Syndrome) cannot be transmitted by social contact such as living or working together; touching; or sharing plates, drinking glasses, or eating utensils.

A terminal objective should have a verb that requires preparation to perform an overt behavior (*state,* in this case). It can also specify what information must be transmitted to make that overt behavior possible. Consequently, the terminal objective makes clear what content the message must present and what can be evaluated to ascertain whether the outcome has been accomplished.

Compare the preceding terminal objective with the following, which is not satisfactory, and some of the crucial differences become clearer:

- Members of the target audience shall know that AIDS is not transmitted by social contact.

A copywriter cannot be certain what constitutes "social contact"; thus important points may be left out of the message. An evaluation researcher would object that "knowing" is a subjective state; the objective should declare what conditions are acceptable for testing its attainment.

Verbs like *state* or *select* solve many problems. For example,

- Members of the audience shall state correctly that Alaska does not export oil to Japan.

or

- Given a choice of four statements, the audience members shall select the correct answer: that Alaska does not export oil to Japan.

What people "know" is not observable, but what people can "state" or "select" correctly is clearly capable of being assessed since each involves an overt behavior.

For these reasons, terminal objectives are not acceptable when they specify subjective outcomes such as "know," "believe," "sense," "hold an attitude," "hold an opinion," "think," "be aware of," and "comprehend." Verbs that satisfy MBO managerial needs specify that audience members must exhibit an overt behavior, such as telling, demonstrating, selecting, listing, ranking, reporting (as in a diary), or stating.

Specification of Measurement Technique. Another way to transform abstract terminal objectives into testable ones is to state what measurement technique should be used to verify attainment. Attitudes, beliefs, opinions, and values mentioned in terminal objectives can be measured—usually, by identifying how the audience members respond to (1) questions; (2) declarations or statements that they are instructed to judge; or (3) information, belief, opinion, or attitude scales.

For example, a terminal objective might deal with a subjective behavior successfully by incorporating reference to measurement of the outcome:

- The members of the target audience shall express attitudinal favorability toward donating to the March of Dimes in response to a question that can be answered with Likert-type categories: agree strongly, agree, neutral, disagree, disagree strongly.

Incorporation of Deadline. A terminal objective might include a deadline as a boundary. For example, a terminal objective might be stated as follows:

- By July 31, members of the target audience shall be able to state correctly the Big Brother Association's slogan—"A Chance in a Lifetime."

Incorporation of a Level of Performance. Many campaigns do not deal with simple dichotomous results. Attainment may be a matter of degree. You can write terminal objectives to deal with partial attainment by specifying a level of attainment as a boundary. The terminal objective can state minimal conditions that must be present to verify satisfaction of the desired outcome.

In communication campaigns, 100 percent of an audience rarely is exposed to a message, and just as rarely does a campaign produce perfect learning. For example, audience members might remember only 2 of 5 facts or assertions in a TV advertisement or only 4 of 15 or more items presented in a radio program. Research or experience may suggest a realistic level of attainment for you to specify in a particular situation. It helps to be familiar with published research relating to your problem.

Unrealistically high levels of attainment in terminal objectives can lead to erroneous assumptions that results are inadequate, which can lead to discouragement on the part of members of the campaign team.

Any objective can be written in several ways. First, the objective might specify that out of five operations, the target audience shall be able to perform at least the essential ones (which would be listed in the terminal objective). For example,

- After being exposed to Alaska's "The Story at the Top of the World," a majority of the audience shall be able to state three of the four following facts: (1) Alaska exports no oil to Japan, (2) North Slope oil reserves are already declining, (3) world oil prices determine Alaskan oil prices, (4) Alaska contributes more to U.S. federal government income than it gets back.

Second, the objective might require a specified percentage of the target audience to be able to demonstrate the behavior. For example:

- At the end of the project, at least 40 percent of the target audience shall be able to state that when most of the fertilizer that is distributed to a plant in the field is deposited on leaves rather than at the base, fertilization is considered ineffective.

Third, the objective might use baseline data against which results would be compared, as in the following example:

- The percentage of registered voters in the contiguous 48 U.S. states who can identify as correct the declaration that Alaska contributes more funds to federal revenues each year than it receives in return shall increase from 15 percent to 35 percent.

USING TERMINAL OBJECTIVES EFFICIENTLY

Relating Terminal Objectives and Messages

Terminal objectives control the development of campaign messages. If the outcome you specify in any terminal objective is to be realized, the messages to be delivered must incorporate content that implements the objective. For example, if a terminal objective specifies that members of a target audience shall demonstrate five behaviors, some message content clearly must transmit information about how to perform these same five behaviors.

Terminal objectives in MBO make it possible to delegate work to copywriters and others in creative services and explain with no ambiguity what information must be incorporated. Also, checking these people's work becomes easier because if you do not find a one-to-one relationship between terminal objectives and the resulting messages, the outcomes specified in the objectives cannot be realized.

Terminal Objectives for Audience Segments.

In cases where a project addresses more than one audience segment, some communications might be addressed to all segments, but some communications are appropriate to only specified segments. As a result, you should subdivide terminal objectives in relation to particular audience segments. In Exhibit 5.1, terminal objectives 1 through 7 are necessary to attain the specified global objective. However, there are two audience segments. Terminal objectives 1 through 3 apply to both target audiences, 4 and 5 apply only to segment 1, and 6 and 7 apply only to segment 2.

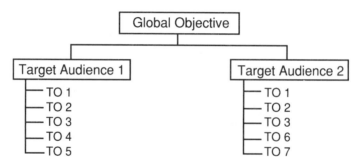

EXHIBIT 5.1. Conceptual Organization of Global and Terminal Objectives for Project with Two Target Audiences
Note: TO represents a particular terminal objective.

Terminal Objectives as a Basis for Copy Pretesting

In an MBO-based communication system, the content and visualization of messages are designed to implement terminal objectives. Therefore, if you want to "copy test" (pretest) the messages before you reach the full execution stage of the campaign, terminal objectives provide the test criteria.

In a pretest, you generally expect to find that people from the target audience segment or segments who are exposed to the messages will be able to satisfy the terminal objectives. Such confirmation should enhance your confidence in the effectiveness of the messages. However, you may find some message content that is not accomplishing the desired results; this information enables you to identify and isolate specific message components that do not work, so you can reformulate or modify them before the campaign is implemented.

SUMMARY

Effective planning of communication projects requires a systematic approach that makes explicit in writing

- The global objectives
- The terminal objectives
- The intermediate objectives

These elements are all part of management by objectives, a planning technique that is used widely in both profitmaking and nonprofit organizations to

- Be explicit about the outcomes to be realized by the campaign.
- State the conditions that guide copywriting and related creative work. When a terminal objective states that a particular outcome must be produced, it is clear both to you and to subordinates what type of message is necessary to attain that outcome. Consequently, there should be absolutely no chance that your campaign creates and presents irrelevant messages or omits relevant content.
- Evaluate whether the specified outcomes are attained after the campaign is complete.
- Manage the work force more effectively since you have a system to inform campaign workers what they must do and what constitutes satisfactory completion. It also enables you to give workers flexibility in the selection of procedures they will use to complete the work specified in an objective.
- Monitor work during the execution stage of the campaign. You always have the option of modifying intermediate objectives in order to complete the project satisfactorily.

Thus, MBO provides an explanatory structure that enables you to inform superiors or clients about the campaign plan, the conduct of the work, and monitoring or evaluation procedures. This information must also be shared with subordinates or team members, so that everyone has full information about the campaign and has a context to comprehend how each individual's work contributes to it.

Mastering MBO requires comprehension and application of a limited body of rules concerning how adequate objectives are formulated.

REFERENCES

E. W. Brody, *Public Relations Programming and Production* (New York: Praeger, 1988).

Russell H. Colley, *Defining Advertising Goals for Measured Advertising Results* (New York: Association of National Advertisers, 1964).

Peter Drucker, *The Practice of Management* (New York: Harper & Row, 1954).

J. E. Grunig and T. Hunt, *Managing Public Relations* (New York: Holt, Rinehart and Winston, 1984).

J. N. Kondrasuk, "Management by Objectives: Past, Present and Future," *Managerial Planning,* May/June 1982.

D. D. McConkey, *How to Manage by Results* (New York: American Management Assn., 1965).

D. D. McConkey, *MBO for Nonprofit Organizations* (New York: AMACOM, 1975).

Paul Mali, *Improving Total Productivity: MBO Strategies for Business, Government and Not-for-Profit Organizations* (New York: Wiley, 1978).

N. R. Nager and T. H. Allen, *Public Relations Management by Objectives* (White Plains, NY: Longman, 1984).

G. S. Odiorne, *Managing by Objectives* (New York: Pitman, 1965).

R. D. Ross, *The Management of Public Relations* (New York: Wiley, 1977).

S. R. Ruth and W. W. Brooks, "Who's Using MBO in Management?" *Journal of Systems Management,* February 1982, pp. 16–17.

W. M. Weilbacher, *Advertising* (New York: Macmillan, 1979).

FURTHER READINGS

D. D. McConkey, *How to Manage by Results,* 4th ed. (New York: AMACOM, 1983).

Paul Mali, *MBO Updated* (New York: Wiley, 1986).

R. F. Mager, *Preparing Instructional Objectives,* 2nd ed. (San Francisco: Fearon, 1975).

R. H. Migliore, *An MBO Approach to Long-Range Planning* (Englewood Cliffs, NJ: Prentice-Hall, 1983).

L. R. Oaks, *Communication by Objective* (South Plainfield, NJ: Groupwork Today, 1977).

G. S. Odiorne, *Management Decisions by Objectives* (Englewood Cliffs, NJ: Prentice-Hall, 1969).

———, *MBO II* (Belmont, CA: Fearon, 1979).

J. L. Riggs and G. H. Felix, *Productivity by Objectives* (Englewood Cliffs, NJ: Prentice-Hall, 1983).

R. S. Sloma, *How to Measure Organizational Performance* (New York: Macmillan, 1980).

CHAPTER 6

Planning the Campaign's Messages

Once you have established your campaign's management by objectives, you must develop plans for your messages. If these communications are not related to the terminal objectives, the campaign is unlikely to attain the desired results.

In the systems approach, (1) analysis of the problem leads to the identification of one or more segments that must be targeted within the general population, (2) the factors controlling the behavior in the segment or segments must be identified and verified, and (3) these factors must then be addressed in terminal objectives that specify the campaign's intended results.

The terminal objectives identify the performance criteria that must be produced by the campaign's messages. For example, if terminal objectives state that audience members must be able to identify five attributes of a client's service, these five attributes must be represented in a campaign message (see Exhibit 6.1). If they are not, the desired results specified in the terminal objectives cannot be attained, and as a consequence, neither can the intended ideal state.

The conceptualization of messages should be not be viewed entirely, or even primarily, as a creative activity. Creativity is a process that takes content specified by the MBO and makes it more effective through imaginative execution.

In planning, the terminal objectives serve as a checklist to control the elaboration of message content, thereby reducing the ambiguity that might affect the successful delegation of work.

Feedback can be used to verify that (1) message themes do relate to terminal objectives and (2) extraneous themes that do not contribute to the

EXHIBIT 6.1. Parity Between Terminal Objectives and
Content Incorporated in Message

Terminal Objectives		Message Content
1	——————>	X
2	——————>	X
3	——————>	X
4	——————>	X
5	——————>	X

Note: Each X indicates that a fact, argument, or assertion that is
represented in a terminal objective is dealt with in the message.

attainment of the objectives are not included (see feedback loop 1 in Exhibit
6.2). Cross-checks help ensure that the campaign will produce the intended
results.

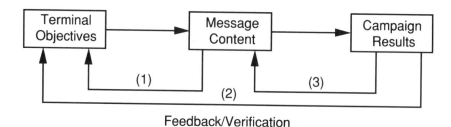

Feedback/Verification

EXHIBIT 6.2. Relationships Between Objectives, Message Content, and Conse-
quent Campaign Results

In the posttest evaluation, it is possible to check the results against both
the terminal objectives (feedback loop 2) and the message content (feedback
loop 3) to ascertain what works or what does not and why.

MAKING AN "INVISIBLE RESULT" VISIBLE

Message planning based on MBO offers an additional advantage when a
campaign fails to produce overt short-term behaviors. Target audience segments often do not implement immediately the practices that are advocated
by a campaign, or only a small percentage might do so. Use of observable
action as the exclusive criterion for campaign results does not consider latent
or "invisible" cognitive results—knowledge, attitudes, beliefs, or affect—
that might predispose individuals to implement the recommended behaviors
later. Terminal objectives identify latent intended results and make their
measurement possible during the evaluation at the end of a campaign.

OPTIMUM CONTENT "LOAD" FOR A MESSAGE

Some campaigns entail a relatively large number of terminal objectives. This raises a question about how many facts, arguments, or assertions should be incorporated into any one message.

Memory's Limitations

Content cannot be acted on if it is not remembered. Research suggests that human memory has limits in regard to any information-processing task.

As noted in Chapter 2, George A. Miller (1957), a psychologist, offers a theory entitled "The Magical Number Seven, Plus or Minus Two," which says that when people encounter a number of objects, phenomena, facts, or assertions, the average number they remember is seven. Most remember between five ($7 - 2 = 5$) and nine ($7 + 2 = 9$)—thus, the "plus or minus two" part of the theory's title.

Such basic memory capacity can be expanded, Miller theorizes, through chunking and super-chunking. Chunking involves the grouping in memory of related objects (which, following information theory, Miller calls "bits"), and super-chunking describes the regrouping of informational chunks into even larger, more encompassing units.

Copy Platform/Copy Points Structure

Miller's theory explains the utility of a message-structure plan advertising uses, but it also can serve other needs. An individual message usually incorporates a limited number of *copy points,* which are facts or assertions that must be transmitted. A *copy platform,* which integrates the copy points, is a chunking device that can take the form of a slogan (see Exhibit 6.3).

When a campaign involves numerous terminal objectives, you might

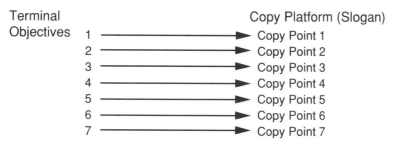

Exhibit 6.3. Terminal Objectives Related to Copy Platform and Message Copy Points

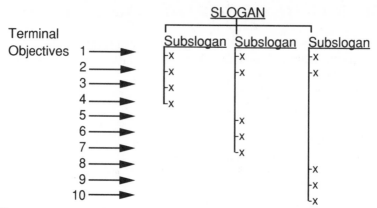

ExHIBIT 6.4. Relationship Between Terminal Objectives and Content Dispersed Across Messages

Note: Each X indicates that a fact, argument, or assertion that is represented in a terminal objective is dealt with in the message.

divide the content across different messages that are chunked under the same slogan, or you might divide the content under subslogans that serve as chunks and then use the main slogan as a super-chunk (see Exhibit 6.4). The structure illustrated in Exhibit 6.4 also can be adapted to a situation in which terminal objectives are divided according to different audience segments.

THINKING ABOUT CREATIVITY

Utilization of managerial techniques such as MBO and the copy platform/copy points structure does not limit persons who handle the creative activities—copywriting, scripting and visualization, and production.

Putting Structure Under Creativity

Efficient management requires that (1) the specifications for message content follow logically from the problem analysis and (2) there are means to determine whether a campaign's messages embody content that directly relates to terminal objectives.

Without such a management structure, creative processes frequently take an independent track; for example, writers might introduce themes that are unrelated to a campaign's terminal objectives or omit important points that they feel do not ''fit'' well with their particular creative approach.

The managerial approach provides specifications that eliminate or at least minimize ambiguities about the delegated creative tasks. Creative specialists still enjoy relatively great liberty in their execution of the actual messages—as long as the final results implement the terminal objectives.

Arousal and Follow-Through

The *AIDA formula*—an acronym for attention, interest, desire, and action—is one of the best known techniques for structuring effective, persuasive communications. However, literature in psychology about cognitive processes suggests that AIDA should be preceded by another *A* for arousal; attention is not likely to result without arousal. For example, in print messages, if arousal is not created by a headline or visuals, the text following it is unlikely to be read. Ogilvy (1985) notes, for example, that headlines are five times more likely to be read than the related text. Typically, effective headlines deal with gratification (human interest or other aspects of affect) or utility (news, benefits, or rewards). Bovée and Arens (1989, p. 342) contend that the opening of video messages must also be relevant to the target audience and pertinent to the problem—another way of saying that arousal is essential.

Competitive Message Environment

One of the biggest challenges confronting a manager or planner is to get messages that create arousal and thereby gain exposure. This is more of a problem than it might seem.

Communication clutter exists for every individual in modern society. Advertising specialists estimate, for example, that a typical city dweller in the United States comes into contact with about 3,400 messages a day. To avoid being overwhelmed by the potential information-processing demand, all people engage in selective exposure, employing subjective criteria—for example, availability, potential utility, congruence with existing attitudes or behaviors, or gratification—to select messages and thereby reduce the communication clutter to a manageable level (see Davison, Boylan, & Yu, 1976, pp. 131–157). Thus, many messages that the various mass media deliver are not received by the intended audience segment.

Gestalt Effects

Information-processing traits complicate the ways in which individuals react to messages—especially those not sufficiently differentiated from others.

Gestalt is a school of psychology that deals with perception and explains differentiation processes (see Berelson & Steiner, 1964). Gestalt theory says that objects or phenomena that are perceived as similar tend to be assimilated or grouped and integrated, thereby providing a simpler information structure. This is the *assimilation effect*. The obverse is the *contrast effect;* when cues indicate objects or phenomena are not similar, they are likely to be differentiated.

Many messages that are part of the communication clutter fail to stand out because of the assimilation effect. Others imitate promotional assertions, formats, or approaches to visualization that the competition also uses. You can prevent this problem by the use of specific techniques.

GETTING THE MESSAGE ACROSS

Fortunately, there are options that can make your messages distinctive.

Unique Selling Proposition

Rosser Reeves (1968) advocated development of a *unique selling proposition* (*USP*). The idea is part of advertising but may be adapted to other information problems. "The proposition must be one that the competitor either cannot or does not offer. It must be unique—either a uniqueness of the brand, product, service or information—or a claim not otherwise made. . . ." (pp. 47–48).

Slogans and headlines, in particular, must do more than provide labels; they must convey concisely some distinctive benefit that "sells" the advantage of exposure to the message. For example, in the face of the AIDS epidemic, a headline that says "7 Facts You Should Know About AIDS" conveys less of a benefit than "These 7 Facts About AIDS Can Save Your Life." Moreover, the USP approach keeps the message focused, and exposure is more likely when the message clearly demonstrates utility in terms that are relevant to an intended audience.

Thus, USP helps create perceptual arousal, which increases the probability of exposure to the message and pursuant attention to the content. However, there are other devices that you might consider and incorporate in your messages.

High-Arousal Cue Words

David Ogilvy (1963) suggests that "magic words" like *new, free, save,* and *win* in headlines or slogans greatly improve the chance of attracting attention to the content that follows.

Ogilvy's notion builds on both selective exposure theory and Reeves' USP concept: Terms that instantly convey a notion of utility and distinctive benefit reinforce the perception of rewards that can motivate audience members to become exposed to a message.

Vocabulary that can be related to the psychological needs identified in Abraham Maslow's hierarchy of needs (1943; also see Weiner, 1980, pp.

412–414) seems to be particularly relevant: physiological (survival), safety, social approval (love), ego (self-esteem), and self-actualization.

When more than one slogan or headline results from the staff's best efforts, you can use copy-testing research to determine which one members of a targeted segment prefer.

Visualization Factors

Research and theory indicate the *visualization* factors that can be used in creative strategies to improve the likelihood of exposure:

1. *Physical size of layout:* Studies indicate that larger ads are more likely to result in the messages being "noted" and "read most" (Baker, 1979, p. 159). However, doubling the size does not guarantee doubled exposure.

2. *Color:* In print media advertisements, use of color increases readership as much as 50 percent over black and white (Baker, 1979, p. 159).

3. *Simple, bold images:* Gestalt theory suggests that simple but bold graphic designs are effective.

4. *Complex images:* A. L. Yarbus's (1967) studies of eye movements indicate that when people scan pictorial objects, their eyes trace and retrace complex detail—especially that which offers informational cues.

5. *Incongruity or exaggeration:* Incongruous images often "stop" viewers or readers, for example, a print advertisement showing a 747 jumbo jet parked in the backyard of a neighborhood, a print advertisement depicting a man's face with no mouth (to dramatize the importance of political speech), and a TV ad showing an automobile driving across the surface of a lake.

6. *Affective images:* Affect in the psychological sense deals with feeling. Visualization that incorporates positive affective images improves message exposure, for example, "grandparent" types, attractive males, attractive females, children, and pets. In brief, good affective images stir human emotions.

Continuity: Unifying
The Different Messages

The different messages in a communication campaign should be recognized as part of the same effort, whether the format is print, radio, television, brochures, or direct mail. This is *message continuity:* Each message serves to reinforce the previous one to which the member of a target audience has been exposed. A "building" effect, which improves memory and learning, is accomplished through message continuity devices:

Slogans. One of the principal reasons for utilizing a slogan—other than to make it easier to remember message copy points—is that the message being examined becomes linked to all other messages in the campaign that bear the same slogan, regardless of the medium of delivery.

Standardized Identity Symbols. One of the most common identity symbols is the "signature" or "logotype" that identifies the organization. It should be used whenever possible in mass media, direct mail, newsletters, and public events.

Personalities. Campaigns often use the same spokespersons or personalities throughout. Well-known individuals enhance the prospects for exposure, and they also become associated quickly with the campaign message and the sponsoring organization. For example, every time an audience sees or hears Bill Cosby in a commercial, there is an implicit cue: "Now here's another message from Jell-O."

Music or Sound Effects. Many campaigns incorporate particular sound effects, jingles, or theme music as message continuity devices. The devices immediately establish that each radio or television message is part of a campaign.

Video Messages

Bovée and Arens (1989, p. 343) offer additional advice regarding messages for video: Elaboration of the message should unfold naturally, without gimmicks. Content should have strong human interest—especially as it relates to the target audience. Sentences should be short and conversational. Verbal content should interpret visual content and prepare the viewer for the next scene, rather than describing what is being seen. The audio and visual portions should be coordinated. Video should avoid static scenes but should not give the appearance of "jumping." The message should appear to be fresh and new.

Using Appropriate Language

Communicators often take it for granted that they and the members of target audience segments share the same vocabulary and language skills. That often is not the case.

Literacy Problems. In the United States, a conservative estimate is that 20 percent of the adult population is not *functionally literate*. Another estimate is that more than 50 percent of the adult population cannot comprehend the written materials they encounter in everyday life.

Traditional estimates of national literacy are based on the percentage of the adult population that has at least four years of formal education, which should provide a basic competence in reading. However, functional tests of reading ability prove that the estimates are erroneous.

Cultural Differences. In many regions, populations comprise *cultural subgroups* that often do not use the "standard" language. Vocabulary, in particular, is often different. Failure to use words and phrases that are familiar to a subgroup can affect both exposure to a message and its comprehension.

When a communicator is part of a subgroup that is accustomed to nonstandard vocabulary—such as those dealing with high technology or government—problems of communication with some audience segments may be great. The use of specialized vocabulary or redefining of familar words often confuses members of some audience segments.

When in Doubt, Test the Copy. *Copy-testing* (pretesting) is increasingly appropriate. In a simple version, it might involve submitting copy to people similar to a target audience segment and asking them to identify words, phrases, sentences, or paragraphs that are hard to understand. At a more technical level, it might involve a methodological *readability analysis,* such as the procedures established by Flesch, Gunning, or Dale and Chall (see Severin with Tankard, 1988, pp. 69–87) Desktop computer software can be obtained to perform such analyses.

THE MESSAGE PLAN

As noted, it is advantageous for a manager or planner to compress the voluminous information that results from managerial deliberations so that essential facts can be stated in an easy-to-follow format that communicates quickly. Some examples are real state and ideal state analyses, force field analysis diagrams, and MBO summaries. A *message plan* should also be summarized in a *format* that puts the essential information in clear perspective. Thus, I recommend the report format in Exhibit 6.5 for these reasons:

1. It leads a manager or planner to reduce the message plan to its essentials.
2. It makes it easy to cross-check for discrepancies—for example, to determine whether the copy platform/copy point content is congruent with the terminal objectives specified for a particular audience segment.
3. It reduces the ambiguity involved in communicating tasks to members of the creative staff and tells them what end results will be tested to determine whether the message does its job.

EXHIBIT 6.5. Format to Summarize Message Plan

──────────────── **Target Audience Segment** ────────────────

──────────────── **Terminal Objectives** ────────────────

──────────────── **Copy Platform/Copy Points** ────────────────

Slogan:
Subslogan (if any):
Copy points:

──────────────── **Formats to be Executed** ────────────────

[ ] News release
[ ] TV spot (time:)
[ ] Radio spot (time:)
[ ] Print media ad (size:)
[ ] Poster (size:)
[ ] Other (specification:)

──────────────── **Language Versions** ────────────────

[ ] Spanish [ ] Portuguese [ ] French
[ ] Other (specification:)

──────────────── **Suggested Treatment** ────────────────

The model format and content specifications can be adapted to the particular needs of any campaign.

The *formats to be executed section* allows you to note situations in which the same basic message must be produced in parallel versions appropriate for different channels of communication. This section can be modified to include speech scripts or slide-tape shows for personal presentation to live audiences as well as to mass media.

The *treatment section* should include suggestions about ways in which the message will be packaged: setting, visualization, casting of personalities, sound effects, music, affect devices, continuity devices, and so on.

In some campaigns, more than one summary sheet may be required, for example, (1) when there is more than one target audience segment and the terminal objectives are different for each, (2) when the campaign in unfolded in stages over time and different terminal objectives are introduced in each stage, or (3) when earlier terminal objectives are repeated but the treatment is changed to prevent overexposure.

SUMMARY

From a managerial perspective, message planning involves stating the criteria that must be met by campaign messages. It also provides a structure that reduces or eliminates ambiguity in work delegation. Moreover, such a structure enables you to copy-test or pretest the executed messages, as well as the campaign results, against the criteria that will contribute to solution of the problem.

Message planning also must take into account constraints imposed by human information processing, particularly as it affects selective exposure and memory. Arousal devices can improve message exposure. A message organization structure called copy platform/copy points, based on theories of memory processes, can improve the memorability of campaign messages.

Message planning also will be more effective when it employs continuity devices that create or increase audience awareness that all messages in a campaign are related. Such devices include slogans, standardized symbols, personalities, and sound effects or music.

It is important to recognize language differences across audience segments and to copy-test or pretest as a way of verifying whether messages are likely to be understood.

Summarizing the main decisions in the message plan makes possible cross-checking of important specifications to ensure internal consistency, minimize ambiguity in work delegation, and explain to the creative staff the criteria that will be used for message evaluation.

REFERENCES

Stephen Baker, *Systematic Approach to Advertising Creativity* (New York: McGraw-Hill, 1979).

Bernard Berelson and Gary Steiner, *Human Behavior: An Inventory of Scientific Findings* (New York: Harcourt, Brace & World, 1964).

C. L. Bovée and W. F. Arens, *Contemporary Advertising,* 3rd ed. (Homewood, IL: Irwin, 1989). An excellent resource for persons who need more detail about production for different message formats.

W. P. Davison, James Boylan, and F. T. C. Yu, *Mass Media Systems and Effects* (New York: Praeger, 1976), pp. 131–157.

Abraham Maslow, "A Theory of Human Motivation," *Psychological Review,* 50 (1943): 370–396.

G. A. Miller, "The Magical Number Seven, Plus or Minus Two: Some Limits on Our Capacity for Processing Information," *Psychological Review,* 63 (1957): 81–97.

David Ogilvy, *Confessions of an Advertising Man* (New York: Athenaeum, 1963).

David Ogilvy, *Ogilvy on Advertising* (New York: Random House, 1985). A source of valuable insights for managers and planners about not only advertising, but also persuasive communication in general.

Rosser Reeves, *Reality in Advertising* (New York: Knopf, 1968).

W. J. Severin with J. W. Tankard, Jr., *Communication Theories,* 2nd ed. (White Plains, NY: Longman, 1988).

Bernard Weiner, *Human Motivation* (New York: Holt, Rinehart and Winston, 1980).

A. L. Yarbus, *Eye Movements and Vision,* trans. B. Haigh (New York: Plenum Press, 1967).

CHAPTER 7

Planning the Message Delivery System

The next task that a manager or planner must confront in a campaign is how to deliver the message or messages efficiently to the targeted audience segment or segments. This chapter deals with media or channel selection, cost analysis, and scheduling for a campaign.

Mastery of a systems approach makes it easier to work through a complicated decision-making process. You must learn how to differentiate among mass media or channels in terms of their ability to reach the desired audience. It is not always true that the larger a particular medium's audience, the more desirable it is as a delivery vehicle; for example, a specific newspaper might serve a large audience yet have only a small percentage of an important target audience. Within a medium's total audience, suppose only 30 percent are in the segment you want to reach; thus if you select that medium you also must pay for the other 70 percent who are of no interest. Other media might offer better penetration or reach.

You must also learn how to analyze the *cost-effectiveness* of the different channels you are considering. For example, mass media base their charges for space or time on their ability to deliver quantity or quality audiences; media selection usually involves analysis and comparison of the costs charged to deliver one message unit to a hypothetical 1,000 audience members.

You must learn how to utilize *message frequency,* or repetition, effectively. Frequency is necessary to ensure exposure to a message because individuals often "drift in and out" of audiences. You can plan to deliver messages concurrently via different media or channels, a strategy called *media mix;* the integrative plan during a time period is called a *media sched-*

ule. This helps prevent the campaign from disappearing because of periodic lack of activity. However, budgets are usually limited, so it is not economically feasible to have messages appearing every day or in all mass media or other channels. Careful planning is essential to ensure the exposure to the campaign's messages across time. Additionally, receivers' learning of message content usually requires repeated exposure; it is rarely sufficient to expose a target audience to a campaign message just once.

Mass media are usually defined as including newspapers, radio, television, movies, direct mail, point-of-purchase (or point-of-decision) displays, outdoor displays, and transit posters.

However, in information campaigns, *other channels of communication* are also available. Corporations and other organizations use conferences, press kits, newsletters, computerized electronic mail, organizational communication videotape systems, exhibitions, public events, speaker bureaus, and satellite TV distribution, including teleconferencing. Marketing and political campaigns use computer-operated phone dialing and message playback. Health communication campaigns sometimes utilize comic books for the delivery of serious messages to language-handicapped audiences. Also "street workers" or teams of community activists are employed in health campaigns for face-to-face contact with hard-to-reach individuals like illicit drug users in urban areas. Puppet theater and mobile cinema or video units are used in various less developed nations, especially in rural areas. Portable cassette recorders are used in some campaigns for two-way communication with farmers. "People's theatre" is utilized in less developed nations to reach audiences often not reached by mass media.

Campaigns often must depend on both mass media and other information channels to advance their goals; moreover, in different situations, receivers may assess their informative potential and credibility. For example, Norton and Hughey (1987) studied the reactions of gay and bisexual men on communication about the AIDS epidemic. There were marked differences in the way they rated sources for information and trustworthiness (see Exhibit 7.1).

USING MEDIA EFFECTIVELY

Mass Media Advantages and Disadvantages

The different types of mass media present identifiable advantages and disadvantages for the development of a message delivery system, as Exhibit 7.2 explains.

Matching Media and Audience Segments

As explained in Chapter 2, target audience segments almost always must be defined in terms of demographics, particularly for the mass media. A manager

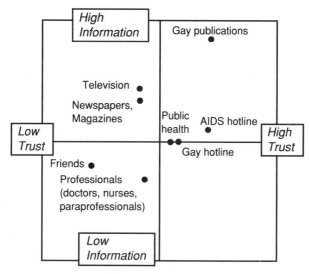

Exʜɪʙɪᴛ 7.1. Source Information Potential, Trustworthiness
Source: Robert Norton and J. Hughey, "Understanding the Exigency in Order to Craft the
Rhetorical Response; Health Promoting Behavior Relating to the AIDS Virus in a Low
Prevalence State," presentation to the Speech Communication Association, 1987.

or planner must then try to identify which medium can "deliver" audiences
that demographically match each target audience segment. This task requires
a basic understanding of how research data support media planning.

Audience Research Reports. Mass media and audience research firms publish
reader, viewer, and listener studies categorized by demographics. Consequently, if you know the demographic profile of your target segment or
segments, you can use audience research reports to find the media that can
deliver such segments. Some audience research firms provide access to
computerized databases of studies for particular networks, making the data
search much more effective.

Primary Research. In some cases, you might decide to conduct independent,
primary research in a population to obtain data on both the target audience
segment or segments and the use of particular media. The resulting data might
look like those in Exhibit 7.3, which presents partial tables that summarize
findings from two cross-tabulation tables regarding different media. To learn
which medium—newspaper A or newspaper B—has the higher readership in
any age segment, you can compare the percentages for a particular age group,
for example, in the columns.

For example, if you need to deliver messages to the 18–34 age bracket
and can afford only one medium, the data suggest that newspaper A (with 85

Exhibit 7.2. Mass Media Advantages and Disadvantages

Advantages	Disadvantages

Newspapers

Advantages	Disadvantages
1. Sense of immediacy. 2. Local emphasis. 3. Flexibility concerning price, production, deadlines. 4. Mass reach. 5. High-fidelity color. 6. Longevity in household for repeated reference. 7. Reach in ethnic subpopulations.	1. National advertising rates are higher than local rates. 2. High cost of buying national coverage. 3. Variation in Run of Press (ROP) color. 4. Small pass-along (secondary circulation).

Magazines

Advantages	Disadvantages
1. Selectivity—special magazines for particular population segments. 2. Fine color reproduction. 3. Long life in household or place of readership. 4. Big pass-along (secondary circulation) audience. 5. Controlled circulation agreements, guaranteeing circulation to specific audience segments.	1. Early closing dates for content. 2. Lack of immediacy. 3. Slow building of reach, e.g., due to delayed reading.

Television

Advantages	Disadvantages
1. Sight and sound enable dynamic presentation. 2. Flexibility in terms of geographic selection. 3. Reach in both selective and mass markets. 4. Cost efficiency through day-part selection.	1. High total cost. 2. Short-lived messages. 3. Limited availability of preferred programs and time slots.

Radio

Advantages	Disadvantages
1. Reach in special kinds of target audiences. 2. Lends itself to high frequency (repetition). 3. Good economical choice as supporting medium. 4. Excellent for mobile populations. 5. Follows mobile people enjoying summer leisure. 6. Flexibility—can be used selectively and message insertions or changes can be made quickly. 7. Local coverage availability.	1. Many stations divide audience in any one market. 2. Short-lived messages. 3. No opportunity to refer back to messages.

Direct Mail

Advantages	Disadvantages
1. Very selective for audience targeting. 2. Response is easy to check.	1. Possibly expensive because of production and mailing costs.

Exhibit 7.2. (*continued*)

Advantages	Disadvantages

Direct Mail

3. Personal medium—can be addressed by name.
4. Geographic and production flexibility.
5. Long life for some mailings.
6. Economy when direct mail enclosed with bills.

2. Mailing lists may be inaccurate or incomplete or difficult to build.
3. Variability in delivery dates.

Outdoor Displays

1. Wide coverage of local markets.
2. High frequency—relative permanence in view, heavy traffic of flow.
3. Largest print message format available.
4. Flexibility in geographic sites.
5. High summertime visibility.
6. Round-the-clock exposure.
7. Effective for simple copy theme and visual identification.

1. Limited to simple messages.
2. High outdoor reach does not assure high recall of messages.
3. Relatively high-cost medium.

Transit Displays

1. Mass coverage in a metropolitan area.
2. High frequency as riders repeat exposure.
3. Relative efficiency: high exposure, low cost.
4. Flexibility—especially selectivity.
5. Reaches people en route to decisionmaking.

1. Limited message space.
2. High competition; audience distracted.
3. Limited to simple messages.

Cable Television

1. Good for homes where local station signals are weak.
2. Opportunity for special pay programming.
3. Can customize coverage for special audiences.
4. Rates tend to be relatively low.
5. Availability of unusual commercial lengths.

1. Weak in major markets.
2. High Cost Per Thousand.
3. Audience demographics scarce.
4. Cable programming tends to duplicate that of networks.

Point-of-Purchase (or Point-of-Decision) Displays*

1. Presents message where decision is made.
2. Great flexibility for creativity.
3. Ability to demonstrate message in use.
4. Good color reproduction.
5. High frequency—can place in path of the people.

1. People who control site might not cooperate.
2. Slow production for elaborate displays.
3. High unit cost.
4. Space availability problems.
5. Shipping problems.

Source: Jack Z. Sissors and Jim Surmanek, *Advertising Media Planning*, 2nd ed. (Chicago: Crain Books, 1982), pp. 172–185. **Reprinted by Permission.**
*Leon Quera, *Advertising Campaigns: Formulation and Tactics* (Columbus, OH: Grid, 1973), p. 72.

Exhibit 7.3. Two Newspapers and Target
Audience Demographic

	Ages of Audience Members				
Read Yesterday	12–17	18–34	35–49	50–64	65+
Paper A	30%	85%	90%	82%	65%
Paper B	20%	65%	80%	85%	90%
Number of cases	50	250	350	250	200

percent of its circulation in that segment "read yesterday") would be a more effective selection than newspaper B (with 65 percent), provided that paper B's total number of persons in that age bracket is not considerably greater.

The Concept of Reach

The preceding example corresponds to a simple notion of print media's *reach*—which is equivalent to a medium's potential to produce exposure to a message in a target audience segment. Another useful definition of reach involves broadcast media: the unduplicated portion of a population that is exposed to a message at least once during a four-week period.

Exhibit 7.4 helps clarify the second definition, recognizing that the composition of broadcast audiences is more changeable than that for print media. Some individuals are not consistently part of an audience; they enter or exit at different times or dates. Moreover, some individuals never become part of the audience.

In this illustration, 50 percent of the population (five out of the ten

Exhibit 7.4. Reach in a Hypothetical Population of Ten Individuals During Four-Week Period

Individual	Week 1	Week 2	Week 3	Week 4
1	X	R	R	R
2	X	—	R	—
3	X	R	R	R
4	—	—	—	—
5	—	—	—	—
6	—	—	—	X
7	X	R	R	R
8	—	—	—	—
9	X	R	R	R
10	—	—	X	R

Note: X indicates a new exposure, R a repeat exposure, and — no exposure.
Source: Adapted from J. Z. Sissors and J. Surmanek, *Advertising Media Planning*, 2nd ed. (Chicago: Crain Books, 1982).

individuals) is exposed during week 1. Another 10 percent (one out of the ten) is exposed for the first time during week 3, increasing the cumulative exposure to 60 percent. Finally, another 10 percent (one out of ten) enters the audience for the first time in week 4, boosting the cumulative reach during the total four-week period to 70 percent. Repeat exposures are not counted.

Television and Reach. The television industry has introduced other useful concepts concerning program reach—(1) rating, (2) households using television (HUT), and (3) share—that must be understood by those who deal with media planning.

Rating refers to the percentage of all households with television that are actually tuned in to a TV program that is being rated. In reporting, the percentage mark is dropped. When a TV program has a rating of 16, it means that 16 percent of the households with television are watching that program.

Rating scores in the teens and twenties are common even for popular programs. With three major TV networks, if there were no other competing programming, you might assume that any one program could gain a 33 rating. However, the TV market is fragmented by local VHF and UHF stations, as well as by cable TV services such as Home Box Office, Showtime, Bravo, Cable News Network, and so on. This competition diminishes the rating that any one program might earn. Moreover, many households with television simply do not have sets that are turned on at any given time.

Households using television (HUT) has a different base for estimations. Only those households using television at the time the research is conducted —as opposed to all TV households—are considered. Thus HUT is used to calculate a second estimation of TV program reach, called share. *Share* expresses a TV program's actual viewership in relation to all households that have TV sets operating at the time the research is conducted—that is, HUTs. Because the number for HUT is always smaller than that for all households owning television sets, share is always larger than rating.

Usually, both rating and share are reported for individual TV programs. However, share may be the indicator that is of greater interest.

The Concept of Frequency

Frequency refers to the number of times within a four-week period that a message is repeated, to enhance potential exposure among members of a target audience segment or segments.

In a technical sense, frequency refers to the average exposure an individual is likely to encounter during a specified time period. That is, in a population, some individuals will be exposed to a message more often than others. It is possible, therefore, to conceptualize frequency in terms of a statistical distribution of possible exposures, the average being identified as the message plan's frequency.

Frequency addresses three basic problems:

1. As Exhibit 7.4 demonstrates, a stipulated frequency of one would fail to reach the maximum potential audience because of the way individuals drift in and out.
2. Even if members of the audience were reached, one exposure to a message would appear to have little or no effect on learning or other behavior (Naples, 1979, pp. 63–79). There is no definitive proof that effective frequency can be defined in terms of an absolute minimum or maximum, but Naples (63–79) suggests that a frequency of three produces minimal conditions for effect. By increasing frequency, he says, you can improve the likelihood of effect, although there is no linear relationship: At some point, effect tends to drop off despite an increase in frequency.[1]

   A major concern with frequency is that message content tends to be learned relatively slowly, over time, and repetition enhances the likelihood that a message will be remembered. A related problem is *memory decay,* or the forgetting of content. Repetition builds *recall,* or retention; without repetition, forgetting begins rapidly—as much as 60 percent of new content is forgotten within half a day—and memory decay tends to level off after a period of four to six weeks).

   Exhibit 7.5 illustrates how exposure or nonexposure affects the response in two situations. One situation is called "easy" because the audience already has some familiarity with the subject and exposure may be less intensive; the other is called "difficult" because the response is complicated by less familiarity with the subject, competition from other sources, and perhaps a hard-driving or intensive media plan that is designed to gain the maximum results in the shortest possible time (Ray, 1982, pp. 390–397).

   The figure illustrates the slow building of response, much like the *S* curve, as a function of repeated exposure; it also shows that response drops off quickly—especially in the "difficult" situation.
3. Where frequency is allocated across different media—the combination of which is known as the *media mix*—the probability of exposure to the message increases since individuals who do not use one medium might be in the audience of another (Weilbacher, 1979, p. 391).

Reach and Frequency Trade-offs

Reach and frequency both operate within the constraints of finite budgets, especially when media time or space must be purchased or when such delivery channels as direct mail or speaker bureaus are used.

---

[1] See Jack Z. Sissors and Jim Surmanek, *Advertising Media Planning,* 2nd ed. (Chicago: Crain Books, 1982), pp. 267–285, for a review of the literature concerning frequency effects.

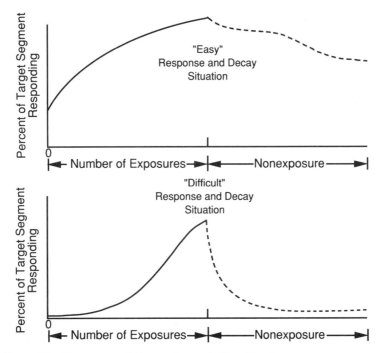

Exhibit 7.5. Exposure and Memory Decay in Two Situations
Source: M. L. Ray, *Advertising and Communication Management* (Englewood Cliffs, NJ: Prentice-Hall, 1982). Reprinted by permission.

If you increase the reach of a campaign, it costs more. If you increase frequency, it costs more. Generally, then, within a finite budget, if reach is increased, frequency must be reduced; if frequency is increased, you can afford less reach. If you cut back too much on frequency, your campaign may produce no effect, as Naples (1979) indicated, because of insufficient psychological reinforcement.

COST-EFFECTIVENESS ANALYSIS

Let us assume that you have been able to identify the mass media that provide adequate reach in a target audience segment. Next, you will want to analyze whether you should favor some media over others because they are more cost effective.

Information about charges for commercial time or space can be obtained from the individual newspapers, magazines, radio stations, TV stations, or other companies. However, in the United States, *Standard Rate & Data Service* (*SRDS*) compiles and publishes such information for the major classes of mass media and updates it periodically. These publications are sold to subscribers like advertising and public relations firms. Some public and university libraries also make SRDS publications available. Similar services exist in some countries outside of the United States.

To evaluate and make intraclass comparisons of mass media cost effectiveness, media planners utilize an analysis technique called *cost per thousand* (abbreviated *CPM,* the *M* representing *mil* or thousand).[2] Cost per mil is the cost to deliver one unit of commercial time or space to a hypothetical 1,000 audience members.

Media CPM can be calculated for both print and broadcast media. However, CPM is used for comparative analysis within a particular medium —such as daily newspapers. Since rate structures differ for each class, cross-media CPM analysis—for example, radio CPM versus newspaper CPM—is not comparable.

The basic formula for cost per thousand is:

$$CPM = \frac{\text{Cost for Unit of Space (or Time)} \times 1,000}{\text{Medium's Reach (in Numbers)}}$$

You must compute the CPM for each medium in every comparison you make.

The cost per unit term in the CPM numerator is fairly self-explanatory: For radio, it might be the cost of a 30-second commercial; a newspaper unit cost might be a column inch of space. The denominator, the number specifying the medium's reach, can be handled in one of two ways, although one or the other should be used consistently as the base for comparison: It can represent either the medium's total circulation or the medium's circulation in the target audience. Circulation and reach are considered equivalent in both cases.

Audience research reports provide information that will enable you to calculate the coverage in terms of numbers of people. Reports for print media give total circulation; if they give percentages, these can be multiplied by the circulation to obtain the number of individuals in subgroups or segments that the medium covers. Reports for broadcast media provide similar information to enable calculation from rating or share to actual numbers of individuals reached. Often the conversion is elementary, such as one rating point being equivalent to a specified number of households.

Continuity, Pulsing, Flighting, and Media Mix

To balance planning against budget, you need to understand and be ready to utilize three strategies: continuity, pulsing, and flighting. The three are shown in Exhibit 7.6.

---

[2] Cost per mil must be differentiated from PERT-CPM, in which the CPM refers to *Critical Path Method.*

Exhibit 7.6. Continuity, Pulsing, and Flighting

	Week 1	Week 2	Week 3	Week 4
Continuity	XXXXXXXXXXXXXXXXXXXXXXXXXXXXXXXXXXXXXXXXXXXXXXXX			
Pulsing	XX XX XXXXXXXXXXXXXXXXX	XX XX XXXXXXXXXXXXX	XX XX XXXXXXXXXXX	XX XX XXXXXXXXXXX
Flighting	XX	XX	XX	XX

Source: Adapted from A. M. Barban, S. M. Cristol, and F. J. Kopek, *Essentials of Media Planning* (Chicago, Crain Books, 1976).

Continuity is a strategy that ensures that the message will appear relatively continuously before the target audience. That is, the target audience segment will not go days, weeks, or months without encountering the message after the previous exposure.

Media other than outdoor displays, which stay in the environment for long periods of time, necessitate continuity and usually relatively high levels of frequency across time. Consequently, continuity tends to be expensive.

Pulsing is a strategy that combines some degree of continuity across time with periodic bursts of greater frequency. The strategy can be useful when frequency is costly and the occasional use of greater frequency is likely to enhance potential exposure or psychological reinforcement.

Flighting is a strategy that uses a medium, discontinues use, reinstates use, discontinues use, reinstates use, and so on. It is useful when limited funds prevent continuity.

Media mix refers to the concurrent use of different mass media. The strategy is used partly to ensure that members of a target audience will be exposed to a message somewhere or at some time during the four-week scheduling period. It also has the effect of supplementing continuity within particular media since it can enhance the potential for exposure (see Exhibit 7.7).

Exhibit 7.7. Flighting Combined with Media Mix to Achieve Continuity in Campaign

Week: Day:	Week 1 1 2 3 4 5 6 7	Week 2 1 2 3 4 5 6 7	Week 3 1 2 3 4 5 6 7	Week 4 1 2 3 4 5 6 7
TV	X	X	X	X
Radio	XXXXXXXXXXXX	XXXXXXXXXXXX	XXXXXXXXXXXX	XXXXXXXXXXXX

MASS MEDIA: MEDIUM AND VEHICLE

The discussion to this point has utilized the terms mass media and medium. However, the technical vocabulary of message planning differentiates between the following terms:

- *Mass media* includes newspapers, magazines, radio, television, movie trailers, direct mail, point-of-purchase (or point-of-decision) displays, outdoor displays, and transit posters.
- *Medium* refers to any one of the mass media mentioned in the previous entry.
- *Vehicle* signifies a specifically named medium—for example, the *Boston Globe,* the *New York Times, Time, U.S. News & World Report,* WNEV-TV, or WBZ-TV.

When media plans are specified, the particular vehicles that will be utilized must always be identified.

THE MEDIA/CHANNEL PLAN

As in most managerial processes, deliberations on media selection tend to be extensive, making it easy to become lost in details. You have seen that managerial techniques such as force field analysis, MBO, and message planning worksheets can be useful in summarizing decision making. Now we will look at other techniques for summing up media or channel planning.

Gross impressions is an index that relates the sum of all audiences that presumably should be delivered by all vehicles that are utilized in a media plan. Because a gross impressions index does not rule out duplicated coverage, it artificially inflates the characterization of reach. As Sissors and Surmanek (1982, p. 51) point out,

> The number of impressions delivered by a media plan usually runs into the millions, and because the number is so large, it is called a boxcar figure. Its value, however, is debatable. Alone, Gross Impressions have limited meaning. But if they can be related to some measure of campaign effectiveness, such as sales volume, brand awareness levels or competitive media plan effectiveness, they can be of more value.

Gross rating points (GRPs) is a term that characterizes the mathematical product of reach and frequency:

$$\text{Gross Rating Points (GRPs)} = \text{Reach} \times \text{Frequency}$$

For example, you know that a TV program's rating is equal to its reach, in terms of all TV households. Suppose you are dealing with a program with a 15 rating. The number of message insertions in that program is equal to frequency. Suppose time is purchased for three messages. Consequently, the GRPs for this situation would be GRPs = $15 \times 3 = 45$.

It is possible to sum GRPs across a week or across a four-week period.

An example of the process, with reach and frequency drawn from a TV example might be as follows:

$$
\begin{array}{rcl}
\text{2 commercials in program with 20 rating} & = & \text{40 GRPs} \\
\text{6 commercials in program with 15 rating} & = & \text{90 GRPs} \\
\text{3 commercials in program with 7 rating} & = & \text{21 GRPs} \\
\text{Total GRPs for week} & = & \text{151 GRPs}
\end{array}
$$

Similar calculations can be made for print media, once you have determined from audience research what percentage of each medium's total audience is made up of the target audience.

GRPS have no absolute, concrete meaning. They are indices of *relative* performance. They can be used, for example, to compare the results of two different media plans that are developed for the same time period, or to verify a media plan that assigns different levels of activity to audience segments or to audience segments in different geographical areas. GRP analysis is suitable for targets differentiated by age, gender, income, education, or any other demographic variable (Sissors & Surmanek, 1982, p. 52).

In reports on media plans, it is common practice to list information about GRPs. Reporting deals most often with total campaign GRPs and GRPs by four-week planning segments, but in some cases weekly GRPs also may be reported.

Media or channel schedule is a graphic format that summarizes the media mix, including information about continuity, flighting, or pulsing strategies applied to each vehicle. The schedule also relates decisions about frequency. A manager or planner needs to make the information comprehensible quickly (see Exhibit 7.8). Although weeks and days constitute the basic reporting unit, the schedule can be adapted to report other units, such as months and weeks for a year's plan. Some managers or planners incorporate information about reach and frequency for each major time period. In Exhibit 7.8, reach and frequency could be reported for each week and then cumulatively for the month. In a schedule for a year, reach and frequency could be reported for each month and then cumulatively for the 12 months.

Reporting of costs is often included for medium/channel use (in the far-left column) with cost subtotals for each medium, and a cost grand total (at the bottom of the column).

Weighting

While the media or channel schedule is being formulated, often the problem being addressed varies over time or across geographic areas. Such cases might dictate that the schedule incorporate *weighting* to increase or decrease communication activity as necessary. Here are some examples:

Exhibit 7.8. Format for Media/Channel Schedule

	Week 1 1 2 3 4 5 6 7	Week 2 1 2 3 4 5 6 7	Week 3 1 2 3 4 5 6 7	Week 4 1 2 3 4 5 6 7
Days:				
Medium:				
Vehicle 1	XXXXXXXXXXXX		XXXXXXXXXXXXXX	
Vehicle 2	X	X	X	X
Cost:				
Medium:				
Vehicle 1		XXXXXXXXXXXXX		XXXXXXXXXXXXXX
Vehicle 2	X X X		X X X	
Cost:				
Total Cost:				
R/F per Period				

Weighting by Consumption Cycles. For example, if the campaign is to promote milk consumption and research shows that consumption peaks in certain months in the fall, winter, and spring but drops during the hot summer months, the media or channel schedule would logically be weighted similarly—with more communication activity in the peak months and less activity in the other months of those three seasons; summer activity would be scaled down even further.

Weighting by Media Use Patterns. For example, in U.S. cities, radio listening is heavier during morning and afternoon "drive time," when people are driving to or from work. An effective media schedule for radio would probably weight the schedule for more communication activity during morning and afternoon drive time, assuming that the desired audience segments are known to be in the station's or stations' audience at those times.

Weighting by Geographical Patterns. Often those who consume a product or service, or who are rated highly as target audience segments, are most prevalent in specified market areas. In such cases a media schedule probably would weight the plan to dictate more communication activity in those high-activity areas and relatively less in others.

ADDITIONAL MEDIA PLANNING CONSIDERATIONS

Message Positioning in Media

To improve the likelihood that campaign messages will gain exposure, you will want to place them in the media where the target audience or audiences will be most likely to encounter them—for example in specific sections or on specific pages of print media, or in specific programs on TV or radio. This can be accomplished by ordering *message positioning within the media*. In some cases, media assess additional charges when position is requested, but the increase in exposure is usually worth the cost.

Public Service Announcements (PSAs)

Nonprofit organizations utilize *public service announcements (PSAs)* to get media exposure, often without cost. Radio and TV routinely carry PSAs without charge, although there is no control over positioning—not even regarding the day or week when a message will be broadcast. Broadcast media usually have a PSA director who can provide information about policies and procedures. Print media are not mandated to carry PSAs, as broadcast media are as part of Federal Communications Commission public service requirements to obtain a station license, but they often do. They also may provide free space in proportion to the amount of space that is purchased by a nonprofit organization. As in the case of broadcast media, you can inquire about policies and procedures of particular print media outlets.

SUMMARY

Media planning is not equivalent to publicity, a field in which the idea of message diffusion is to get a message out to the largest possible number of persons. Media planning begins with the idea of a target audience segment.

For the most communication with that segment, the media planner works to

1. Maximize coverage, or reach, in each target segment and minimize waste coverage
2. Determine what repetition (or frequency) is sufficient to (1) ensure exposure to the message; (2) prevent the campaign from disappearing periodically—that is, provide sufficient continuity; and (3) maximize the probability that content will be remembered or learned and, preferably, acted on
3. Make clear through gross rating point (GRP) analysis (1) that reach and frequency are adequate or (2) that when alternative media/ channel plans are considered or when such plans are weighted (such as by segment, time, or geographic area) it will be possible to verify that the GRPs that are produced are consonant with the specified weighting goals
4. Determine through cost per thousand (CPM) analysis that choices of mass media—or more correctly, specific vehicles—are cost effective
5. Present a succinct summary of the message delivery plan in a simple, easy-to comprehend format known as a media/channel schedule: The schedule also may present costs, both by medium subcategories and by total, as well as reach and frequency statistics for each major period of the campaign. The scheduled communication activities can be weighted to be as efficient as possible in relation to time and geographic differences. The media/channel schedule also employs continuity, pulsing, and flighting to ensure that there will be sufficient activity in each subperiod to provide psychological reinforcement in the target audience segment.

REFERENCES

Arnold Barban, S. M. Cristol, and Frank J. Kopek, *Essentials of Media Planning: A Marketing Viewpoint* (Chicago: Crain Books, 1976).
Robert Norton and J. Hughey, ''Understanding the Exigency in Order to Craft the

Rhetorical Response; Health Promoting Behavior Relating to the AIDS Virus in a Low Prevalence State,'' presentation to the Speech Communication Assn., Boston, 1987.

M. J. Naples, *Effective Frequency: The Relationship Between Frequency and Advertising Effectiveness* (New York: Association of National Advertisers, 1979).

Leon Quera, *Advertising Campaigns: Formulation and Tactics* (Columbus, OH: Grid, 1973).

M. L. Ray, *Advertising and Communication Management* (Englewood Cliffs, NJ: Prentice-Hall, 1982).

J. Z. Sissors and Jim Surmanek, *Advertising Media Planning,* 2nd ed. (Chicago: Crain Books, 1982). An exceptional resource for managers and planners who want to improve their mastery of media planning.

W. M. Weilbacher, *Advertising* (New York: Macmillan, 1979).

CHAPTER 8

Planning with PERT-CPM

The planning and later execution of a campaign involve a large number of activities or tasks. As a manager or planner, you need a managerial system that enables you to define campaign activities and their relationships in order to plan, delegate, monitor, and control effectively. *Program Evaluation and Review Technique—Critical Path Method (PERT-CPM),* provides such a system.

Some of the advantages of PERT-CPM are the following:

1. *Defining activities and objectives:* A manager or planner must have a written work plan. Without one, it often is found, usually too late to make needed changes, that some crucial activities were badly defined or omitted unintentionally to the detriment of the campaign. PERT-CPM builds on management by objectives (discussed in Chapter 5) to define and organize information about activities and execution times.
2. *Resource management:* All campaigns have more than one sequence of tasks. In planning, you must be able to identify the sequences that can jeopardize the deadline. When such problems exist, you need a system that helps you cope efficiently—reallocate resources rationally or make reasoned cuts—to meet your deadline. Without PERT-CPM, the complexity of campaigns is so great that your ability to pinpoint and solve such problems is problematic.
3. *Work scheduling:* PERT-CPM provides a basis to delegate work that is necessary to the objectives and reduces ambiguity in assignments. This helps ensure that the campaign can be completed either by a specified deadline or in the minimum time.

4. *Evaluation:* With PERT-CPM you can verify whether objectives are being met as scheduled. Without such a system, monitoring is very difficult.

PERT-CPM was developed as part of the planning and administration involved in construction of the first U.S. nuclear submarine. Although PERT-CPM meets the needs of exceptionally complex projects or programs, it also can meet the needs of less complex work. For example, you could use PERT to plan and administer a research project with multiple operations, such as sampling, questionnaire design, interviewer training, interviewing, data collection, processing, analysis, and report writing. Some of these tasks, such as sampling, may involve complex subroutines, which can also involve PERT. Moreover, in a campaign, you can also get better control over execution stages with the aid of PERT.

PERT TERMS AND SYMBOLS

Developing a Pert Vocabulary

You must master a basic vocabulary before working with PERT:

Activity designates one or more tasks that must be executed to complete an objective. Activity will be stated in terms of *doing* something—for example, *contracting* an artist, *designing* the layout for a publication, *applying* an attitude scale, *reading* and *summarizing* reference sources, *interpreting* results of a research project, *writing* a report, or *proofreading* the manuscripts.

Objective signifies a marker of progress. It can represent the beginning or the end of an activity. An objective does not require utilization of time or resources; it simply tells what will have been completed provided things are going well. I recommend that the term should be associated with the end product of a specified activity; consequently, a PERT objective is conceptually equivalent to an MBO intermediate objective, as explained in Chapter 5. For that reason, a PERT objective will constitute a criterion to verify whether tasks associated with it have been completed. Examples of objectives are: opinion leaders *interviewed,* survey research sample *designed,* brochures *printed* or secondary research publications on daily newspapers *read* and *summarized.*

Predecessor identifies an objective that is to be completed before an activity relating to another objective begins.

Successor identifies an objective on which work cannot begin until a specified prior objective or set of objectives has been completed.

Concurrent objectives signifies objectives that may be accomplished in the same time period. For example, suppose your team has two research specialists and must develop a questionnaire and design a sampling plan; the activities for the questionnaire (questionnaire design completed) could be completed by one person while the other works on the sampling design (sampling design completed). Therefore, the objectives can be treated concurrently.

Time refers to a standard time unit that is used for all PERT estimates of how much time is required to complete each objective. You may express times in days or hours or minutes but you cannot switch units within PERT operations. If partial units must be specified, such as a day and a third, they can be represented as fractions or decimals—for example, $1\frac{1}{3}$ or 1.33.

Begin signifies initiation of work on all of the activities and objectives in a campaign.

End represents the conclusion of all the objectives in a campaign.

PERT network is a graphic that shows how a campaign's activities and objectives fit together. Beginning, activities, objectives, times, and ending are represented by graphic symbols arranged in a design that shows sequence and concurrent operations. The resulting design is called a PERT network, although some persons use *flowchart* interchangeably; that term is not considered correct in this book because it is associated primarily with computer programming.

Basic Pert Symbols

PERT utilizes graphic symbols that enable you to visualize operations that constitute a network. These are the standardized symbols you must learn:

Begin is the point at which PERT activities and objectives are all initiated and is signified by the word *begin* written in capital letters and enclosed in a box:

$$\boxed{\text{BEGIN}}$$

Objectives are represented by numbers in circles. The numbers will be used to link each symbol in a network with the written description in a planning worksheet. An objective symbol looks like this:

⑮

Activity is symbolized by a line to the left of the circle containing the objective number. The length of a line representing an activity has no particular significance; it may be as long as necessary to serve the needs of network design. An activity symbol looks like this:

Time is represented by a number in parentheses. Time will be written above the activity line to which it corresponds:

End is signified by the word *end* in capital letters, enclosed in a box:

DESIGNING A PERT NETWORK

The basic steps in designing any PERT network are the same:

1. List each objective.
2. Give each a unique identifying number.
3. Use symbols for objectives and organize all of the objectives into logical sequences.

In a network, PERT objectives do not have to be ordered numerically. An objective's number serves only two simple purposes: to identify the objective and to distinguish it from all the other objectives. Some managers or planners like to list objectives in a logical sequence according to the order in which they would usually occur and then assign numbers in sequence. However, although that system can make it easier to read a complex PERT network, it is not necessary.

In the following pages are a series of tasks for you to complete to help you understand the basic concepts and processes of PERT-CPM. Each task will be followed by a *model response,* to allow you to check your own response to the question or problem posed. Without looking at the model response, use PERT symbols and create a network to represent these objectives:

1. Draft of article written
2. Final copy typewritten
3. Manuscript edited
4. Final copy duplicated
5. Topic researched
6. Topic for paper identified

Model Response A

Next, without looking at the model responses, answer these questions:

1. Which are *successor* objectives to 1?
2. Which are *predecessor* objectives to 4?
3. Can objective 3 be completed before predecessor objectives 1, 5, and 6?

Check your answers against the model responses.

Model Response B

1. Objectives 3, 2, and 4
2. Objectives 2, 3, 1, 5, and 6
3. No

Now examine the PERT network in Exhibit 8.1.

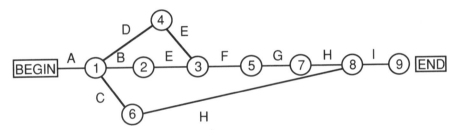

EXHIBIT 8.1. Sample PERT Network
Note: Activities in a PERT network are not identified by letters. However, to facilitate answering the following questions, letters are used here to make references to specific activities easier.

Without looking at the next model response section, answer these questions:

1. What activity is associated with objective 3?
2. Is an activity related to an objective depicted to the right or the left of that objective?
3. What activity is associated with objective 8?
4. What activities are predecessors to activity E?
5. What activities are successors to activity B?
6. Does the network depict concurrent objectives or activities?

Model Response C

1. E
2. Left
3. H
4. A, B, D
5. C, D, E, F, G, H, I
6. Yes (activity D with objective 4 and activity C with objective 6 are both realized concurrently with others on the main line running through the network)

You must understand the concept of *necessary predecessor*. It is impossible to design a network for a campaign without being able to identify necessary predecessor objectives—those that must be completed for activities relating to a succeeding objective to be initiated.

Predecessors could be listed all the way back to the "begin" symbol. However, a necessary predecessor is different in that it is the one immediately prior to the objective being considered. For example, in the previous network, objectives 1 and 2 are predecessors to objective 3, but only objective 2 is a necessary predecessor to 3.

As your next task, design a PERT network for the following objectives. Remember to consider whether some objectives might be executed concurrently with others.

1. Topic defined
2. Project topic approved by supervisor
3. Topic researched
4. Supplies (paper, pens, etc.) purchased
5. Manuscript draft completed
6. Final manuscript's typist contracted
7. Manuscript edited
8. Final copy typewritten
9. Final copy reproduced

After you have completed your PERT network, compare it to the following model response.

Model Response D

Examine the PERT network in Exhibit 8.1. Compare your solution with that illustration. Note that objectives 4 and 6 can be accomplished concurrently with others.

Pert Time

The next step is to refer to the times needed to complete the activities and insert them into the PERT network. Time for an activity is displayed as a number in parentheses, and the information is placed adjacent to (usually over or beside) the line that represents the activity and to the left of the associated PERT objective symbol.

Suppose you have two objectives related to the production of photographic slides for an audiovisual show. One is "text originals typed" and requires 1.5 hours. The second is "originals photographed" and requires 1 hour. The segment of the PERT network representing the objectives, related activities, and times would look like this:

Once again, note that both the activities and the times relating to objectives are expressed to the left, or in front of, the circle representing the objective.

Now examine the information in Exhibit 8.2 about objectives in the preparation of a brochure for a conference and the time estimated to complete the activity related to each objective. Suppose this particular project must be completed within 19 days, and it must not impede other phases relating to the mounting of a conference. Can the work be accomplished in 19 days? Clearly, there is not sufficient structure in the information to enable us to decide just by looking at the time estimates for individual activities. A PERT network provides the needed structure.

EXHIBIT 8.2. Objectives for Conference Brochure

Objective Number	Objective	Time (Days)
1	Conference theme and topics OK'd	3
2	Conference and promotion budget OK'd	1
3	Brochure content specified	1
4	Graphic design completed	2
5	Guest speakers contracted	8
6	Printing bids obtained	3
7	Brochure text completed (naming guest speakers)	2.5
8	Brochure printed	3
9	Mailing list completed	2
10	Mailing completed	2

Now look at the PERT network in Exhibit 8.3 and insert the times in the parentheses; follow the rules given earlier and use the information provided about the objectives and their estimated completion times. After you have your solution, refer to the next model response.

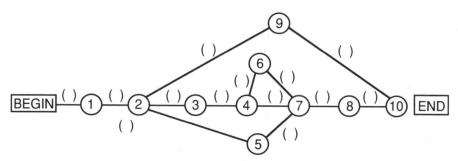

EXHIBIT 8.3. PERT Network for Conference Brochure Preparation

Model Response E

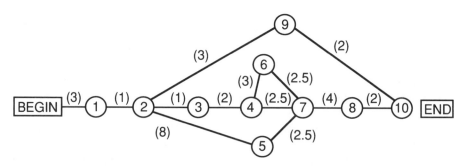

Identifying Network Paths

You probably have observed that PERT objectives are grouped along particular lines in a network. These are called *paths,* which are particular sequences of objectives and related activities that run from left to right through a network. Necessary predecessors determine which objectives constitute a particular path. The utility of paths, one of the most powerful features of PERT analysis, is explained later.

To be sure you understand how to identify paths, refer back to Model Response E. Note that there are four paths:

- Path 1: Objectives 1, 2, 3, 4, 7, 8, 10
- Path 2: Objectives 1, 2, 9, 10
- Path 3: Objectives 1, 2, 5, 7, 8, 10
- Path 4: Objectives 1, 2, 3, 4, 6, 7, 8, 10

It might help if you trace each network path with a finger as you read the list of objectives for each path.

Once you can identify each path in a network, it becomes easy to obtain the *total path time* by adding the individual time estimates that lie along the path. The first few times you do this, you should write the objectives for each path, then put the time underneath each objective so that you will know which time estimates to add. If you do so, you will probably make fewer errors while learning the procedure.

Refer to the network in Model Response E. List each path objective, record the related times, and then calculate the total path time for each path:

- Path 1   Objectives: _____
            Times: _____
- Path 2   Objectives: _____
            Times: _____
- Path 3   Objectives: _____
            Times: _____
- Path 4   Objectives: _____
            Times: _____

Check your answers against the next model response section.

Model Response F

- Path 1   Objectives: 1,   2,   3,   4,   7,   8,   10
            Times: 3 + 1 + 1 + 2 + 2.5 + 4 +   2 = 15.5
- Path 2   Objectives: 1,   2,   9,   10
            Times: 3 + 1 + 3 +   2 = 9
- Path 3   Objectives: 1,   2,   5,   7,   8,   10
            Times: 3 + 1 + 8 + 2.5 + 4 +   2 = 20.5
- Path 4   Objectives: 1,   2,   3,   4,   6,   7,   8,   10
            Times: 3 + 1 + 1 + 2 + 3 + 2.5 + 4 + 2   = 18.5

Note: Total path times represent work days or portions of work days—the same time units used earlier in estimating the time required to complete the PERT events in the network.

CRITICAL PATH METHOD

Now you are ready to relate total path times to the PERT concept of *critical path*.

If no deadline is set, a critical path can be defined as that path (or those paths) in a network that require the longest time to complete. Consequently, a critical path is significant because it specifies the shortest time in which an entire campaign can be completed. In some cases, paths may be tied on total path time; in this case, there would be more than one critical path.

When there is a deadline for completing a campaign, the critical path method enables you to determine which path or paths might jeopardize a satisfactory conclusion. For example, suppose a client specifies that a campaign must be "in the field" in three weeks (15 work days) but a PERT analysis turns up a critical path with 18 work days. Thus the campaign cannot meet the deadline unless changes are made in the work plan. The critical path in this case also helps with decisions about changes because it suggests where modifications could be made to meet the deadline—only in objectives or activities lying along the critical path. Usually, modifications involve decisions about time allocation (allow less), assignment of resources (add an extra person to help with the work), or substitution of a new approach (find another way to solve the problem or redefine tasks relating to certain objectives).

To check your understanding about the critical path method, answer these questions about the paths in the previous network:

1. Which is the critical path? (Identify it by number and total time.)
2. Is there more than one critical path in the problem?
3. As things now stand, is it possible to complete the project in 19 days?
4. What does knowledge about the critical path suggest to you about possible modifications if you answered no to the previous question?

Check your answers against the next model response section.

Model Response G

1. The critical path is 3. It requires a minimum of 20.5 days to complete. None of the other paths requires as much time.
2. There is only one critical path in the problem. The total time of the critical path is not tied with any other path total.
3. The time allowed is 19 days. The critical path, or the one detailing activities in the network that require the longest time to complete, is 20.5 days. Therefore, it is impossible to complete the whole project in less than 20.5 days, as it is now planned.
4. Some modifications must be made in the activities and objectives along path 3. One possibility is that the time required for the activities for objective 5 (guest speakers contracted) might be reduced by having an additional person work on the tasks involved.

IMPROVING PERT TIME CONTROL

Locating Slack

The PERT network and critical path analysis give you greater control over a campaign's planning. However, the benefits do not end there. Another feature of PERT helps in work delegation or monitoring; that is, it makes it possible for you to determine which objectives must be completed on time, allowing for no deviation, and which ones allow for *slack,* or extra, time. When critical path analysis indicates that modifications must be made in activities or objectives in a path, knowledge about slack enables you to make better decisions about where human resources do not have to be tightly controlled; reallocation of human resources might make it possible to ensure that work on all the objectives in all of the paths is concluded by the deadline. Moreover, in delegating work, information about slack enables you to inform workers whether any specified objective must be completed on a particular date or could be completed on a later date without compromising successor objectives or the entire campaign.

To calculate slack, you begin by determining both the *earliest time* and the *latest time* that every objective in a campaign's network can be attained. Examine the network in Exhibit 8.4; beside each PERT objective symbol you will see two numbers separated by a comma. The number to the left of the comma indicates the earliest time. The calculations to obtain the earliest time are simple. Consult the path that includes objectives 1, 2, 3, and 4. "Begin" represents 0 (zero) time. Add the time for the activity associated with objective 1, obtaining 6 (the earliest time for that objective). Then add the time for the activity related to objective 2, obtaining 11 (the earliest time for objective 2). Then add the time for the activity associated with objective 3, obtaining 15 (the earliest time for objective 3). Finally, add the time associated with activity 4, obtaining 18 (the earliest time for objective 4). If you repeat these operations, you can determine the earliest times for the path containing objectives 1, 5, 6 and 4. In summary, then, to obtain the earliest times for each objective, add cumulatively each objective from left to right in each path.

To obtain the latest time for each objective, work backward from right to left in a network, beginning with "end." Find the total path time, then work backward, progressively subtracting each activity time.

Look at the objectives in the path 4, 6, 5, 1. Begin with 18, the latest time for objective 4. (It is the number to the right of the comma.) Then subtract 3, the time for the activity associated with objective 4, obtaining 15. That number is written above objective 6 and to the right of the comma. Next,

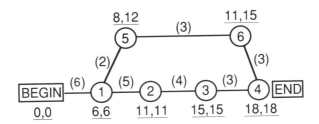

EXHIBIT 8.4. Sample PERT Network

Note: The earliest time and latest time for each objective are underlined in the network.

subtract 3, the time for the activity related to objective 6, obtaining 12. That number is written above objective 5 and to the right of the comma. Repeat the same operations to obtain the latest times for the objectives 4, 3, 2, 1, and "begin."

Once the earliest time and latest time are recorded for each objective in the network, you can calculate the slack—which some managers or planners also call *total float*—in the network by subtracting the earliest time from the latest time for each objective, as illustrated in Exhibit 8.5.

ExHIBIT 8.5. Calculating Total Slack

Objective	Calculation of Slack
1	6 − 6 = 0
2	11 − 11 = 0
3	15 − 15 = 0
4	18 − 18 = 0
5	12 − 8 = 4
6	15 − 11 = 4

Exhibit 8.5 shows that for objectives 1, 2, 3, and 4, which are along the critical path, there is absolutely no slack. If these objectives are not accomplished on time, there is no way that the project can be completed in the 18 days specified. For objectives 5 and 6 work could extend up to four days beyond the time allowed, and the campaign could still be completed on time.

A second type of slack, *activity slack,* questions whether there is any slack time in the completion of activities, and if so, how much can be utilized before the successor objective is jeopardized. Some managers or planners also call this type of slack *free float,* which can be computed with the following formula:

Activity Slack = Latest Time − (Earliest Time + Estimated Activity Time)

If you calculate the activity slack for the preceding network it would look like Exhibit 8.6. The zero activity slack findings indicate that each objective in the critical path must be completed within the time specified or the next successor objectives in that path cannot be completed on time. However, in the last three cases, each objective can use up to four days more than the specified time without compromising the related successor objectives.

More Accurate Time Estimation

When things must be done on a tight schedule, they rarely go either as well as hoped or as badly as feared. We tend to guess about how much time will be

Exhibit 8.6. Calculating Activity Slack

Activities	Calculation of Activity Slack
BEGIN − 1	6 − (0 + 6) = 0
1 − 2	11 − (6 + 5) = 0
2 − 3	15 − (11 + 4) = 0
3 − 4	18 − (15 + 3) = 0
1 − 5	12 − (6 + 2) = 4
5 − 6	15 − (8 + 3) = 4
6 − 4	18 − (11 + 3) = 4

needed, estimating the most likely outcome on the basis of experience regarding the worst scenario, the best case, and the most probable outcome. PERT provides both a simple and a weighted approach to address the need for improved estimates.

To begin, three types of time estimates must be differentiated. They are needed in calculations later.

- T_O The most *optimistic time estimate* (remember T for *time* and O for *optimistic*): This is the time in which an activity could be completed if everything does go as well as hoped.
- T_L The most *likely time estimate* (remember T for *time* and L for *likely*): This is the time that we think is most realistic—considering both things that might go well or badly.
- T_P The most *pessimistic time* estimate (remember T for *time* and P for *pessimistic*): This is the time in which an activity might be completed if various things, expected or unexpected, go wrong. The possibility of crises and catastrophes is considered here.

Commonsense estimation considers a subjective average figured across these three factors. If you were to calculate an arithmetic average for three scores, you would add the three figures and divide by the number of scores. Similarly, you can calculate an arithmetic average for multiple PERT time estimates for any objective—a figure designated as "T_E" (remember T for *time* and E for *estimate*)—with this formula:

$$T_E = \frac{T_O + T_L + T_P}{3}$$

Study Exhibit 8.7 and calculate T_E for each of the four activities. Do not consult the model responses until you have your own answers.

EXHIBIT 8.7. Calculating Time Estimates

	T_O	T_L	T_P	T_E
Activity 1	6	5	9	_____
Activity 2	3	6	9	_____
Activity 3	3	6	7	_____
Activity 4	5	6	7	_____

Model Response H: Averaged Time Estimates for Each Activity

- Activity 1 = 6.67
- Activity 2 = 6
- Activity 3 = 5.67
- Activity 4 = 6

A problem with an arithmetic mean, also called "simple average" by some, is that extreme estimates like T_O or T_P may have more impact than T_L. PERT recognizes this fact and compensates by weighting T_L (the most likely estimate) more heavily, as in this formula:

$$T_{E/W} = \frac{T_O + (4)\,(T_L) + T_P}{6}$$

The formula says, in effect, that whatever the estimate of T_L, it should be weighted double—multiplied by a factor of 4—and to keep the weighting factor in balance, the denominator must be modified, making it 6. To help make the process clearer, suppose a member of your planning staff estimates the three times for a campaign activity this way: $T_O = 4$, $T_L = 8$, $T_P = 10$. Calculate your answer for the representative time estimate:

$T_{E/W} =$ _____

When you have your answer, compare it with the next model response.

Model Response I

$$T_{E/W} = \frac{T_O + (4)\,(T_L) + T_P}{6} = \frac{4 + (4)\,(8) + 10}{6}$$

$$= \frac{4 + 32 + 10}{6} = \frac{46}{6} = 7.67$$

Whenever the planning is important enough to require the best estimate of time required, you should use the weighted formula $T_{E/W}$.

PLANNING LARGE PERT NETWORKS

We have thus far discussed PERT techniques for relatively small problems that generate relatively small networks. However, as a manager or planner you are likely to deal regularly with campaign problems involving larger numbers of activities; mastery of some additional techniques can enable you to cope with these cases.

First, list the activities, then group them into coherent clusters, each with some objective in common as a culmination. For example, consider these activities: (1) getting bids for the printing of a brochure, (2) selecting a printer, and (3) delivering the copy to the favored printer. They terminate in one objective: "Brochure copy delivered to the printer."

Next, use a PERT worksheet format, like that in Exhibit 8.8. List the activities and objectives, to which you will assign numbers. The numbers in the example are sequential, but that is not absolutely necessary.

Next, enter the time estimates; either simple or weighted. Remember, however, that consistent units of time must be used—for example, hours or eight-hour work days; a mixture of units is not acceptable.

Then specify the necessary predecessors for the objectives. Remember that in PERT a necessary predecessor is one that must be completed immediately prior to the accomplishment of the activities associated with the next objective. For example, in Exhibit 8.8 note that the activities related to objective 2 would not be initiated before the completion of objective 1. Consequently, objective 1 is a necessary predecessor to objective 2. Also only a predecessor that immediately precedes a specified objective must be listed; there is no reason to list every predecessor all the way back to "begin." Fill in the necessary predecessors in Exhibit 8.8, then check the model responses.

After you have verified your list of necessary predecessors and made any necessary corrections, take a sheet of paper and work out a network based on the information in the worksheet.

As you develop the design, remember that you may create paths that bow outward, but you cannot have activity lines that cross.

Compare your work with the next model response and verify whether your network is viable. One way to do so is to work your way backward through each path to determine that each supposed necessary predecessor is, indeed, necessary. Your network might vary from the model response. Occasionally, different managers or planners can produce networks that are not the same but are equally viable.

Exhibit 8.8. PERT Planning Worksheet

Activity	Objectives	Number	Time	Predecessors
Get client approval for campaign	Client approval obtained	1	10	
Write newspaper ad copy				
Design newspaper ad				
Deliver ad to newspapers	Newspaper ad completed	2	3	
Contract for ad publication	Newspaper ad contracted	3	1	
Write TV PSA script				
Develop PSA storyboard				
Obtain slides for PSA	TV PSA completed	4	5	
Deliver PSA to TV stations	TV PSAs delivered	5	1	
Write radio PSA script	Radio PSA written	6	7	
Deliver PSA to radio stations	Radio PSAs delivered	7	1	
Write brochure text				
Design brochure layout	Brochure copy completed	8	2	
Get brochure bids from printers				
Select printer				
Deliver copy to printer	Brochure copy delivered	9	2	
Define brochure distribution points				
Pick up brochures from printer				
Distribute brochures	Brochures distributed	10	5	
Design poster	Poster copy completed	11	2	
Get poster bids from printers				
Select printer				
Deliver poster to printer	Poster copy delivered	12	2	
Define poster distribution points				
Pick up poster from printer				
Distribute posters	Posters distributed	13	5	
Allow 4-week exposure time	Exposure completed	14	20	
Run campaign evaluation				
Analyze evaluation result				
Write evaluation report	Evaluation completed	15	10	

Model Response J

Activity	Objectives	Number	Time	Predecessors
Get client approval for campaign	Client approval obtained	1	10	BEGIN
Write newspaper ad copy				
Design newspaper ad	Newspaper ad completed	2	3	1
Deliver ad to newspapers				
Contract for ad publication	Newspaper ad contracted	3	1	2
Write TV PSA script				
Develop PSA storyboard				
Obtain slides for PSA	TV PSA completed	4	5	1
Deliver PSA to stations	TV PSAs delivered	5	1	4
Write radio PSA script	Radio PSA written	6	7	1
Deliver PSA to radio stations	Radio PSAs delivered	7	1	6
Write brochure text				
Design brochure layout	Brochure copy completed	8	2	2
Get brochure bids from printers				
Select printer				
Deliver copy to printer	Brochure copy delivered	9	2	8
Define brochure distribution points				
Pick up brochures from printer				
Distribute brochures	Brochures distributed	10	5	9
Design poster	Poster copy completed	11	2	8
Get poster bids from printers				
Select printer				
Deliver poster to printer	Poster copy delivered	12	2	11
Define poster distribution points				
Pick up poster from printer				
Distribute posters	Posters distributed	13	5	12
Allow 4-week exposure time	Exposure completed	14	20	3, 5, 7, 10, 13
Run campaign evaluation				
Analyze evaluation result				
Write evaluation report	Evaluation completed	15	10	14

Model Response K

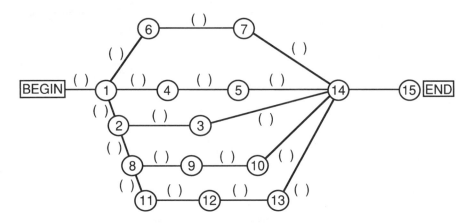

Note that the network in Model Response K has parentheses in which time estimates must be inserted. Refer to the worksheet in Exhibit 8.8 and locate the time for each objective in the network, then enter the figures. Then compare your work to the next model response section.

Model Response L

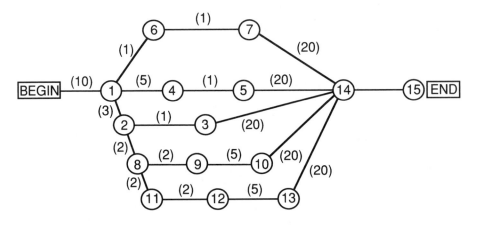

Finally, calculate the path times and locate the critical path or paths. Refer to the network in Model Response L and identify the paths, listing the objectives as you learned to do earlier. Then copy the times, recording them beneath the objectives in the paths to which they pertain, and sum the times for each path that you identify. Identify the critical path or paths. When you have completed these tasks, check against the next model response.

Model Response M

- Path 1   Objectives: 1,   6,   7,   14,   15
            Times: $10 + 1 + 1 + 20 + 10 = 42$ days
- Path 2   Objectives: 1,   4,   5,   14,   15
            Times: $10 + 5 + 1 + 20 + 10 = 46$
- Path 3   Objectives: 1,   2,   3,   14,   15
            Times: $10 + 3 + 1 + 20 + 10 = 44$
- Path 4   Objectives: 1,   2,   8,   9,   10,   14,   15
            Times: $10 + 3 + 2 + 2 + 5 + 20 + 10 = 52$
- Path 5   Objectives: 1,   2,   8,   11,   12,   13,   14,   15
            Times: $10 + 3 + 2 + 2 + 2 + 5 + 20 + 10 = 54$

            Critical path = path 5

Managers or planners customarily darken the activity lines for the critical path in a network, which makes them easy to see in a network diagram.

PERT AND THE GANTT CHART
WORK CONTROL SYSTEM

In addition to the advantages already discussed, PERT can be used as input for the development of a *Gantt chart,* a work delegation and control technique used widely by effective managers. A case example serves to illustrate the process.

Suppose you have a problem that includes the PERT objectives specified in Exhibit 8.9.

The objectives result in a PERT network like that in Exhibit 8.10.

To obtain start and end dates for each PERT objective, use the proce-

Exhibit 8.9. PERT Objectives for Speech

Number	Objective	Time
1	Speech theme specified	1 day
2	Research conducted	2
3	Script written	2
4	Speech rehearsed	1
5	Slides produced	2
6	Slides edited and keyed to script	1
7	Site setup checked	1
8	Speech presented	1
9	Evaluation completed	1

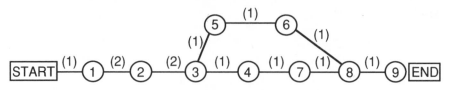

EXHIBIT 8.10. PERT Network

dures discussed earlier to calculate slack; the calculation of start and end times, you might recall, were used to figure slack estimates. Here, we use output from a PERT-CPM computer program instead. Refer to Exhibit 8.11 (and remember that a PERT objective can be called a PERT event, and that slack can also be called float).

EXHIBIT 8.11. Computerized PERT-CPM Analysis for Network

Start Event	End Event	Start Time	End Time	Job Time	Free Float	Total Float	
Begin	1	0	1	1	0	0	CP
1	2	1	3	2	0	0	CP
2	3	3	5	2	0	0	CP
3	4	5	8	1	0	2	
3	5	5	7	2	0	0	CP
4	7	6	7	1	2	2	
5	6	7	8	1	0	0	CP
6	7	8	9	1	0	0	CP
7	8	9	10	1	0	0	CP
8	9	10	11	1	0	0	CP

The begin and end event entries in each line show the individual nodes in the network; the entries in the end event column correspond to the circled objective numbers in the network. The job time column contains the information about the execution time for each end event, line by line. The free float column tells whether the objective identified in the end event column in that line can go over the specified job time without interfering with work in the next objective; a zero entry means there is no float for the objective (or no activity slack), but a figure above zero indicates that additional time is available. Similarly, the total float column tells whether the objective identified in the end event column in that line can go over the specified job time without causing the entire project to go over the maximum time specified in the critical path (which might mean that it would go past the deadline); a zero entry means there is no total float (or no total slack), but a figure above zero indicates that additional time is available.

Add the times for the two paths in the network in Exhibit 8.10; you will find that the total time is 11 days; the critical path is made up of objectives 1,

2, 3, 5, 6, 7, 8, and 9. If you examine Exhibit 8.11, you will find that each line that contains one of those objectives (in the end event column) has a *CP* notation at the end, which means that the objective, or end event, lies on the critical path.

You can use the information about start time, end time, job time, free float, and total float to set up a Gantt chart, as in Exhibit 8.12.

The Gantt chart can be used for three purposes: work delegation, work tracking, feedback.

Work Delegation

The chart shows to whom work is assigned, the objective (a criterion for completion), when the work can begin, and when it should be finished. The figures in parentheses show whether there is any float or slack—which indicates what the consequences are if a deadline is missed. For example, objective on lines with two zeros in parentheses must be completed; failure to meet the scheduled deadline means that neither the next objective nor the entire project can be completed. These objectives lies along the critical path. The float figures (in parentheses) for objective 7 indicate two days of free float and two days of total float; Exhibit 8.11 provides information that work on this objective could be initiated two days earlier than scheduled. The float figures for objective 4 show that there is no free float (i.e., activity slack), but there is total float amounting to two days. If the early start option for objective 7 is exercised, objective 4 cannot run past the specified time without interfering with work on the next objective; yet we learn from total float that if objective 4 runs over by two days, the project could still be completed within 11 days (e.g., by ruling out an early beginning on objective 7).

Work Tracking—Monitoring and Control

The Gantt chart can be expanded, as in Exhibit 8.13, to permit a manager to record information about what happens when the campaign goes into the execution stage. Shaded bars or colored lines can be entered in a line underneath the original lines. The additional information is useful in monitoring, coaching, and evaluating employees.

Feedback

The Gantt chart provides corrective information about time estimates to make future plans more accurate.

Although it is possible to use the procedures for estimating slack (see pp. 164–169) to obtain the information to develop a Gantt chart, the major project planning software packages with PERT-CPM that are available for desktop computers can also produce Gantt charts. Some of these software

EXHIBIT 8.12. Gantt Chart Based on Network

Responsible	Objective	Dates:	Week 1 1 2 3 4 5	Week 2 1 2 3 4 5	Week 3 1 2 3 4 5	Week 4 1 2 3 4 5	
Harris, Smith	1 Speech theme specified		X	. . . . .	. . . . .	. . . . .	(0,0)
Tait	2 Research conducted		. X X . .	. . . . .	. . . . .	. . . . .	(0,0)
Smith	3 Script written		. . . X X	. . . . .	. . . . .	. . . . .	(0,0)
Harris, Smith	4 Speech rehearsed		. . . . .	X * * . .	. . . . .	. . . . .	(0,2)
Wilson	5 Slides prepared		. . . . .	X X . . .	. . . . .	. . . . .	(0,0)
Wilson	6 Slides edited, keyed to script		. . . . .	. X . . .	. . . . .	. . . . .	(0,0)
Tait	7 Site setup checked		. . . . .	. * * X .	. . . . .	. . . . .	(2,2)
Harris	8 Speech presented		. . . . .	 X	. . . . .	. . . . .	(0,0)
Donohue	9 Evaluation completed		. . . . .	. . . . .	X	. . . . .	(0,0)

Note: Examples in parentheses in each line indicate float. The number before the comma reports free float (activity slack); the second gives total float (total slack). Asterisks in the calendar indicate where there is float.

packages also provide a monitoring capability, like that demonstrated in Exhibit 8.13. (For information consult Fersko-Weiss, 1987, 1988.)

SUMMARY

Program Evaluation and Review Technique, or PERT-CPM, is a form of managerial network analysis; it is a work planning technique based on the identification of managerial objectives like MBO. In fact, PERT objectives correspond to MBO intermediate objectives when they specify the end point or outcome for some task or activity.

The development of a PERT network leads to a graphic representation of sequences of activities and objectives. It also leads to an objective consideration of whether work must be done in sequential order or can be accomplished concurrently with other work.

Once managers or planners have learned basic rules for identifying paths in the PERT network and calculating path times, they are able to ascertain the total time required to complete a project. If the result is not satisfactory, the PERT network provides insights about where revisions might be made in the work plan. The identification of slack or float is particularly useful in that regard.

PERT-CPM can be applied to relatively complex projects by grouping tasks or activities that have some common objective as an end point, thereby reducing the number of objectives that must be entered into a network.

The PERT planning worksheet, which can serve as the basis for work assignments, requires identification of tasks and estimated work times. It can also be used to formulate a work assignment and tracking system, such as a Gantt chart. The analysis of PERT slack or float time can help make the work assignments even more specific, by determining whether tasks must be completed on an exact date, or can allow for flexibility (whose limit also can be determined by the PERT system). Work that is delegated and monitored with a Gantt chart tends to reduce workers' frustrations since there is minimal ambiguity about assignments, deadlines, and leeway.

Gantt charts are exceptionally useful to managers and planners because they make it easier not only to delegate work and track it but also to obtain feedback about time use for future planning.

REFERENCES

Henry Fersko-Weiss, "Project Management Software," *PC Magazine,* September 29, 1987, pp. 153ff. An extensive analysis of new computer software dealing with PERT-CPM, Gantt work charts, and budgeting.

Henry Fersko-Weiss, "One Project, 3,000 Tasks: High-End Project Managers Make

EXHIBIT 8.13. Gantt Chart Work Tracking

Responsible	Objective	Dates:	Week 1 1 2 3 4 5	Week 2 1 2 3 4 5	Week 3 1 2 3 4 5	Week 4 1 2 3 4 5	
Harris, Smith	1 Speech theme specified		X				(0,0)
Tait	2 Research conducted		X				(0,0)
Smith	3 Script written		X X				(0,0)
Harris, Smith	4 Speech rehearsed			X * *			(0,2)
Wilson	5 Slides prepared			X X			(0,0)
Wilson	6 Slides edited, keyed to script			X			(0,0)
Tait	7 Site setup checked			* * X			(2,2)
Harris	8 Speech presented			X			(0,0)
Donohue	9 Evaluation completed				X		(0,0)

Note: The bars beneath the original Gantt chart lines are entries noting when the assigned work on objectives is accomplished.

178

the Plans,'' *PC Magazine,* May 16, 1988, pp. 155ff. Analysis of more powerful (and more expensive) project planning software for large projects: Open Plan, Plantrac, Primavera Project Planner, Qwiknet Professional Planner, SSP's Promis and View-Point.

FURTHER READINGS

Paul Barnetion, *Critical Path Planning* (Princeton, NJ: Brandon/Systems, 1970).

Federal Electric Corp., *A Programmed Introduction to PERT* (New York: Wiley, 1963).

Ian Holding and P. K. McIlroy, *Network Planning in Management Control Systems* (London: Hutchinson Educational Ltd., 1970).

S. M. Lee, G. L. Moeller, and L. A. Dignon, *Network Analysis for Management Decisions* (Boston: Kluwer Nijhoff, 1982).

J. J. Moder and C. R. Phillips, *Project Management with CPM and PERT* (New York: Reinhold, 1964).

George Odiorne, *Management by Objectives* (Englewood Cliffs, NJ: Prentice-Hall, 1969).

CHAPTER 9

Preparing a Campaign Budget

All managerial endeavors operate with finite resources—a vital one being money. Consequently, as a manager or planner, you must understand the logic and structure of *budget* formulation. Although some people believe that a budget serves exclusively to determine the total cost of a campaign, it actually is a vital part of a powerful managerial evaluation and control process. As such, it also involves

1. Comparative analysis of *cost/benefit factors* for a particular campaign when other campaigns are competing for the same resources
2. Analysis of possible *alternatives*—for example, an optimum plan versus a more conservative plan, each of which would imply different financial factors
3. Analysis of cost/benefit factors within a particular campaign proposal as they relate to the attainment of stated goals and objectives
4. Evaluation of the cost effectiveness of individual expenditures in a campaign proposal, such as allocations for mass media, staff, consultants, and materials
5. Attribution of productivity and related costs to particular activity areas, individuals, teams, or departments
6. Administration of the budget, once the campaign is under way, to make sure that available resources are used in a cost-effective manner and that execution of the campaign does not exceed the allowed resources

AVAILABILITY OF CAMPAIGN FUNDS

A campaign manager or planner would like to believe that a proposed plan and its budget can gain funding based on its own merits. That often is the case when a campaign's MBO goals and terminal objectives are clearly related to the organization's problems, there is substantial evidence that the plan can attain the goals and objectives, the cost/benefit analysis is favorable, and there is proof that individual expenditures are economical. However, there is a latent issue concerning how much an organization is willing to spend on communication activities like promotions, campaigns, or educational programs.

Weilbacher (1979, pp. 102–114) comments that there are various approaches, not one of which is universally accepted since "American business is heavily dependent on rule-of-thumb methods in setting advertising [or other communication] allocations" (p. 105).

Approaches to allocation decisions, cited by Weilbacher (1979), include

1. *Arbitrary methods,* which may involve spending whatever the chief executive officer feels is appropriate or whatever funds are not otherwise committed
2. *Rule-of-thumb methods,* which often are expressed in terms of (a) a percentage of organizational income, (b) a standard expenditure per unit reached or per case sold, (c) a task method that mandates an expenditure sufficient to ensure accomplishment, or (d) a share of market sales
3. *Market experience methods,* which try to systematize feedback from campaign activities but which depend on market testing and projections
4. *Theoretical methods,* which involve statistical models based on data gained through actual experience: Such methods are suspect, either when they are adopted without adequate testing from other fields, largely because similar processes seem involved, or when no convincing proof of predictive validity is presented; it is less satisfactory to theorize that an expenditure of X dollars will produce the outcome Y than to offer firm proof that a stated expenditure actually has attained a stated outcome in an acceptable number of cases.

If a campaign is to be executed with funding from your own organization, upper-level managers will usually suggest or discuss boundaries for a budget total. Alternatively, if you work in an advertising agency, public relations firm, or another organization that deals regularly with campaigns, your company or colleagues will usually have a fairly realistic idea of whether a budget total would be considered unreasonable by a client. This information often is brought up in the first meetings of a campaign manager or planner and in-house executives who are concerned with a project. Moreover, as a manager or planner, you can gain valuable insights about expenditures in different situations by gleaning information from trade journals, conferences, and colleagues, especially those from different organizations.

GENERAL CONSIDERATIONS ABOUT BUDGET DEVELOPMENT

Making an early start on a budget marks an effective manager or planner. A sufficient reason for beginning work as early as possible is that preparation of a managerially defensible budget may require almost as much time as most of the other planning activities combined.

Moreover, the consequences attached to an inadequately prepared budget can be disastrous. An unrealistically high budget may cost you a job in competitive bidding or might reduce the relative merit rating enough to drop it below the "definitely fund" cutting point. An unrealistically low budget might be considered a strength when managers rate the proposal; but if it is accepted, it still might produce a disaster when the campaign administrator discovers that the allocated funds are not sufficient to complete the campaign. Unanticipated cost overruns not only make clients and upper-level management unhappy but also can undermine a manager's or planner's credibility and future effectiveness.

An organization is fortunate if it has a budget officer who is experienced in the regular "costing out" of campaign expenditures; such a person often has a relatively current idea of cost factors and suppliers, and also usually has reference materials or budgets from other, similar projects within easy reach. This person might have much of the needed information stored in computer files that are readily accessible and capable of being copied into a new budget record file. Moreover, the computer-experienced budget officer might use either spreadsheet software[1] or project planning software[2] that includes spreadsheet features. Such software not only makes it easier to input and correct individual information but also can accomplish even routine tasks like

---

[1] Spreadsheet software supports budgeting operations that are useful for campaigns and other projects. See Graham (1986) and Taylor (1987) for details.

[2] Various project management software packages provide integrated management tools: PERT-CPM analysis, Gantt charts, and budgeting assistance. Some also provide work load analysis, including detection of overloads or other conflicts, and support for administrative monitoring of campaigns whose execution has already begun. See "Project Management Software Report Card" (1988) for a comparative analysis of several major packages. Computer magazines routinely contain advertisements for other, less expensive (though usually less powerful) project management software.

column alignment by decimals and calculations of subtotals and the total. If a budget item error is found—for example, an incorrect salary charge for a person who is involved in different parts of a complex campaign—the software can be ordered both to make corrections in every place the particular item is mentioned in the budget file and to recalculate the budget subtotals.

For individuals and small organizations that either do not have a budget preparation specialist or deal with campaigns infrequently, budget preparation is time-consuming and must not be put off until the last minute. Usually, the collection of budget information can be initiated fairly early in the planning process. For example, as soon as the message plan is relatively firm, you will have some clear ideas about creative and production factors; as the media or channel schedule takes shape, you can consider costs concerning the designated delivery vehicles; and after the PERT-CPM worksheet is completed, you will have additional information about factors that might not have been detected earlier. Considerable inefficiency will result if you or your subordinates take the position that work on a budget should not begin before all these sections have been completed.

The previous two paragraphs suggest that a managerially effective budget contains extensive detail. Yet many budgets have been brief, perhaps only a page or less. The apparent discrepancy depends on the uses of a budget.

Management Use

A manager or planner must know not just the grand total and section totals but also cost factors for specific expenditures. To assess the real costs of a campaign, you need detailed information on all the budgeting factors. Without that information, it is not clear whether the subtotals and total are relevant, accurate, and trustworthy and whether substantial elements have been omitted. Moreover, there can be no confidence that individual expenditures are cost effective.

Administrative Use

As a manager or planner, you may be charged with the administration of a campaign after a decision has been made to fund it. With a detailed budget, you have more control, and you are able to set up some form of accounting system that tells how much is available for each cost category. Perhaps more important, you can monitor expenditures and prevent cost overruns for individual categories; or if managerial rules permit, you may be able to shift financial resources between categories during a campaign when an overrun is foreseen and prevent a cost overrun for the entire campaign.

Presentation Use

In some cases, the persons who will make the decision about whether a campaign will be funded indicate that they want only the "bottom-line" information—summary information, rather than a detailed budget. However, more cost-conscious clients or upper-level managers tend to want a detailed budget. Like a campaign manager or planner, they want to know the real costs of a campaign, whether there are alternative versions with related budgetary options, and the cost effectiveness of a particular plan.

In summary, to be an effective campaign planner, manager, or administrator, you must develop or order a detailed budget. If your client or upper-level managers prefer a skeleton budget in a presentation, that is something you must address. You should attempt to clarify these expectations well before the actual date of the presentation.

BUDGET CATEGORIES

You will find that most budgets for campaigns have relatively standardized, recurring categories. Among them are the following:

1. *Key personnel:* administrators, staff, and projected needs for newly hired individuals
2. *Temporary employees:* persons who work fulltime but are contracted to do staff work for a limited time only and part-time employees hired to supplement the regular staff
3. *Contracted personal services:* consultants and independent contractors who may provide services such as research, copywriting, graphic design, production, envelope stuffing and mailing, and hand delivery of materials
4. *Fringe benefits:* various benefits to which employees are entitled by contract or that are mandated by government, including FICA contributions, retirement plan payments, and health plan benefits
5. *Production services:* any specialized production that cannot be done in-house, including services like typesetting; audiovisual production; duplication of sound tapes, videotapes, or slides for mass distribution; and printing and production of electrotypes or mats
6. *Maintenance services:* repairs to equipment related to the campaign—computers or printers, audiovisual equipment, or other vital equipment that tends to break down at the most inconvenient times
7. *Disposable materials:* supplies and materials that are expected to be completely used up by the end of the campaign—paper, pens, photocopies, rub-on type, and so on

8. *Capital acquisitions:* typewriters, desktop computers and related hardware, fax machines, tables, chairs, file cabinets, and similar "hard goods" whose life will extend beyond the campaign
9. *Mass media time or space charges:* may also be presented in the media or channel schedule
10. *Traffic costs:* mailing or other distribution of materials—delivering press kits; mailing sound tapes, videotapes, or slides and scripts to broadcast media and so on.
11. *Transportation costs:* intra- or intercity expenditures for cabs, trains, or plane as well as per diem expenses for out-of-town trips
12. *Communication costs:* expenses for basic phone service, WATS and other long-distance or international phone service, facsimile transmission, courier or air-express delivery, and postal expenses; could also include a "hotline" or automated response or message-delivery system, space satellite distribution services, and access to computer data banks or information-retrieval systems
13. *Office or other work space:* rental of additional space when necessary for offices, work space, conferences, meetings, or trade show exhibitions
14. *Entertainment:* working lunches or dinners, catering services for meetings, and other work-related entertainment necessities
15. *Contingency reserve:* "emergencies" of various types; usually a percentage of the total budget, perhaps 5 to 15 percent.

When a campaign will be implemented by an in-house group, it is important to list costs for both existing resources and additional expenditures that will be incurred. Remember that managers, planners, and administrators must have accurate information about the real costs of a campaign—individual expenditures as well as the total. Also, if you do not account for existing resources, it will not be obvious to others who might count on the same resources that a conflict that could undermine several activities might be in the making. If all costs are listed and a manager or planner needs to demonstrate the real costs, but also the new expenditures (ones that are outside of existing resources), it is possible (1) to list existing resource costs in parentheses, making it possible to show all costs, and (2) to recalculate subtotals and the total to show only the additional costs (excluding those costs that are enclosed in parentheses).

INCORPORATING THE PROFIT FACTOR

Except for campaigns that will be run by an in-house organization, you will have to decide how profit is incorporated into a budget. There are three basic approaches.

Commission on Mass Media Orders

Mass media may certify advertising agencies as "commissionable"; that is, the agencies are entitled to a percentage of the advertising costs that they generate for a vehicle (a particular newspaper, magazine, radio station, or TV station) by including it in the media or channel schedule and buying insertions. The logic is somewhat similar to the travel industry's funding of travel agents: You do not directly pay the travel agent who spends time answering your questions and searching the best routes, times, and fares on a computerized reservation system; the airline that gets your business returns money to the travel agency in the form of a commission for the agency's having served, in effect, as an adjunct to the airline's sales staff and having generated more business and potential profit. (Unfortunately, the commission system often encourages clients to believe that they are entitled to other "free" services—which would siphon off profits. This is likely to be the case for advertising agencies that also do public relations work; the commission for advertising does not compensate an agency when a client insists on PR services, which are not covered.)

Fee for Service

This is an approach in which the organization is charged a percentage of the budget or a percentage of service charges to cover the cost of planning and/or executing a campaign. In many respects, the fee system is superior from a management perspective because it educates clients and other managers about the real cost of campaigns, rather than creating an illusion that services are "free."

Inclusion of Profit in Human Resource Charges

Profit is factored across hourly rate charges for key personnel who conduct a client's account work. A possible risk is that a client who is unaccustomed to the practice may react adversely after encountering an hourly rate for a campaign manager that is considerably higher than hourly pay for a manager in the client's own organization. However, in urban markets where the practice is established and accepted, this approach may generate less controversy than debating justifications for a particular fee.

A BUDGET FORMAT

As in several other cases discussed earlier, a manager or planner needs a concise summary of decisions regarding budgeting. A *budget format* serves this purpose.

Exhibit 9.1 presents a budget format that will serve, with relatively minor

EXHIBIT 9.1. Model Format for Budget Summary

Categories	Unit Costs	Total Costs
01. Administrative and staff salaries		
(1) Person 1 (details)	$XXXXX	$XXXXX
(2) Person 2 (details)	XXXXX	XXXXX
(3) Person 3 (details)	XXXXX	XXXXX
(4) Person 4 (details)	XXXXX	XXXXX
Subtotal		XXXXX
02. Temporary or part-time staff		
(1) Person 5 (details)	XXXXX	XXXXX
(2) Person 6 (details)	XXXXX	XXXXX
Subtotal		XXXXX
03. Fringe benefits		
(1) Person 1 (rate)	XXXXX	XXXXX
(2) Person 2 (rate)	XXXXX	XXXXX
(3) Person 3 (rate)	XXXXX	XXXXX
(4) Person 4 (rate)	XXXXX	XXXXX
(5) Person 5 (rate)	XXXXX	XXXXX
(6) Person 6 (rate)	XXXXX	XXXXX
Subtotal		XXXXX
04. Contracted personal services		
(1) Consultant (details)	XXXXX	XXXXX
(2) Researcher (details)	XXXXX	XXXXX
(3) Designer (name and details)	XXXXX	XXXXX
Subtotal		XXXXX
05. Production		
(1) Typesetting (details)	XXXXX	XXXXX
(2) Printing (details)	XXXXX	XXXXX
(3) Duplication of sound tapes (details)	XXXXX	XXXXX
(4) Duplication of videotapes (details)	XXXXX	XXXXX
Subtotal		XXXXX
06. Media budget		
(1) Vehicle 1 (details)	XXXXX	XXXXX
(2) Vehicle 2 (details)	XXXXX	XXXXX
(3) Vehicle 3 (details)	XXXXX	XXXXX
Subtotal		XXXXX
07. Traffic/distribution costs		
(1) Item 1 (details)	XXXXX	XXXXX
(2) Item 2 (details)	XXXXX	XXXXX
(3) Item 3 (details)	XXXXX	XXXXX
Subtotal		XXXXX
08. Travel costs		
(1) Travel (occasion/details)	XXXXX	XXXXX
(2) Travel (occasion/details)	XXXXX	XXXXX
(3) Travel (occasion/details)	XXXXX	XXXXX
(4) Per diem (rate/details)	XXXXX	XXXXX
(5) Per diem (rate/details)	XXXXX	XXXXX
Subtotal		XXXXX

EXHIBIT 9.1. (*continued*)

Categories	Unit Costs	Total Costs
09. Communication costs		
(1) Local phone service (details)	$XXXXX	$XXXXX
(2) Long-distance phone service (details)	XXXXX	XXXXX
(3) Air courier service (details)	XXXXX	XXXXX
(4) Postage (details)	XXXXX	XXXXX
Subtotal		XXXXX
10. Supplies & materials		
(1) Category 1 (details)	XXXXX	XXXXX
(2) Category 2 (details)	XXXXX	XXXXX
(3) Category 3 (details)	XXXXX	XXXXX
Subtotal		XXXXX
11. Capital equipment		
(1) Item 1 (details)	XXXXX	XXXXX
(2) Item 2 (details)	XXXXX	XXXXX
(3) Item 3 (details)	XXXXX	XXXXX
Subtotal		XXXXX
12. Contingency		
(Details)	XXXXX	XXXXX
Subtotal		XXXXX
13. Grand Total		**$XXXXX**

modifications, for most campaigns and can be modified for complex campaigns that segment budgets by either the time period (month, quarter, semester, or year) or major activities.

Once you have decided on the major categories, you should group information according to the individual category to which it relates. You should list unit costs for each item, where appropriate—for example, $350/hr. Then you should calculate totals for items and also category subtotals. Finally, you should calculate the grand total, the sum of all subtotals.

EXPLANATIONS TO CLARIFY THE BUDGET

Although costs in a budget are usually self-explanatory, some that are unusual may necessitate justification. Upper-level managers usually work with budgets often enough that they have a mental picture of how costs for most factors should look; if any budget item appears either too high or too low, it is as though a mental warning flag pops up. When Robert McNamara was U.S. secretary of defense, for example, he reportedly ordered slides in data presentations to be stopped and run back because he wanted to verify out-of-the-norm statistics or those that conflicted with others.

On many occasions, expenditures that are out of the norm may be acceptable—provided they are justified. A particular celebrity to be used in testimonials may demand and get higher than normal fees, for example; this merits explanation. Or a higher-quality, heavier-weight, coated printing paper may be a good choice despite higher costs, but the advantages should be noted. Terse explanations, where necessary, can be grouped in a section entitled "Explanations," following the budget summary pages, each explanation keyed by a number to the cost item with which it corresponds. It is not a good idea to insert explanations within the budget form (Exhibit 9.1); this would be analogous to a storyteller's interrupting a dialogue repeatedly with parenthetical digressions, not all of which are uninteresting but cumulatively disrupt the audience's attention.

SUMMARY

Preparation of a budget for a campaign is much more complicated than simply assembling a page or two of cost estimates. In management, a budget is part of a system that involves extensive and complex decision processes.

In formulating a budget, you must be certain that it covers the main cost factors essential to a campaign, clearly contributes to attainment of the campaign's goals and objectives, and does so in the most cost-effective manner.

A budget must be crafted carefully. Brody (1988, p. 34) comments,

> Detailed price tags must be attached to every component. They must include all costs involved. Labor, fringe benefits and other overhead must be specified together with any and all production and out-of-pocket costs for each component of the proposed program. Production cost factors should be based on multiple vendor estimates, rather than practitioner "guesstimates." At all times "no unpleasant surprises" should be a cardinal guideline in budget preparation.

The amount of work that goes into the collection and verification of information is so extensive that a budget should be initiated at the earliest possible time—usually as soon as the message strategy is relatively complete.

Upper-level managers will analyze the budget to determine whether the campaign will be funded, although some mandated programs will be funded even though budget factors are not favorable. These managers seek answers to questions about whether a campaign contributes to the organization's goals and objectives, seems capable of attaining the campaign's goals and objectives, offers an acceptable cost/benefit ratio, and demonstrates cost-effective use of resources. The merits of a campaign proposal and its budget are always weighed against alternative possibilities that the money might be used better in other ways, such as investment, other new projects, or continuation of old projects.

If a campaign is funded, management then counts on a budget as a vital tool for administration. A budget supports effective monitoring of expenditures and makes possible decisions about control and reallocation of resources to prevent cost overruns.

Budget preparation may be made easier by either desktop computer spreadsheet packages, designed specifically for budgeting, or integrated project manager software packages that include budgeting.

Budget information must be presented in a format that makes it possible to scan and comprehend the information rapidly; it should be possible to grasp the full picture but also cross-check both for balance among major categories and for discrepancies, either of which may reflect serious problems. Where implementation of a campaign is a for-profit activity, as opposed to a campaign that is conducted by a group within the organization as part of normal work activity, profits are addressed in different ways. Advertising agencies' profits are mainly based on commissions from mass media from whom they buy time or space. Other approaches are a fee for service, usually a fixed percentage of the overall budget, or inclusion of profit in hourly billings for campaign personnel.

Finally, unusual budget costs require explanations. Unanswered questions may distract the client or upper-level managers during the evaluation of your proposal or may lead to an unfavorable decision if no one raises the questions or answers them by chance during a face-to-face presentation.

REFERENCES

E. W. Brody, *Public Relations Programming and Production* (New York: Praeger, 1988). Extensive discussion of factors relating to PR budgeting decisions.

Neill Graham, *The Mind Tool; Computers and Their Impact on Society* (St. Paul, MN: West, 1986), pp. 213ff. In Chapter 9, "Electronic Spreadsheets," Graham provides detailed conceptual information about this class of software.

"Project Management Software Report Card," *Info World,* May 23, 1988. A comparative analysis of Harvard Total Manager II 2.0, Microsoft Project 4.0, Superproject Expert 1.0, and Time Line 3.0.

Jared Taylor, "Challenging 1-2-3 on Price and Power," *PC Magazine,* October 27, 1987, pp. 94ff. A comparative analysis of several spreadsheet programs.

William M. Weilbacher, *Advertising* (New York: Macmillan, 1979). Extensive insights about factors affecting budgeting decisions in advertising.

FURTHER READINGS

James E. Grunig and Todd Hunt, *Managing Public Relations* (New York: Holt, Rinehart and Winston, 1984).

Norman R. Nager and T. Harrell Allen, *Public Relations; Management by Objectives* (White Plains, NY: Longman, 1984.)

CHAPTER 10

Evaluating Campaign Results

Anticipating the eventual completion of a campaign, you must decide how the campaign's implementation and results should be evaluated. An *evaluation plan* for a campaign is necessary to

- Determine whether the communication vehicles that you employ actually reach the targeted audience segment or segments, creating the potential for exposure to the campaign's messages
- Ascertain whether members of the desired segment or segments actually hear, see, or read the messages and attend to their content
- Find out whether members of the desired segment or segments demonstrate the intended knowledge, affect, motivation, or practices (KAMP) that the campaign MBO specifies should be produced
- Determine that you can rule out alternative explanations for the campaign's results, including extraneous sources or previously existing behaviors in the audience segment or segments.

Additionally, where PERT-CPM planning and other work control management systems are employed, evaluation may address another need: It can test whether the work activities instrumental to the implementation of the campaign were accomplished in the most time- and cost-effective manner.

When a managerial systems approach is not used, it is problematic how campaign impacts and the actual planning and implementation of the work can be evaluated. Most intuitive approaches to campaign evaluation, although appealing to common sense, tend to be ineffective. Unfortunately,

193

this observation applies to many evaluation schemes that enjoy broad acceptance among communication practitioners.

Some examples of deficient evaluation procedures serve to illustrate commonly encountered problems. For example, some communication practitioners report *gross impressions,* suggesting that campaign impact is equal to the number of messages placed in a media vehicle (i.e., frequency), multiplied by either the reported circulation or reach of the vehicle or the circulation or reach of the vehicle in the intended target segment. The great flaw in this scheme is that exposure might not have occurred—many persons are not in an audience when messages are published or broadcast; others will engage in selective exposure and avoid the messages. Moreover, the reporting of gross impressions does not prove whether the MBO terminal objectives have been met. If outcomes like those intended are observed in target audiences, you cannot be certain factors other than the campaign do not account for part or all of the results.

Some practitioners employ *clipping or broadcast monitoring services,* particularly in communication campaigns that use publicity or other forms of nonpaid media insertions like public service announcements (PSAs). The volume of message use by the mass media is presented as though it were proof of a campaign's impact, although it is not.

Many practitioners specify *observable behaviors* as the exclusive criterion against which to test campaign results. Some examples are the number of persons actually showing up at a designated site to give blood after a campaign to promote donations, the increase in requests at designated clinics for vaccinations following publicity about inoculation against an impending influenza epidemic, or the purchase volume at specified stores for an article of clothing featured in an advertisement. However, this approach does not deal with the first three KAMP outcomes—knowledge, affect, or motivation. Short-term overt responses can be suppressed by a variety of contingent conditions such as time pressures affecting potential respondents, inconvenience of the location or operating hours of the organization making the offer or request, or individuals' inability to respond immediately because of a lack of funds. Evaluations based only on criteria of overt or observable practices at a specified time fail to recognize that messages function mainly to *build cognitive readiness or motivation* to act when the enabling conditions that control the behavior become present.

In evaluation, practitioners might be tempted to attribute outcomes or results to their campaigns, although more than one campaign is operating concurrently in the environment. Moreover, there might be other complicating inputs from extraneous sources, such as news reports or information transmitted through social networks, that might account for some, most, or all of the observed results. Consequently, there is no way to know whether the campaign produced the results, unless there is some way of ''untangling'' and ruling out these other effects.

Evaluation research provides a methodology, based on MBO, for testing whether a campaign has, indeed, attained its objectives. Moreover, the results of the evaluation research can be used as corrective feedback to improve the next round of planning, either in a current campaign or in others that follow.

THE TWO-STAGE EVALUATION PROCESS

The formulation of evaluation research involves two basic stages:

1. *Specification of measurement criteria:* You must state in very explicit terms the criteria you intend to use. This usually involves *operationalization*—explaining how the intended impacts will be measured or observed in the evaluation research.
2. *Specification of research design:* You explain how the actual research will be conducted within the audience segment, what groups you intend to test and under what conditions, and how you will execute the data analysis.

Specification of Criteria

A great advantage of MBO, other than to control the development of the message plans and work assignments, becomes evident as you begin to work on evaluation research.

Terminal objectives specify evaluation research test criteria. These objectives deal with the knowledge, affect, motivation, practice, and situational factors that control the problem that your campaign addresses.

Exhibit 10.1 shows that the MBO terminal objectives dictate the key

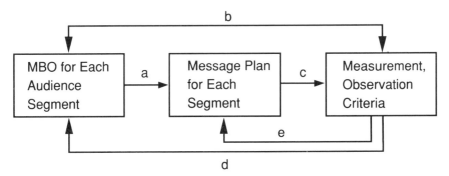

EXHIBIT 10.1. Conceptual Relationship of MBO to Both Message Plan and Evaluation Criteria

Note: Loops a, b, and c are proactive—that is, prescribing what must be accomplished in the connected future stage. Loops d and e are feedback loops, making it possible to check resulting work against the criteria transmitted through the proactive loops.

messages in the message plan (proactive loop a) and the criteria for the variables that must be operationalized in the evaluation research design for eventual testing (loop b). If you need information beyond that provided by the MBO to refine the operationalization of the test criteria, additional details are provided by the message plan (loop c).

Once your operationalization of the test criteria is ready, you can test the statements against, first, the MBO terminal objectives for each segment (loop d) and, second, the message plan specifications (loop e).

Case Study. Suppose you are dealing with information about the AIDS epidemic and the lack of human immunodeficiency virus (HIV) transmissibility by specified means.

Exhibit 10.2 illustrates the relationship of MBO terminal objectives, the message plan, and evaluation research criteria regarding the related information. One copy point exists for each terminal objective in the MBO section. Note that there is an operationalization for each outcome that the MBO terminal objectives specify.

When your MBO plan contains extensive terminal objectives, you might decide to (1) test each one or (2) test only the ones that are most crucial to the success of your campaign.

Quite often, the writing of evaluation research measurement items, like those in Exhibit 10.2, follows the same rules advocated in Chapter 4 for survey research questionnaire items, including measurement scales. These items can also be organized in a questionnaire format.

If you intend to test a large number of objectives, you might want to pretest your evaluation instrument, for example, a questionnaire, to verify that interviewees are willing to collaborate in a long interview. This pretest may also provide a basis for estimating interviewing time and costs, including data processing.

Exhibit 10.2. Systemic Relationships in Planning—MBO, Message Plan, and Evaluation Criteria

Management by Objectives

Members of the target audience will express agreement with the following:

The AIDS virus is not known to date to be transmitted by social contact, including by the following means:
1. Sneezing or coughing
2. Shaking hands
3. Kissing
4. Sharing of eating utensils

The AIDS virus is not known to date to be transmitted by mosquitos.

The AIDS virus is not known to date to be transmitted by contamination of toilet seats.

Exhibit 10.2. (*continued*)

Message Copy Points

In approximately seven years of experience with the virus that causes AIDS, world reports on epidemiology have not revealed even one case of HIV infection caused by

Sneezing or coughing. Reason: The virus that causes AIDS is not airborne.

Shaking hands. Reason: The virus is spread through the exchange of body fluid, which does not occur under normal conditions while shaking hands.

Kissing. Reason: Although the AIDS virus is known to exist in the saliva of infected persons, the evidence is that transmission does not occur, because (1) the amount of virus is extremely limited and (2) chemical properties of saliva are believed to make the virus less viable. Caveat: If a noninfected person has bleeding gums and kisses an HIV carrier, there might be some element of risk, however small.

Sharing of eating utensils. Reason: In no case where family members are caring for an AIDS victim has anyone been known to have become infected, although they share eating utensils. The AIDS virus is not known to be viable on exposed surfaces, and high temperatures during dish washing evidently kill the virus.

Mosquitos. Reason: In lab experiments, the AIDS virus has not been found to be viable within mosquitos because the mosquito as host does not provide the body temperature range needed for the virus to survive.

Toilet seats. Reason: The AIDS virus is not known to be viable on exposed surfaces. Moreover, disinfectants used in cleaning kill the virus.

Operationalization of Evaluation Research Criteria

Respondents will be asked to respond to a series of declarations about transmissibility of the AIDS virus, in terms of the following categories: (1) disagree strongly, (2) disagree, (3) don't know/uncertain, (4) agree, (5) agree strongly. Despite whether the declarations are stated in positive or in negative form, the respondents should, when the scoring is corrected for direction, essentially demonstrate correct knowledge. A score of 5 will be given for the most correct answers. (Note: The correct answers that are expected if the objectives are met are marked with a letter *X*.)

The measurement items would take the following form:

I am going to read you a series of statements about how people might or might not become infected with the virus that causes AIDS. Tell me whether you agree strongly, agree, disagree, or disagree strongly with each statement. If you don't know or are uncertain, please tell me.

The AIDS virus can be spread by casual social contact—that is, everyday types of activities conducted in public.
[ ] Agree Strongly   [ ] Agree   [ ] DK/UN   [X] Disagree   [X] Disagree Strongly

Sneezing or coughing *cannot* spread the AIDS virus.
[X] Agree Strongly   [X] Agree   [ ] DK/UN   [ ] Disagree   [ ] Disagree Strongly

The AIDS virus can be spread by shaking hands.
[ ] Agree Strongly   [ ] Agree   [ ] DK/UN   [X] Disagree   [X] Disagree Strongly

The virus that causes AIDS can be spread by kissing.
[ ] Agree Strongly   [ ] Agree   [ ] DK/UN   [X] Disagree   [X] Disagree Strongly

The sharing of eating utensils *cannot* spread the AIDS virus.
[X] Agree Strongly   [X] Agree   [ ] DK/UN   [ ] Disagree   [ ] Disagree Strongly

The AIDS virus can be spread by mosquitos.
[ ] Agree Strongly   [ ] Agree   [ ] DK/UN   [X] Disagree   [X] Disagree Strongly

The AIDS virus can be spread by toilet seats.
[ ] Agree Strongly   [ ] Agree   [ ] DK/UN   [X] Disagree   [X] Disagree Strongly

Research Design

Beyond being specific about what should be evaluated, you need to learn and to apply evaluation research design principles. Research design enables you to separate impacts of your campaign from those of other forces operating in the environment of the target audience segment or segments; sometimes these forces may be viable alternative explanations for the same outcomes. For example, although you may find that interviewees demonstrate a comprehension of information that your campaign conveys, this might not prove that the campaign is the sole cause; often, preexisting knowledge or exposure to other information sources might account for that comprehension. In *experimental research methodology,* which serves as a foundation of evaluation research, this problem is called *confounding;* it is a situation in which effects of some variable that is of interest are intertwined with effects of others. Without an adequate research design, you cannot be sure what produces the observed outcomes.

The most accepted research designs are those that employ *random assignment* of subjects to treatment conditions. The designs also may include control groups to help sort out other variables or conditions outside of the campaign that might create confounding.

The reason for randomization, which uses random numbers tables such as those discussed in Chapter 4, is that it enables you to be sure that all test groups are set equal on personal variables at the outset. Random assignment puts people in groups purely by chance: If there are people who know about the issues related to a campaign who are assigned to one of two test groups, there is a predictable chance that similar people will also be assigned to the second test group. Similarly, if people with high IQs (and presumably better information-processing skills) are assigned by chance to one group, there is a predictable chance that similar people will be assigned to the second test group.

Random assignment is one of the most effect ways to rule out many confounding variables prior to the testing. *Matching* of subjects is another way to try to set conditions equal among groups. This technique is used in many types of evaluation, for example, an advertising campaign in which two communities are matched on demographics and market buying patterns that relate to an advertised product. The advertising campaign is introduced in one of the matched communities. If at the end of the evaluation, there is more knowledge about the product in the test market where the campaign is conducted, the assumption is that the campaign produced the result. In effect, the pairing of communities on the basis of similar age groups and similar income levels as well as similar consumption patterns is an intuitively appealing way of setting equal particular variables that might, along with the ad campaign, affect outcomes.

Matching is not entirely satisfactory, however, because unknown variables other than those used in the matching might affect outcomes, but they might not have come to the evaluation research designer's attention. For example, there might have been a product liability lawsuit years earlier that reflected negatively on a particular brand, or there might have been consumer reports in the local newspaper or some similar less than obvious influences that introduce confounding and affect response patterns.

Random assignment is superior in that, as a general rule, it factors out both obvious and less obvious confounding variables. Then, control groups can be introduced to help isolate the effects of other specific variables that might influence the results, so they, too, can be factored out during data analysis.

It might be helpful to work through some examples to illustrate the logic of research design.

Suppose someone advocates a *posttest-only design* for evaluation. In Exhibit 10.3, C represents the exposure to the campaign, a horizontal line represents the time span of the campaign, and *posttest* represents the testing against the MBO criteria.

EXHIBIT 10.3. Posttest-Only Design

_____ C _____ Posttest

The assumption is that the campaign explains the effects observed in the posttest. However, suppose you are running an information campaign on international issues. If your evaluation research test group comes from a high-education area, the subjects are more likely than the general population to follow international and policy issues. Thus this tendency becomes confounded with the effects of the campaign. It is not easy, therefore, to prove that your campaign produces the outcome.

Another case is the *pretest/posttest design,* such as in Exhibit 10.4. It also is deficient. This is a form of matching design. By using a pretest, you obtain data on some specific group against which you can compare the posttest results, obtained after exposure to the campaign. At least there is a sense that the personal variables, called *subject variables,* are set equal. However, the design does not rule out whether the pretesting, itself, might sensitize the individuals to awareness of the topics that the campaign presents, and thereby affect the outcome. Neither does it rule out other confounding variables that might exist in the community but are not represented by the subjects in the test.

EXHIBIT 10.4. Pretest/Posttest Design

Pretest _____ C _____ Posttest

You can factor out the possible effects of the pretest by adding a control group—specifically, one that is not pretested, as in Exhibit 10.5.

Exhibit 10.5. Pretest/Posttest Design with Control

Pretest _____ C _____ Posttest
_____ C _____ Posttest

The assumption here is that if the pretest contributes a confounding effect, there should be a difference in the posttest scores. However, a new problem becomes evident: With the introduction of the control group (the one with no pretest), you have a second group, one that is not set equal with the first group; the posttest results still might be misleading because of different personal or subject variables—for example, prior knowledge or IQ—in the two groups. Very much like the test markets and ad campaign example, you might try to solve this problem by matching.

Matching always is based on variables, or characteristics, that can have some impact on the outcome. Frequently, the matching characteristics are age, education, or IQ, all of which affect information-processing capabilities. This might produce a research design like Exhibit 10.6.

Exhibit 10.6. Design Based on Matched Groups

Pretest _____ C _____ Posttest
_____ C _____ Posttest

Note: The *M* represents the matching of subjects or groups on the basis of critical variables that might have been confounding.

This design still confronts you with the problem of which variables to use to match subjects or groups; a mistake might not identify the important ones that create confounding in the posttest results.

Usually, designs using randomization produce superior results, as already explained. The most basic *random allocation design* is illustrated in Exhibit 10.7. This design ensures that prior knowledge does not affect the outcome since that variable is factored out by randomization. Persons with

Exhibit 10.7 Design Based on Groups Formed by Randomization

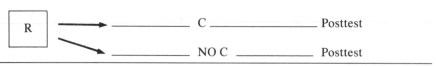

_____ C _____ Posttest
_____ NO C _____ Posttest

Note: *R* indicates that subjects or groups have been allocated through the use of a random numbers table.

prior knowledge have an equal chance of being assigned to either group. Also, IQ would not affect the outcome, for the same reason: Persons with higher or lower IQs have an equal chance of being assigned to either group. Statistically, it can be proved that observed differences between subjects in the two groups that exist after the randomized assignment are inconsequential statistically; they are not patterned or not systematic since they occur purely by chance. Presumably, only the influences of the campaign remain as systematic effects. Other, more advanced research designs are discussed by Campbell and Stanley (1963) and Kerlinger (1973).

Randomization designs are much more difficult to plan for applications in the field—that is, where the targeted audience segment or segments live or work—than in an experimental laboratory setting. (A "laboratory" in this context may be an auditorium or a room where individuals can be exposed to messages and tested.)

Because of the pervasiveness of mass media, implementation in the field often proves to be difficult when the major media are the principal vehicles for the campaign. Forming "treatment" (those who will be exposed to a campaign, for example) and "no treatment" (those who will *not* be exposed) groups is difficult because of the likelihood that most people have been exposed to the media. Effects of "small media"—direct mail, selectively distributed brochures, and posters—constitute less of a problem in that regard. Otherwise, laboratory experiments might be considered.

Another substantial problem of all evaluation designs is the sampling of subjects to be included in test groups; this affects the external generalizability of the results. Evaluation research must be done among members of the targeted audience segment. Some researchers substitute other types of persons or areas to make their work easier or to speed up data collection—unacceptable practices.

Statistical correlation is sometimes advocated as a substitute for an adequate evaluation research design. It can obtain evidence by comparing levels of knowledge on specific themes among those in the sample who are exposed to the campaign and those who are not. However, for evaluation purposes, this approach usually is deficient despite the use of a widely acknowledged methodology like survey research. You cannot be sure that confounding variables are ruled out unless you utilize statistical analysis to factor out their effects—for example, partial correlations or test factors or control variables with cross-tabulation analysis (discussed in Chapter 4 in connection with multivariate tables). Moreover, the effects of other variables can be tricky: Sometimes they suppress effects; sometimes they artificially magnify effects; and sometimes, like jokers, they even cause relationships to appear to be the reverse of what they actually are. Even so, the irreducible problem is that you often cannot be sure you have accounted for and measured all the confounding variables that might explain or otherwise affect and distort the data about the outcomes.

Analysis of Data. A manager or planner may often rely on visual inspection of data—differences in proportions, percentages, or arithmetic means—to ascertain whether there is a difference in test groups' scores. However, since campaigns often produce results of limited magnitude, visual inspection might not provide satisfactory evidence that observed differences are greater than might occur by chance. Consequently, awareness of statistical tests may be important.

You can measure differences between two arithmetic means with a statistical t-test; differences among three or more means require examination with *analysis of variance (ANOVA)* tests. You can measure differences between two percentages or proportions with either a z-test or a median test, which is based on the chi-square statistic. The median test also is appropriate for tests involving three or more proportions or percentages. Brown, Amos, and Mink (1975) explain the basic concepts underlying tests in a way that does not even require a calculator. Roscoe (1975) provides easy-to-follow explanations and models and step-by-step instructions for the calculation of statistics. Guilford (1973) gives additional information for readers who wish to move beyond the first stage of statistical mastery.

EVALUATING INTERMEDIATE OBJECTIVES

Gantt charts, which are discussed in Chapter 8, provide a technique for monitoring work related to intermediate objectives (see Exhibit 10.8). You can track and record the attainment of individuals while a campaign is being conducted; the tracking information usually is indicated by shaded or colored bars in lines placed immediately beneath work assignment lines. If you desire, you can add an additional column to the format for comments—for example, why things worked out better or worse than expected in regard to particular tasks or individuals.

SUMMARY

An effective managerial system provides for evaluation, first, of how efficiently a planned campaign or project functions to produce desired results. Second, by gaining feedback, management can improve its practices over time, improving efficiency and reducing waste.

Evaluation research must conform to reputable and widely accepted procedures to produce satisfactory results and enhance the credibility of the planning and implementation effort in the eyes of the sponsor.

Management by objectives provides a viable structure to control the design of messages, but it also serves in a later stage to make clear the criteria for evaluation. Research design is another indispensable component of mana-

Exhibit 10.8. Gantt Chart Work Tracking

Responsible	Objective	Dates:	Week 1					Week 2					Week 3					Week 4					
			1	2	3	4	5	1	2	3	4	5	1	2	3	4	5	1	2	3	4	5	
Harris, Smith	1 Speech theme specified		X	.	.	.	.	.	.	.	.	.	.	.	.	.	.	.	.	.	.	.	(0,0)
Tait	2 Research conducted		.	X	.	.	.	.	.	.	.	.	.	.	.	.	.	.	.	.	.	.	(0,0)
Smith	3 Script written		.	.	.	X	X	.	.	.	.	.	.	.	.	.	.	.	.	.	.	.	(0,0)
Harris, Smith	4 Speech rehearsed		.	.	.	.	.	X	.	*	*	.	.	.	.	.	.	.	.	.	.	.	(0,2)
Wilson	5 Slides prepared		.	.	.	.	.	X	X	.	.	.	.	.	.	.	.	.	.	.	.	.	(0,0)
Wilson	6 Slides edited, keyed to script		.	.	.	.	.	.	.	X	.	.	.	.	.	.	.	.	.	.	.	.	(0,0)
Tait	7 Site setup checked		.	.	.	.	.	.	*	*	X	.	.	.	.	.	.	.	.	.	.	.	(2,2)
Harris	8 Speech presented		.	.	.	.	.	.	.	.	.	X	.	.	.	.	.	.	.	.	.	.	(0,0)
Donohue	9 Evaluation completed		.	.	.	.	.	.	.	.	.	.	X	.	.	.	.	.	.	.	.	.	(0,0)

Note: The bars beneath the original Gantt chart lines are entries noting when the assigned work on objectives actually is accomplished.

gerially effective evaluation research because it helps ascertain whether observed results can be attributed to the campaign rather than to confounding by environmental or other factors that might produce the same results. If the design is effective, results can be projected to the targeted audience segment.

Matching designs are relatively less trustworthy than randomized designs, but they can be acceptable, especially if the evaluation report is candid. That is, you must point out that although the evidence suggests that the major possible confounding variables are set equal or factored out, there is a possibility that other variables might affect the end results.

This chapter identifies statistical tests that are likely to be useful in analysis of evaluation research data. Also, when evaluation must track work during the execution stage of a campaign, Gantt charts provide a technique to meet that need.

REFERENCES

F. L. Brown, J. R. Amos, and O. G. Mink, *Statistical Concepts: A Basic Program,* 2nd ed. (New York: Harper & Row, 1975).

D. T. Campbell and J. C. Stanley, *Experimental and Quasi-Experimental Designs for Research* (Chicago: Rand McNally, 1963). A classic work regarding experimental research design.

J. P. Guilford, *Fundamental Statistics in Psychology and Education,* 5th ed. (New York: McGraw-Hill, 1973).

F. N. Kerlinger, *Foundations of Behavioral Research,* 2nd ed. (New York: Holt, Rinehart and Winston, 1973). An excellent, less technical explanation of adequate and less adequate research designs.

J. T. Roscoe, *Fundamental Research Statistics for the Behavioral Sciences,* 2nd ed. (New York: Holt, Rinehart and Winston, 1975).

CHAPTER 11

Presenting the Campaign Plan

By this time, it is assumed that as a manager or planner, you have completed the *plan book,* the campaign plan manuscript that forms the core of your *presentation* to either your client or upper-level managers. The plan book should be concise, have an attractive format, and be completely error-free. Most managers, and especially major managers, believe that sloppy preparation of the plan book and presentation is a cue that the execution of the campaign would also be sloppy. Moreover, some clients or upper-level managers regard poorly edited plan books as a personal affront.

Any effective campaign presentation begins with a meticulous editing of the plan book, each member of the management or planning team being required to read both intermediate drafts and the final version critically, so that the writing will be as concise as possible and all errors will be corrected. This attention to the plan book will also help make the planning of the face-to-face presentation more effective by familiarizing every team member with the entire completed package.

This chapter will discuss the planning of a presentation session. Almost all presentations are based on variations of the same basic framework:

1. Review of the plan book
2. Content planning—formulation of a presentation strategy and plan and selection of presenters
3. Audiovisual support planning
4. Setup—scouting the presentation site and facilities, especially existing equipment or that which will be needed
5. Rehearsal

6. Completion of the setup for the presentation—verifying that everything needed is at hand, projection materials are in order, electrical
outlets are located, projection equipment is functioning correctly,
light switches and dimmers are located, and so on
7. Presentation of the proposal—opening, documentation, and closing
8. Completion of the question and answer (Q & A) session
9. Delivery of "leave-behinds" that enable those who will decide on the
proposal to review the details

EVEN PROFESSIONAL PRESENTERS
CAN MAKE ERRORS

One important goal of a good manager or planner is to avoid even one major
problem, insofar as humanly possible. However, when it comes to presentations, persons who take a cavalier approach to management may literally
kill the chances of their plan being adopted because of inadequate preparation. Schultz, Martin, and Brown (1984, p. 467) observe:

> In too many cases, the presentation is treated like a bastard child. It gets whatever
> scraps of time are left over once everything else is done. Perhaps in one day or a
> night, a hundred slides are shot, developed and then thrown into a carousel. We
> rationalize that the stuff is so great, it won't matter how we present it, the audience
> will rave over it. Foolish thinking. Most clients expect to see evidence of great care
> and concern on their behalf. Magnificent work can easily be ignored if it is presented
> in beggar's clothing.

In reviewing comments of communication professionals about campaign
presentation weaknesses, Ron Hoff of Foote, Cone & Belding encountered
the following criticisms (Schultz, Martin, & Brown, 1984, pp. 465–467).

Planning

- "Why doesn't anybody start with a short summary of the problem, the
research, the strategy, the promise, the media . . . *three minutes'
worth?*" (David Ogilvy).
- "The purpose of personal presentation is to leave the prospect with the
feeling that each of the presenters . . . is the brightest, most professional, most capable person in the agency business. Precious few of
our presenters leave that impression" (John O'Toole).

Setup

- "We don't pay attention to lighting. Should be carefully set up and
tested" (Harvey Clements).

Rehearsal

- There is ". . . no evidence that the presenter has taken great pains with his presentation" (Ogilvy).
- "Our presenters lack presence, authority" (David Ofner).
- "Too many extraneous slides" (Clements).
- "Too many presenters—amount of detail" (Bryan Putnam).
- "Too much time on everything" (David Berger).

Presentation

- "No explanation at the start of *why* we are gathered here. No clear agenda" (Ofner).
- "The general failing is treating the presentation as yours, instead of the audience's. Presenting what *you* did, rather than what *they* need" (Berger).
- "They [the presentations] just don't sell; lack of support for what you're recommending" (Arthur Schultz).
- "I don't know whether to read what he's *showing* or listen to what he's *saying*" (Ogilvy).
- "In terms of research, this [a weakness] means emphasizing the study rather than the problem and the solution. In terms of media it means counting Gross Rating Points, instead of conveying a sense of *how much* [of the message] people will encounter" (Berger).

Question and Answer

- ". . . Listen before you talk" (Ogilvy)
- "We don't plan for involvement by the audience" (Clements).

The lesson—which is a vital one—to be learned from these criticisms? All could have been prevented by careful preparation.

COMMUNICATING WITH CLIENTS AND UPPER-LEVEL MANAGERS

These criticisms also suggest that there is a difference in understanding between major managers and persons who are mainly communication practitioners about the purpose and criteria for presentations. To be effective in presentation, persons involved with creative processes like conceptualization, writing, graphics, editing, and production and specialists like researchers need to understand how major managers think about campaigns and presentations. Effective communication and problem-solving often involve *empathy,* which Lerner (1958) defined as the ability to put yourself mentally in another person's shoes—that is, learning to think as though you were the other person.

Behavioral Perspectives

A beginning step involves an understanding that an interpersonal communication process is, itself, like a transaction (Bauer, 1969). Your intended audience will give its attention, provided you can give the audience something it wants. If you do not understand the criteria that are important to clients and upper-level managers, you are at a severe disadvantage in planning a presentation. The discussion in Chapter 2 regarding salience, centrality, selectivity, and the value-expectancy theory of motivation supports this point of view.

Attention to mastery of both the conceptual structure and the details of a campaign plan is also important. Theory and research suggest that effective interpersonal communication depends substantially on interpersonal attraction and relational maintenance (Littlejohn, 1983, pp. 201–216). This process affects both communication and persuasion. *Source credibility* is one of the principal factors, and Atkin (1981, p. 275) reports that two of the main criteria are the trustworthiness and the expertise or competence of the communicator—a finding that has particular significance in business since both criteria are linked to managerial concerns with capability and risk reduction. The third most important criterion is dynamism and attractiveness (p. 275).

Other studies support the proposition that *empathy* (Katz, 1963; Howell, 1982) may be important, especially as it creates a basis for psychological rapport. Empathy relates to an individual's ability to think as though he/she were another person; ability to perform that task with relative accuracy is another dimension of empathy. The better your understanding of major managers' thinking and concerns, the more effective your communication is likely to be. Moreover, empathy may affect perceptions of *homophily,* in which an individual or audience perceives similarities with a communicator ("He is like me"). Homophily usually improves the potential for communication and persuasion. On the other hand, *heterophily* ("He is *not* like me") can be a liability (Rogers with Shoemaker, 1971, pp. 210–212). Newcomb's earlier coorientation theory (1961) provides an elaborated context that aids understanding of homophily and heterophily.

HOW CLIENTS AND UPPER-LEVEL MANAGERS THINK ABOUT PROJECTS

Throughout the planning of virtually every campaign, there is an implicit concern about the merit of the effort: Should work begin on a campaign? If someone—a client, an upper-level manager, or other—believes a campaign ought to be conducted, that does not ensure that it will be. Since resources in an organization are considered finite, a crucial criterion is whether the project can earn a priority high enough to justify *any* expenditure. One of the clearest examples of this type of managerial thinking is *zero-base planning,* founded in the belief that no project has more than a priority of zero until justification is presented and accepted (see Pattillo, 1967; Stonich with Kirby, 1977).

Proposal Categories

Zero-base planning assumes that campaigns or other projects fall into one of two basic categories:

1. *Mandated programs* are those that must be undertaken, even though your client or organization might actually prefer to spend the money on something else, for example, projects required by government agencies or campaigns that are necessary to maintain a position within a market.
2. *Relative merit programs* are those that must compete for funding because finite resources could be used in more than one way. For example, funds might be put into short-term investments; used to support other projects or campaigns; or available only if other projects or campaigns are deferred, canceled, or scaled down to release resources. Most campaigns are judged on the basis of relative merit since their claim on funding depends initially on whether they are assigned a greater or lesser priority than other potential uses of an organization's resources.

Rating Process

Zero-base planning, which also may be known as zero-base budgeting, requires managers to rate a single project or campaign proposal or to make a comparative rating of two or more competing proposals—for example, a situation in which two outside organizations are bidding competitively as providers of a proposed campaign, or there are competing proposals in an organization to start a magazine for an external audience, run a general corporate image campaign, or mount a membership campaign.

The rating process requires managers to articulate and agree on the rating criteria they will use.

Criteria for Rating. Some typical criteria are these:

- Contribution of the project to the organization's goals (as distinguished from a campaign's goals)
- Appropriateness of the stated goals and objectives and the likelihood they can be attained

- Total cost
- Cost/benefit ratio: Benefits can be defined in various ways—from relatively firm indicators related to problem solving, such as sales, brand loyalty, attitudinal measures, and knowledge measures, to relatively soft indicators, such as community service and good will.
- Timeliness: There must be assurance in many cases that a campaign will be implemented within a particular time frame in order to have a salutary impact on the problem it addresses.
- Effective employment of human resources, equipment, materials, and other expenditures: This category may also reflect whether individual factors are cost effective—such as whether hourly or daily charges of consultants are in line with prevailing market costs, whether purchase costs of materials are within reasonable bounds in terms of prevailing market costs or in view of superior quality, and cost per thousand (CPM) for media-buying selections.
- Adverse consequences that would result from a decision not to implement the project or campaign

Because several managerial criteria are involved—more than just dollar-related decisions—I prefer the term *zero-base planning* rather than *zero-base budgeting,* although the logic of the latter is the same: If a proposal does not earn relatively high ratings across all criteria (including cost factors), it might not gain an implementation budget.

Rating Procedures. The zero-base management rating system requires (1) developing a written declaration of the rating criteria, (2) developing a format for a rating card—usually a $5\frac{1}{2} \times 8$-inch card with slots for each rating criterion listed across the top—and (3) stating the rating procedure—usually to assign a number from 0 to 10 (zero indicating no merit) for each criterion. An arithmetic average is calculated for all evaluators' rating scores for each category, and the information is recorded for future reference or discussion. Then a grand average is calculated—an arithmetic average calculated across the averages for the different criteria. The grand average will result in a score between 0 and 10. Finally, it is necessary to set "cutting points"—for example, proposals with ratings of 4 or below will not be funded, those with ratings of 5 to 7 might be funded if financial conditions permit, and those with ratings of 8 or above almost certainly will be funded.

GETTING YOUR ACT TOGETHER

The general framework for presentation planning at the beginning of this chapter serves to organize all the major steps that can contribute to a successful session.

Content Planning

Careful review of the plan book is mandatory, and gathering information about the persons to whom the presentation will be made may be advisable to formulate your presentation's positioning strategy—how you make the campaign plan, itself, relevant and desirable.

The same structure that organizes this book also can provide most of a presentation's structure. The presentation, itself, can be seen as nine segments:

Segment 1. The real state/ideal state analyses provide a concise introduction to the problem that your campaign must address as well as the proposed solutions, including overviews of the segmentation strategy and main communication strategy. This step will help meet Ogilvy's demand for a concise opening statement to orient the listeners.

Segment 2. The force field analyses provide a crystallization of the behaviors or other factors that must be addressed in each audience segment, and verification research provides proof that the analyses are realistic and trustworthy. The analyses also provide a platform for MBO.

Segment 3. MBO focuses the information about what the communication impacts of the campaign will be and how they relate both to the motivating variables just discussed and to the copy platform and copy points that will follow.

Segment 4. The media schedule provides a summary of what will be done to maximize audience exposure and attention to the messages, including how individual vehicles contribute to that aim. The schedule also can be used to demonstrate that the campaign does not "vanish" and that both frequency and the media mix optimize exposure. Moreover, costs and cost-effectiveness explanations are integral to presentation of the media and channel planning.

Segment 5. PERT-CPM provides a basis for explaining the work and timing that will be implemented, as well as the potential for effective work delegation, monitoring, adaptation, and completion.

Segment 6. The overall budget provides a summary of cost factors. Subtotals and totals from the budget usually will be sufficient, although more details might be included for media costs.

Segment 7. The evaluation section provides a basis for explanations about the importance of evaluation, how MBO contributes to the process, and how it will be implemented.

Segment 8. A persuasive closing statement should be developed; at a minimum, it would mean a summary of the benefits and costs. Enthusiasm is helpful, but it is no substitute for evidence that you have done your homework.

Segment 9. Preparations must be made for the presentation's question and answer session. A useful exercise is to take the roles of the major managers and attempt to anticipate and answer the questions they might raise.

Presentation Staffing

Customarily, the team members who have shared the major responsibilities for developing the campaign plan will join in making the presentation; sometimes only the manager or planner and some other key person will participate.

Individual team members who are "low key" in social interaction might prove to be a liability; however, if these same persons are experts and have sufficient and well-organized facts to present, that can establish their credibility and make them invaluable in a presentation—especially in the Q & A session.

The person who will serve as the main presenter should have concise, current biographical sketches for each person; these sketches will be used during introductions at the outset of a presentation.

Audiovisual Support Planning

Projection slides or other visuals should be prepared well in advance to allow sufficient time for editing. Individual visuals should not have too much content. Extensive text in any visual can undermine a presentation. First, content should be grasped in about three to six seconds, so that a presentation does not become boring. Second, complex content should be broken down over several visuals to facilitate rapid comprehension and not divert listeners' thoughts from what the presenter is saying.

A presenter should read all the copy on each visual to the audience. When the content of a visual is not read, most audience members will find it difficult to listen to a presenter and read and attend to the visuals at the same time. Having each presenter read each slide aloud as the presentation progresses integrates the oral and visual elements, enhancing the probability that focused attention, memory, and learning will result.

A good general rule is to avoid presenting complex graphic designs in visuals—especially when, even though an image is projected, text is either difficult or impossible to read clearly and quickly. Eye camera studies of individuals' perceptual scanning of complex visuals prove that they trace and then repeatedly retrace details in complex illustrations (Yarbus, 1967). Even when a presenter explains a complex diagram, there is a possibility that the listener may attend to the diagram only. (Kahneman, 1973, provides an extensive discussion of cognitive processes involved in attention and allocation of effort when individuals encounter competing stimuli.) In most cases, because of perceptual limitations relating to complex visual figures, a wiser decision may be to produce a series of text visuals as substitutes when the information must be covered. One possible exception might be the media schedule visual, although even that should be simplified as much as possible —limiting the graphic to the work-date scale; a list of vehicles and bars or other symbols to represent decisions on continuity, pulsing, and flighting; and the media mix. Information from the plan book's media schedule form about frequency, average frequency, and costs would be shifted to follow-up text visuals.

Color should be used with reservation. A typical problem is that text and graphics in projected visuals are difficult to comprehend when there is insufficient contrast between the content and its background (e.g., light yellow on white; lighter shades of brown on white or tan; and black on medium-to-dark shades of blue, green, red, or brown). Also, content is difficult to perceive when superimposed on backgrounds that are either visually complex (e.g., printed over pictures or artwork) or otherwise intense (e.g., bright red). These observations are based on the Gestalt theory of perception and deal with predictable interactions between ground, or background, and field, the superimposed content (See Berelson & Steiner, 1964).

Most presenters seem to favor 35mm color projection slides as opposed to other forms of visuals such as show cards, flip charts, overhead projector transparencies, and opaque projector materials. One reason is that high-quality slides can be produced quickly and simply, for example, by typing content and using a camera with a macro (close-up) lens and a copy stand. Also more elaborate slides can be produced efficiently with a desktop computer, graphics software, and a transparency-maker machine; images created on a computer can be transferred directly to film, which would then be processed. Another major consideration is that show cards, flip charts, overhead projection transparencies, and originals designed for opaque projection are often clumsy. As Murphy's Law predicts, anything that can go wrong usually does. A corollary rule is that it usually occurs at the worst possible time. Consequently, adequate planning will involve every reasonable effort possible to anticipate and prevent problems.

Sufficient time should be allowed for processing and for editing. Excess visuals that divert attention should be eliminated. Images should be crisp and readable at a distance. Where slides are used, blackout slides should be inserted to coincide with those times that visuals are off-screen—for example, when all attention should be focused on the oral content. Also, no visual should be upside-down or reversed.

The Setup

It is very important to check out the presentation site and facilities, including equipment if that is provided. Locations of electrical plugs and light switches should be noted. Light dimmers, where they exist, should be found and tested. Equipment should be checked, particularly sound amplification equipment. Notes should be made about things that might be required but are not available at the site—a lectern, a tripod for visuals, a projection screen, extra light bulbs (especially for projectors), marker pens, and extension cords.

Rehearsal

An invaluable investment of time is the rehearsal, which offers a final chance to prune and focus the presentation. The entire presentation should be timed; usually all but the Q & A segment can be completed in 15 to 20 minutes. Also, the time allocated to any segment should not be excessively out of balance with that for the others, although more time might be required by segments 1, 3, 4, and 5. The tendency to give skimpy treatment to segments 2 and 7 should be resisted since the related content gives the listeners convincing reasons why the proposed campaign is likely to work and explains how the impacts will be tested. These are factors that underscore your mastery of managerial techniques and give you an edge over competitors who base their plans' merits mainly on "trust in us" arguments or give little or no attention to testing after a campaign to see if the trust was merited.

During rehearsal, someone in the campaign team should be appointed devil's advocate to analyze very critically what is being done and even argue the case that other presentation strategies, tactics, or visuals might be better. Typical problems that merit surveillance include lack of organization, fuzzy explanations, visuals that are not coordinated with what is being said, visuals that are not relevant or that are hard to follow for one reason or another, things that divert attention (too many people on the platform at one time; visuals that are "left up," causing distractions from oral content), and "wall-papering" with visuals (putting up all visuals at once—which would be helpful in a planning session but not in a presentation because the latter must be highly focused). Other personal performance problems include lack of enthusiasm; hesitation or uncertainty regarding content; turning one's back on listeners while reading or pointing to visuals; repeated use of jargon, pet phrases, or stock answers; and displays of idiosyncratic body language, such as gazing into the distance, slouching, scratching, or nervous gestures.

Presentation

Getting off to a good beginning is important. Self-effacing comments and jokes fall into the category of stale ploys from an outdated manual on public speaking; they do not constitute a good start. From the standpoint of transactional analysis (Berne, 1964, 1976), discussed in Chapter 3, such openers are more suggestive of a child eager to please a parent than an adult-to-adult transaction. A better strategy is to initiate the transaction from an "I'm OK—You're OK" position, indicating that the team takes both the client or upper-level managers and the problem seriously and that the team feels it is competent to handle the job.

Introduction of members of the campaign team or all persons who will make the presentation by name and, especially, by title and credentials can help impart that "I'm [or we're] OK" cue; team members should strive to create or reinforce perceptions of trustworthiness and expertise and competence.

Provided that the planning, staffing, and rehearsal criteria have been addressed, the actual presentation should progress smoothly.

Closing

Some form of closing is advisable, but that does not include presentation clichés that try to pump up enthusiasm—in the vein of "Now this *fantastic* campaign is your guaranteed *rocket ride to success!*" A more successful approach is to highlight the main points about the problem, solution, impact, cost effectiveness, and match-up with the client's best interests. The emphasis should be on "you," not "us."

Q & A

All presenters must have familiarized themselves thoroughly with every aspect of the campaign plan book; answers about aspects on which individuals worked usually are more meaningful when related to the efficiency and the total impact of the proposed campaign.

Schultz, Martin, and Brown (1984, p. 480) offer several suggestions for what they call "question time."

- Encourage questions.
- Be truthful, simple, to the point.
- Listen to the question.
- Don't hedge or waffle.
- Don't minimize problems; acknowledge them.
- Make them laugh.
- Don't knock the competition.
- Watch for signs of boredom.
- Make sure you don't all reply at the same time.
- Don't make promises you can't deliver.
- Be ready to offer a list of names of clients [if you are in an agency or organization bidding for an account].
- Be ready to deal with the usual objections.

Leave-Behinds

At the conclusion of the presentation, you should deliver a bound copy of the campaign plan book. If you are in an agency or organization that was contracted either to do the planning but not the execution or to deal with both, you should consider using a binder with a cover or title page indicating for whom the campaign plan was prepared or to whom it was presented. Whether the page should include individual names is a matter for your personal judgment.

If you are bidding for an account, you might include with the plan book a supplementary sheet listing some of your satisfied former clients, with names, addresses, and phone numbers. Even if the references are not checked, this practice suggests that you are willing to have your previous performance examined, enhancing your credibility.

SUMMARY

After all the time, scientific research and other information collection, intellectual ferment, strategy formulation, writing, editing, and preparation that go into a development of the campaign book—not to mention costs—it would be a major managerial disaster to have the resulting product turned down because of inadequate preparation for the presentation.

You should make an early beginning on the planning and preparation of any presentation. First, however, it is equally important to be sure that the campaign plan book, itself, is edited meticulously.

A basic understanding of behavioral principles underlying social interaction in an organizational context explains why and how attention to structure and detail may make communication between you or your campaign team, on the one hand, and your client or your upper-level managers, on the other, more effective—to improve rapport, enhance your team's credibility, and optimize a presentation's persuasion potential.

Also, this chapter illustrates the thinking underlying clients' and upper-level managers' evaluation of proposals for projects and their funding, explaining a technique called zero-base planning or zero-base budgeting; the mode of thinking embodied in this technique is fairly universal.

The planning steps provide a framework for organizing the presentation. To simplify the matter further, this chapter suggests how the presentation units can be grouped into clusters that interlock with other activity segments vital to an effective presentation.

In the planning of a presentation, careful attention to preparation and execution must extend from the very first activities to the minute the campaign plan book is put into the hands of those for whom it was developed.

REFERENCES

C. K. Atkin, "Mass Media Information Campaign Effectiveness," in R. E. Rice and W. J. Paisley (eds.), *Public Information Campaigns* (Beverly Hills, CA: Sage, 1981), pp. 265–271.

R. A. Bauer, "The Obstinate Audience: The Influence Process from the Point of View of Social Communication," in W. G. Bennis, K. D. Benne, and Robert Chin (eds.), *The Planning of Change,* 2nd ed. (New York: Holt, Rinehart and Winston, 1969), pp. 507–519.

Bernard Berelson and G. Steiner, *Human Behavior* (New York: Harcourt, Brace and World, 1964).

Eric Berne, *The Games People Play* (New York: Grove Press, 1964).

Eric Berne, *Beyond Games and Scripts* (New York: Grove Press, 1976).

W. S. Howell, *The Empathic Communicator* (Belmont, CA: Wadsworth, 1982).

Daniel Kahneman, *Attention and Effort* (Englewood Cliffs, NJ: Prentice-Hall, 1973).

R. L. Katz, *Empathy: Its Nature and Uses,* (New York: Free Press, 1963).

Daniel Lerner, *The Passing of Traditional Society* (New York: Macmillan, 1958).

S. W. Littlejohn, *Theories of Human Communication,* 2nd ed. (Belmont, CA: Wadsworth, 1983).

T. M. Newcomb, *The Acquaintance Process* (New York: Holt, Rinehart and Winston, 1961).

J. W. Pattillo, *Zero-Base Budgeting: A Planning, Resource Allocation and Control Tool* (New York: National Assn. of Accountants, 1967).

E. M. Rogers with F. Shoemaker, *The Communication of Innovations,* 2nd ed. (New York: Free Press, 1971).

D. E. Schultz, D. Martin, and W. P. Brown, *Strategic Advertising Campaigns* (Chicago: Crain Books, 1984).

P. J. Stonich with J. C. Kirby, *Zero-Base Planning and Budgeting* (Homewood, IL: Dow-Jones-Irwin, 1977).

A. L. Yarbus, *Eye Movements and Vision,* trans. B. Haigh (New York: Plenum Press, 1967).

FURTHER READING

Muriel James, *The OK Boss* (Reading, MA: Addison-Wesley, 1975).

Glossary

Adoption curve. A graphic depiction of the rate of adoption of new information, practices, or techniques that is virtually the same as the learning curve. The major difference is that the maximum impact in adoption is usually far less than 100 percent. See **Learning curve.**

Adopter types. A categorical classification of people who enter the information diffusion and adoption process in successive stages: innovators, early adopters, early majority, late majority, and laggards; this is one of the explanations why campaign effects build slowly in any population.

Affect. The feelings that communications evoke in people who receive them.

AIDA formula. A simple model for persuasive copywriting: It contends copy should attempt to build attention, interest, desire, and action.

Analysis of variance (ANOVA). A statistical test used to verify or locate significant differences between three or more arithmetic means such as those resulting in different groups from exposure to different campaign message treatments in evaluation research.

Assimilation effect. In Gestalt psychology, a phenomenon that causes people to see things that are similar in design or close in proximity as part of a perceptual whole.

Attention. The likelihood that individuals will attend to and process information such as that conveyed through mass media or other channels.

Attitude. A mental or neural predisposition, organized through experience, enabling individuals to react in response to messages or other stimuli; a ''frame of reference.''

Attitude change theory. A class of theories, the dominant ones of which contend that attitude changes as a result of persons' encountering an interruption of homeostasis, a steady psychological state. Some of the major theories are those regarding balance, homeostasis, cognitive congruity, and dissonance.

Belief. A subjective probability estimation regarding phenomena or likely outcomes of actions. This concept also helps explain individuals' internal rule systems controlling behaviors.

Bias (in sampling). Systematic over- or under-representation of some types of people, for example, by gender, while sampling; bias invalidates the representativeness of data obtained through sampling.

Budget. A managerial device used to explain total and component costs of a campaign or project and to relate the cost-efficiency of decisions; it may reflect use of existing materials, facilities, and human resources, as well as proposed new expenditures.

Capacity model of attention. Daniel Kahneman's notion that people approach perceptual situations with a limited capacity for attention; if arousal is sufficient, they can either allocate additional capacity, or seek and employ strategies for coping.

Causal reasoning. Elementary rules from philosophy concerning the logic to test whether an outcome or event is produced by a specified phenomenon, or more appropriately, might be attributed to other factors.

Centrality. Individuals' perception that some issue is linked to beliefs or values they hold to be very important; compatible messages may find increased acceptance, while opposing messages may meet strong resistance.

Channels (message delivery). Means, other than the institutional mass media institutions, that may be employed to disseminate information. Examples are human information networks, social or work organizations, mimeographed documents, tape-recorded messages, and "people's theater," in which people create *ad hoc* dramas to convey messages or instruct about ways to solve problems.

Check-data. In sampling, this usually refers to questionnaire data obtained through sampling that pertain to demographics and which may be compared to trustworthy external data such as census reports to confirm a study's sampling error estimates.

Chi-square test. A nonparametric statistical test used with data contingency tables, in which frequency (response tally) and percentage data are displayed in row and column cells; this is used to verify assumptions that a relationship, association, or correlation exists between variables.

Closure. In Gestalt psychology, a phenomenon in which individuals tend to "fill in" missing parts of a visual image to produce a coherent, meaningful whole.

Cognitive plan. Part of the cognitive process, dealing with individuals' learning, application, and refinement of internal rules for dealing with problems, including recognition and classification of phenomena, analysis and memory storage, and recall.

Cognitive process. The study of how people process information, including perception, memory and recall, information integration, thinking, and selection of strategies or plans for action.

Cognitive structure. Conceptualization of the process by which people classify, organize, and integrate information mentally to support memory, thinking, and action.

Communication clutter. The excessively large volume of communications vying for individual's exposure and attention, particularly in urban centers. The failure of an individual to reduce the complexity can lead to entropy, or uncertainty. See **Entropy.**

Confidence limits. In the projection of data obtained by sampling, this expresses the bounds of estimation. For example, when there is a finding that 40 percent of a population supports an issue and the sampling error is plus or minus three points, as given in the sample size/sampling error table in this book, one can be 95 percent confident that the true value is not more than 43 percent (40% + 3) nor less than 37 percent (40% − 3), the confidence limits.

Confounding. In research, the intertwining of effects from different variables that may complicate attempts to attribute results, as in a campaign, to specific presumed causes. Research design in evaluation research helps control confounding.

Continuity (in media planning). A message plan that results in the potential for continuous exposure to a message over time.

Continuity (in message planning). Devices incorporated in different messages or varying message formats across mass media to make it easy for audience members to recognize the messages as part of the same campaign; examples of continuity devices are use of the same copy platform and copy points, the same voices, the same graphics devices, or the same theme music.

Contrast effect. In Gestalt psychology, a phenomenon that causes people to see objects that are dissimilar or not in close proximity as being different perceptual entities.

Control variables. In research data analysis, variables that are manipulated statistically to determine whether they, in combination with other variables, might help explain results that are being investigated.

Coorientation theory. Social psychologist Theodore Newcomb's notion that when two people perceive they have things in common, communication and influence between them are more likely to be successful. See **Homophily** and **Heterophily.**

Copy platform. A technique used to organize messages, or copy points, in support of a central theme, or slogan.

Copy points. Specific facts, assertions or arguments that will be incorporated in a message.

Cost per thousand (CPM). In media planning, the cost to deliver a standard unit of advertising via a particular mass media vehicle to a theoretical audience of 1,000; in the acronym CPM, the final letter indicates "mil" or thousand. This is used for inter-class media cost efficiency comparisons, e.g., one newspaper versus another.

Defender role. In campaigns that are intended to introduce change, this characterizes behaviors of persons who resist in order to protect, in their view, the institution or existing behaviors; sometimes the resistance indicates the proposed change is, indeed, flawed or unworkable.

Demographics. A scheme for classification of markets or audience segments in terms of census-type characteristics such as age, gender, education, income, race geographic location, and occupation.

Diffusion of innovations. The study of how new knowledge, practices, or techniques are spread through communication to bring about adoption.

Dummy data tables. Fully labeled research data tables with row and column cells in which frequency counts and percentages will be displayed eventually. These tables serve to help plan what information must be collected and how the resulting data will be analyzed.

Empathy. The ability, as Daniel Lerner expresses it, to put oneself in another's shoes and think as though you were that person.

End-state values. Social psychologist Milton Rokeach's notion of a limited number of long-term goals in life that any individual holds to be important; also called terminal values.

Entropy. Uncertainty, usually encountered in communication situations, as a result of an information overload.

Evaluation research. An indispensable component of campaign management that is employed to determine whether results specified in campaign management by objectives (MBO) statements have been met and whether factors other than the campaign can be ruled out as alternative causes of the results.

Exposure. The likelihood that members of a market or target audience will come into contact with a message transmitted through a specified mass media vehicle.

Field and ground. A Gestalt principle describing phenomena that result from an interaction between a visual background and designs or images imposed on it—e.g., complex backgrounds tend to interfere with perception of the superimposed image; dark images superimposed on light backgrounds seem to recede, and light images superimposed on dark backgrounds seem to emerge from the visual frame.

Flighting. In media planning, alternation between periods of message exposure through some mass media vehicle and no exposure; a technique to eke out a media budget.

Focus group research. Extensive nondirective interviews conducted with a small group of individuals who have knowledge or experience related to a subject being investigated.

Force field analysis. A graphic analysis technique, based on the work of psychologist Kurt Lewin, designed to identify the principal motivating variables or forces (driving or restraining) that control specified behaviors.

Frequency (media planning). The number of exposures to a message that a media plan will produce in a market or target population during a specified time, usually four or six weeks.

Frequency (research). The number of persons responding with a specific answer to some question in a questionnaire.

Functional literacy. Individuals' ability to read and explain what they have read; literacy levels detected by functional literacy tests usually are much lower than for traditional measurement. See **Literacy.**

Games (behavioral). Eric Berne's notion that many interactions between individuals are predictably patterned as though they are part of a game in progress; anyone who recognizes such a game usually can then develop strategies for coping with the problems that emerge.

Gantt chart. A graphic technique for displaying and tracking work assignments and progress toward completion of assigned tasks; may be developed manually or through use of computer project management software.

General systems model. A group of elements, functionally interrelated within some boundaries in the service or attainment of specified goals. Communication provides both linkages and tension that energize the system; it is also used to help the system manage to keep tension at an acceptable or productive level, including by reducing entropy or uncertainty.

Gestalt. A school of psychology that contends humans have an inborn predisposition to organize perceptions in terms of configuration—generating rules about how people will respond to stimuli relative to assimilation, contrast, field and ground, closure, and other consistent behaviors.

Global objective. A form of management by objectives (MBO) that defines major intended results of a campaign or project; similar to the notion of a goal.

Gross impressions. In media planning, the total number of potential exposures to a message created by a media plan; a very inexact index of a plan's effectiveness.

Gross rating point (GRP). In media planning, the mathematical product of reach and frequency for planned message insertions in a specified mass media vehicle— e.g., a message repeated six times (frequency) in a vehicle, such as the *Boston Globe*, with 40 percent reach in a specified market or target audience would yield $6 \times 40 = 240$ GRPs. GRPs may be summed across vehicles in a class of media, such as television.

Heterophily. Audience members' perception that a communicator is unlike them, which can impede communication and influence.

Homophily. Audience members' perception that a communicator is somehow similar to them (e.g., in interests), which can improve communication and influence.

Household utilizing television (HUT). In media planning and research, the number of households with sets actually in operation at the time a program or program segment is broadcast.

Individual focus sessions (IFS). A variation of focus group research in which extensive nondirective interviewing is done with individuals, rather than with groups.

Information-retrieval systems. Computerized systems to obtain information selectively from various types of electronic data bases.

Intention. A cognitive plan to engage in particular ways to solve some behavioral situation or problem.

Intermediate objective. A form of management by objectives (MBO) that defines end-results of work activities or tasks.

Instrumental values. Milton Rokeach's notion of individuals' relative ratings of the acceptability or desirability of courses of action that might be used to attain desired goals in life, for example, what he calls end-state or terminal values. See **End-state values.**

Learning curve. A stretched-out "S" curve that depicts the typical progress of learning: It rises very slowly at the outset, rises rather rapidly for a time, then peaks and once again ceases to rise more than in modest increments; this suggests that it is usually unrealistic to expect marked short-term changes from a campaign. See also **Adopter types.**

Lifespace analysis. Psychologist Kurt Lewin's notion that behavior, including motivation, can be explained jointly by individuals' store of experience, which they use to interpret situations (i.e., their "lifespace") and their inclination to move purposely to attain a valued (i.e., "valenced") reward when lifespace suggests it is attainable.

Life-style. A scheme to classify members of a market or a target audience by overt behavioral patterns, such as purchasing, traveling, participation in causes, or hobby.

Literacy. A proxy or stand-in measure for the ability to read; many countries treat completion of four years of formal education as being equivalent to being literate. This is contrasted with functional literacy. See **Functional literacy.**

KAMP variables. An acronym describing the major classes of information variables a campaign may affect: knowledge, affect, motivation, and practice.

Knowledge gap phenomenon. A proposition, supported by research, that in any population where information is equally available to individuals, some will predictably learn more and some less.

Magical number 7 plus or minus 2. Psychologist George A. Miller's notion that on an average, most people can remember seven items from an array, while a lesser number will recall as many as nine or as few as five.

Management by objectives (MBO). A planning technique requiring the statement of observable or measurable results that will be produced by work; MBO also controls work delegation, tracking, and evaluation.

Marketing curve. A graphic depiction of the rate at which people make decisions to accept marketing propositions, virtually identical to a learning curve. However, the maximum impact to be gained in marketing usually is far less than 100 percent. See **Learning curve.**

Mass media. Major institutions such as radio, television, newspapers, magazines, outdoor advertising, and direct mail, that convey information, editorial opinion, entertainment, or advertising to the mass public.

Matching design. In experimental and evaluation research, the establishment of test groups that are matched on extraneous variables that might influence results. See also **Confounding.**

Media mix. In media planning, the composite of mass media vehicles that are selected and integrated to transmit a campaign's messages to a market or to one target audience or more.

Media schedule. In media planning, a graphic that depicts the media plan, including the media mix, decisions on continuity, flighting and pulsing, average frequency per period, and media costs.

Median test. A nonparametric statistical test designed, like the chi-square test, for use with data contingency tables in which data are presented in row and column cells; this is used to test differences between percentages in two or more groups.

Memory decay. Individuals' forgetting of messages to which they have been exposed.

Motivation. The study of the process whereby people act in order to attain desired outcomes or to avoid or prevent noxious ones. See **Lifespace analysis, Force field analysis,** and **Value-expectancy theory.**

Multistep flow of communication. Similar to the two-step flow of communication, the multistep flow recognizes that communications in many situations are retransmitted several times along a human chain or network after having been received from the mass media. See **Two-step flow of communication.**

Network analysis. The study of human communication chains that reveals aspects of flow patterns, groupings or cliques, dependencies, and linkages between cliques.

Nondirective interviewing. A form of interviewing used in focus group research and individual focus sessions. It requires the interviewer or moderator to engage in a flexible dialogue with interviewees, suggesting leads for elaboration or new discussion rather than reading standardized questions, as in survey research.

Nonverbal communication. Forms of nonverbal communications or cues regarding behavioral predispositions, usually involving facial expressions, head and body positioning, and gestures.

Operationalization. In research, a technique that explains the procedures that will be implemented to measure a specific variable.

Opinion leader. Any person sought by others for information, interpretation, or advice and therefore believed to be influential in human communication networks.

PERT. Program Evaluation and Review Technique.

PERT activity slack. A PERT planning term. See **PERT free float.**

PERT-CPM. Program Evaluation and Review Technique—Critical Path Method; a planning technique used to plan work activities in campaigns and other projects.

PERT critical path. A sequence of activities in a PERT network that takes the longest time to complete and thereby determines the earliest completion of a campaign or project or, in a case when a deadline is set, either matches or exceeds the amount of time allowed—which may necessitate either the careful monitoring of work or a revision of the plan.

PERT event. A marker that distinguishes the end-point of some related tasks or activities; also called a PERT objective, it is similar to a management by objectives system intermediate objective.

PERT free float. A calculation to determine whether work on tasks or activities related to some PERT event or objective (equivalent to an instrumental objective) may exceed the time allowed without causing the next objective not to be completed on schedule; also called activity slack.

PERT network. A graphic depicting the sequencing of PERT events, with their related tasks or activities, in a work plan.

PERT objective. Synonymous with PERT event. See **PERT event.**

PERT path. In a PERT network, a series of PERT events linked by relational dependencies, for example, necessary predecessor events, that contribute to the completion of a work plan.

PERT predecessor event. In PERT-CPM planning, an event or objective that must be completed before work on tasks or activities related to the next event or objective can be begun.

PERT total float. A calculation to determine whether work on tasks or activities related to some PERT objective or event (equivalent to an instrumental objective) may exceed the time allowed without causing the entire campaign or project not to be completed on schedule; also called slack.

PERT slack. A PERT planning term synonymous with total float. See **PERT total float.**

Plan (management). A specific set of operations that can be implemented to solve a particular problem or attain a particular objective or goal.

Plan (memory). An individual's scheme for storing information in memory in such a way that it can be retrieved efficiently on demand.

Plan book. A written record that articulates an entire campaign plan, including documentation of the problem analysis, strategy, objectives, recommendations for implementation and evaluation, and budget.

Population. In sampling, a subset of a universe that is of interest to a researcher; similar to a target audience segment as part of a total audience. See **Universe.**

Positioning (messages). A plan to describe an offered product, idea, or service as unique in its ability to produce benefits for members of a targeted audience.

Positioning (messages in media). Placement of a message in a specific program or time slot in broadcast media or in a specific section or page in print media, to maximize the likelihood of audience exposure.

Primacy effect. In memory, the greater likelihood that all things being equal an individual will remember the first things presented in a list or series (e.g., messages or television advertisements in a cluster).

Problem-solving activity plan. A subset of cognitive plan, as implied in the TOTE unit, that enables an individual to identify means of coping with specified problems. See **TOTE unit.**

Project management software. A class of computer programs designed to support campaign or project management. They typically support PERT-CPM analysis, Gantt charts, project tracking and revision, and budget elaboration, tracking, and revision.

Psychographics. A scheme for classification of members of markets or a target audience according to relatively enduring psychological traits that predispose them to action.

Public service announcements (PSAs). In broadcast media, free advertising time provided to nonprofit organizations in fulfillment of federal government licensing requirements for public service; print media also may make PSAs available, but sometimes provide free space in some proportion to purchased advertising space.

Pulsing. In media planning, alternation between periods of greater use of frequency in message delivery in a mass media vehicle and lesser use of frequency; ensures minimal exposure continuity and helps eke out a media budget.

Questionnaire. In survey research, a uniform list of standardized questions to be read to all persons picked to be interviewed.

Random numbers table. A table of numbers, usually generated by a computer, that have no meaningful relationships. This is used in survey sampling to ensure representativeness as a result of an equal chance of selection, used in assignment of individuals to groups in evaluation research to nullify differences on personal characteristics in the groups that might affect the research results, and used in random telephone number generation for sampling.

Random telephone number generation. A sampling technique used in survey research that is based on a random numbers table and makes it possible to develop phone numbers by chance, which gives telephone households an equal opportunity to be picked and also reaches unlisted or unpublished numbers.

Randomized design. In experimental or evaluation research, the assignment of persons to test groups through use of a random numbers table. The method cancels out the confounding effects of subject variables. See also **Subject variables** and **Confounding.**

Rating (radio). Radio listenership, expressed as a percentage of total listenership during a specified time period—for example, hour, quarter hour or day-part such as morning or afternoon urban ''drive time'' (commuting hours)—in a specific market.

Rating (television). Television program viewership, expressed as a percentage of all households with television in a specific market.

Reach. In media planning, the unduplicated proportion of a market or target audience that is exposed to a message delivered by a mass media vehicle or media plan during a specified time, usually four or six weeks.

Readability analysis. Calculation of formulas for written text that indicate how difficult it will be for individuals to comprehend the meaning of that text. Among the major formulas are Dale-Chall, Flesch, and the Gunning "fog index." Computer software is available to implement readability analysis.

Real state/ideal state analyses. Managerial inquiry formats that focus on what can be learned about a problem through a review of the history of successes, failures and related insights (real state analysis), and a systematic exploration of what must be changed or affected in order to attain the desired outcomes (real state analysis).

Recall. The likelihood that persons will remember messages when asked about them after having been exposed.

Recency effect. In memory, the greater likelihood that, all things being equal, individuals will remember the last things presented in a list or series, such as messages or television advertisements in a cluster.

Reliability. In research, the ability of some instrument such as a question or scale to measure the same thing in repeated applications.

Research design. In evaluation research, the specification of how the testing of objectives will be implemented with members of a target audience or audiences after the researcher has explained how the measurement of the variables or objectives will be operationalized.

Rules (behavioral). In cognitive process, an individual's personal beliefs on how behavior should be conducted concerning both specific routine daily life activities and exceptional situations.

Salience. Individuals' perception that some issue is relevant to concerns that they have at the time, as opposed to enduring concerns reflected in centrality. A message's salience may improve the likelihood of exposure and attention. See also **Centrality.**

Sampling (nonprobability). A form of sampling that is relatively less used in survey research, because it may be affected negatively by subjective decisions on the part of researchers, interviewers, or even interviewees about who will become part of a sample; this tends to produce biases that make samples nonrepresentative.

Sampling (probability). In survey research, a methodology based in statistical probability theory to select a representative group of individuals or units from an unworkably large mass, thereby facilitating data collection, analysis, and projections; representativeness is ensured because the methodology provides all persons in the mass an equal or known chance of being included in a sample.

Sampling error. The theoretical discrepancy between data obtained by sampling and data that might be obtained by interviewing the entire population from which the sample was drawn.

Sampling frame. A description characterizing a population from which a sample is drawn. The sampling frame makes it possible to be certain from whom the obtained data can be generalized.

Scale. In research measurement, an instrument that is usually composed of six or more submeasures, such as questions or declarations, to cope with more complex phenomena that involve multiple decisional aspects.

Segmentation. A technique to break down a large population into components and identify those components that are likely to have the greatest importance to problem solving or predisposition to respond to a campaign's messages. Such components are targeted audience segments.

Selective exposure. The tendency of individuals to avoid contact with information. See **Selectivity.**

Selectivity. A process in which individuals select some information for processing, disregarding other information. This affects perception, memory, recall, and thinking. Education, perceived utility, and other gratifications have been cited as decisional factors affecting selectivity.

Share. Television program viewership, expressed as a percentage of all households in a defined market whose sets are in use at the time viewing is tested.

Source credibility. Such credibility is found to be attributable largely to audience perceptions of the communicator's trustworthiness and expertise or competence.

Spreadsheet software. A class of computer programs that makes it possible for lay users to input, format, revise, and monitor complex budgets. Such programs may permit breakdowns by organization sectors, profit centers, activities, or personnel.

Standard Metropolitan Statistical Area (SMSA). A series of statistical reports published by the U.S. Bureau of the Census concerning demographic patterns in urban areas with a population of 70,000 or greater. Such reports are vital in marketing, segmentation, media buying, and sampling work.

Statistical software. A class of computer programs that makes it possible for lay users to input and analyze research data, including work with statistical tests and results.

Strategic planning. A results-oriented approach to planning that requires employment of objective managerial methods that are systemically integrated in a way that maximizes the efficiency and impact of a campaign or project. Campaigns using this model make extensive use of problem-solving methods or techniques, research, behavioral theory, management by objectives (MBO), techniques to optimize mass media and other channel message delivery planning, work control systems, budget analysis and evaluation research.

Subject variables. The variables that individuals bring with themselves (i. e., subject variables) in experimental and evaluation research design into the test situation and that may affect results and confuse interpretation. Examples are differences in IQ, education, or experience.

Survey research. A methodology for conducting research in large populations. It customarily employs sampling, questionnaires, and statistical analysis.

System. A group of elements, functionally interrelated in the service or attainment of specified goals. Related to general systems theory. See **General systems model.**

Terminal objective. A form of management by objectives (MBO) that defines a specific end-result of campaign or program activities which, when combined with others, will bring about the attainment of a specified global objective, which is more encompassing.

Test criteria plan. A subset of cognitive plan, as implied in the TOTE unit, that enables an individual to identify means of testing whether activities that have been selected to cope with specified problems produce satisfactory solutions. See **TOTE unit.**

TOTE unit. A notion by Miller, Galanter, and Pilbram that explains a cognitive plan for problem solving: test (identify the problem), operation (pick and implement a strategy or plan), test (verify whether the operation succeeded), and exit (provided success is obtained; otherwise, return to try again).

Transactional analysis. The study of interpersonal communication, based on the notion that persons communicate from parent, adult, or child ego states and that unbalanced or mismatched states may lead to blockages.

***t*-test.** A statistical test used to verify whether there is a statistical difference between two arithmetic means. This may be used to test response treatments in evaluation research when two groups are exposed to different message treatments.

Two-step flow of communication. A model by Elihu Katz and Paul Lazarsfeld that reflects findings that much information from mass media flows in two steps: from the media to opinion leaders, who mediate, and from them to the eventual end audience members.

Unique selling proposition (USP). Rosser Reeves's notion that any product, service, or claim should be presented to a target audience as unique in the benefits it can offer. This is a form of message positioning. See **Message positioning.**

Universe. In sampling, a very large group of people, all of whom have some characteristic or characteristics in common.

Validity. In research, the ability of some instrument such as a question or scale to actually measure what it purports to measure.

Value-expectancy theory. A class of motivational theories generally based on the notion that people tend to act as a function (expectancy) of beliefs that some outcome is involved that has personal attractiveness (value or valence) and that some course of action can lead to the outcome's attainment (instrumentality).

Values. A concept characterizing what individuals rate, in a relative sense, as important or acceptable goals and behaviors in their lives. See also **Instrumental values** and **End-state values.**

Vehicle. A specified, individual mass medium, such as KSTP-TV, WRKO radio, the *Washington Post,* or *Business Week.*

Weighting (media planning). A decision to put more media plan resources where the payoff is likely to be the greatest, such as spending more of a milk advertising budget in nonsummer months, when consumption is the greatest.

Zero-based budgeting. A variation of zero-based planning.

Zero-based planning. A methodology developed by Texas Instruments Corp. that is based on the premise that in each budget period, no proposed project has more than a zero probability of funding until its merits are clearly established in a competitive rating that pits it against other projects vying for the same funds. This is based on objectively identified rating criteria.

z-test. A statistical test like the *t*-test that is used to verify whether a difference exists between two arithmetic means, but versions also exist to test for a difference between two means or two percentages. This may be used in evaluation research to verify differences between two groups exposed to different message treatments. See also *t*-test.

Index